THE MINIMUM STATE

THE MINIMUM STATE

BEYOND PARTY POLITICS

BY

BRIAN CROZIER

HAMISH HAMILTON
LONDON

First published in Great Britain 1979 by
Hamish Hamilton Ltd
Garden House 57–59 Long Acre London WC2E 9JZ

Copyright © 1979 by Brian Crozier

British Library Cataloguing in Publication Data

Crozier, Brian, b. *1918*
  The minimum state.
  1. Political parties   2. Democracy
  I. Title
  351   JF2061
  ISBN 0–241–10242–1

Printed and bound in Great Britain at
The Camelot Press Ltd, Southampton

CONTENTS

FOREWORD

My well-known preoccupation with the problems of insecurity and political violence led me, many years ago, to a search for forms of political organisation that would be less unsatisfactory than existing options. I have discussed these matters in a number of articles and in two previous books: *The Masters of Power* (1969) and *A Theory of Conflict* (1974). The time had come to devote an entire book to the theme of bad government and the possibility of improvement. I have called it *The Minimum State* both because I believe improvement must lie in the direction of drastically reducing the activities of government and because there has been a widespread trend, strongly propelled by the play of party politics, away from the criteria that justify the existence of the State: the safety and security of the citizens, defence against external enemies, and preservation of the value of money.

Many people (but far fewer than, say, ten years ago) will doubtless agree with my diagnosis and analysis but dismiss my proposed remedies as unlikely to command a sufficiently wide acceptance to influence the course of events. To such friendly sceptics, I offer the following advice:

—Do not assume that because you were born and have lived under a party political system it is necessarily there for ever: historically, it is of very recent origin.

—Do not disregard the overwhelming evidence (much of it assembled here) that the party system is not providing good government: if a breakdown is on the way, the time to think about the future is now. If the breakdown does come, it is better to be prepared than to allow a drift into autocracy and tyranny. (The last chapter, appropriately, deals with 'disaster scenarios'.)

A last preliminary word, about the past and the future. Some books are for amusement, others for instruction and contemplation. I would not deny that there is a didactic element in this one, although I hope it will occasionally provide wry amusement. But it is emphatically for action, not contemplation. In 1724, when English customs were fashionable in France, the *Club de l'Entresol* (literally, the Mezzanine Club) was founded in Paris. Its members, however, used the club for the rather un-English purpose of political discussion.

Later came the *Club des Américains* (1785) and (in 1788) the *Société des Amis des Noirs* or Society of Friends of the Blacks. Indeed, 1788 was the year when political clubs multiplied and flourished in France. It is scarcely a coincidence that the Bastille was stormed in 1789: the discussions of the political clubs played a central role in creating the revolutionary climate that swept away the *ancien régime*.

What I am advocating is nothing so drastic as the French Revolution, but a radical rethinking of pluralist premises and purposes. I hope this book may provide food for political debates in various countries, and that the debates may help to create a climate receptive to the view that our democratic systems are in grave danger, not only from their avowed enemies, but from their inherent weaknesses and contradictions; and that the looming collapse can be averted, or at least something saved from the wreckage only if sensible alternatives are discussed while there is still time. In other words, it is a plea against intellectual inertia, emotional blindness and the unquestioning acceptance of received political wisdom.

If *The Minimum State* contributes to this end, I shall not have written it in vain.

BRIAN CROZIER
London, May 1979

ACKNOWLEDGMENTS

I thank the following: Mr Richard Sim, for his prompt and able research assistance; my personal assistant, Mrs Barbara Rose, for her intelligent typing and supplementary research; Mr Theo Haller, the veteran Swiss journalist, for his critical reading of my chapter on Switzerland; and Mr Martin Bendelow, of the Centre for Policy Studies in London, for his stimulating suggestions and comments. I alone, of course, am responsible for the book as it stands, including any errors that may unhappily have survived repeated scrutiny.

BC

PART I

DIAGNOSIS

ONE

THE GUILTY PARTY

The era of party democracy is nearing its close. Henceforth, two imperative tasks await men and women of goodwill. First things first: top priority must be given to survival—that is, the preservation of a threatened way of life against external and internal enemies.*

Having survived, and if we do, the second imperative task is the search for a viable alternative to the system now in its prolonged death throes. The search should be calm, conscious and dispassionate, and the time to undertake it is *now*. It is no good waiting until the long totalitarian night descends upon us, for by then it will be too late. Nor is it sensible to wait for the alternative, but temporary, unpleasantness of an authoritarian military take-over. For the authoritarian climate is not conducive to free enquiry. Too often, authoritarian rule merely seeks to perpetuate itself, failing in the end and reverting to the chaos which justified a military intervention in the first place.

At the moment, and allowing for an infinity of local variations, there are really only three political alternatives. One is the democracy of universal suffrage and political parties which is familiar to us in the West. As Churchill once put it, party democracy is the worst system, except for all the others. Its attractions are many, but it carries with it the seeds of its own destruction. The point of the enquiry is to preserve the attractions and discard the self-destructive aspects. At present, the alternatives are unenticing. Every Marxist regime in the world is a totalist tyranny, and this is true not only of the Soviet Union and the Chinese People's Republic, but to an even

---

* I have already dealt with this problem in my last book, *Strategy of Survival* (Temple Smith, London, 1978, £5.50), in which I described in some detail the Third World War, a unilateral war of aggression waged by the Soviet Union against the rest of the world, styled the Target Area. This war, which began in the 1940s immediately after the end of World War II, is fought by proxy, by terrorism, subversion, psychological war and other covert techniques. In the late 1970s, the aggressors were within sight of victory. Neither appeasement, nor even passive resistance, was sufficient to stave off defeat for the free and prosperous societies of the Target Area. But the tables could be turned by recognising the threat for what it is, adopting a counter-offensive spirit and exploiting the enemy's weaknesses with his own techniques, and at home by taking energetic though temporary measures against subversion.

greater degree of the newer Marxist regimes in Cambodia and
Ethiopia. In countries where the tyranny has been made less pervasive, such as Hungary or Yugoslavia, the improvement is due to
the partial retreat from Marxist–Leninist principles. Do not be
swayed by the blandishments of the fashionable socialists who are
currently so free with their criticisms of the Soviet bureaucracy but
whose collectivist theories would yield in the end the tyranny they
profess to wish to avoid. Communism, by whatever name it wishes
to be known, is the product of an exploded theoretical fantasy of a
century ago, of a collapsed peasant empire and of a fanatical and
highly effective technique for the seizure of power. It offers nothing
save darkness and death. Much the same can be said of the horrible
twin of communism—the ugly and perverted doctrine of fascism,
another road to more darkness and more death. Although Fascists
normally denounce Communists and vice versa, the doctrine of each
has far more in common with that of the other than either has with
the pluralist and representative societies now under threat. Both are
collectivist tyrannies, whose objectives cannot be fulfilled except by
the destruction of our liberties.

The other alternative to party democracy at present on offer is a
period of military and authoritarian rule. This, too, can be exceedingly unpleasant, and may be accompanied, especially in the early
phases, by brutalities and arbitrary injustices. Yet it is on other
counts far preferable to the totalitarian nightmare. For one thing,
even though it may last decades (as in Spain and Portugal) it is in
the end impermanent, unlike the Marxist–Leninist tyrannies, which
apparently go on for ever, or the Fascist ones which collapse only
as a result of a general war. Moreover, as I have frequently pointed
out, such authoritarian regimes tend to soften with time, and offer
a wide range of individual freedoms, including that of marriage,
travel, private property and a choice of employment. This in itself
tends to shorten their term of life; and so does the fact that authoritarian regimes, as distinct from totalist ones, are non-ideological,
resting primarily on the prestige and force of the man or men at the
top. Military rule may be inevitable, and military intervention is
certainly justified when a country is sliding rapidly into revolutionary
anarchy (as in Chile) or is the victim of unrestrained terrorism (as in
Argentina), but it can never, in itself, be desirable. It is a drastic
remedy which may save the patient *in extremis*, but at considerable
cost. Can it be avoided? If it comes, can it be made to yield, in the
end, to a system that would preserve the advantages of party
democracy, without its fatal flaws?

If our search is to be productive, it will have to take a long hard look at what is wrong with existing systems. It is unfortunate but true that bad government has become the rule, not the exception. It is not an exaggeration to say that all the major Western countries, and Japan, are badly governed. Yet all are grossly over-governed. The paradox is disturbing. Among the major countries, I can discern no exception to the rule. The variations in badness are matters of degree. Among the smaller countries, however, there are one or two shining exceptions—of which by far the most striking is Switzerland.

The phenomenon of bad government has reached disaster-levels over the past few years. It threatens the survival of our pluralist and representative societies. For government is central to the whole concept of the State: when government breaks down and anarchy takes over, the State is in the process of disintegration. In a previous work,* I gave reasons for the necessity of the State and examined competing philosophical conceptions of it, with examples. The moral justification of the State is that it offers the weak protection against the strong. But there is more to it than that. Various criteria have been named or postulated, for the subject is one which has agitated many minds. My own selection consists of three criteria only: the safety and security of the people (the defence of the weak); defence against external enemies; and the preservation of the value of money. In my view, that is to say, these are the minimum requirements, the *raison d'être* of the State. It follows, if the criteria are accepted, that any government which fails on any of these points, or any two of them, or all three, is a bad government.† But it may be objected, what about education? And Welfare? Housing and sport? Culture

---

* *A Theory of Conflict* (Hamish Hamilton, 1974).

† In a speech on 6 May 1978, Mrs Margaret Thatcher, the British Conservative leader, lumped internal security with defence as one item; listed welfare as another; and put economic management where I would put money. I find these criteria less than satisfactory as a list of *essentials*. It is instructive to compare these lists (Mrs Thatcher's and my own) with a more famous selection—that of Adam Smith in scattered passages of Book V of *The Wealth of Nations*. For Smith, the first duty of the sovereign (his synonym for our State) is 'protecting the society from the violence and invasion of other independent societies'; the second duty is that of 'protecting, as far as possible, every member of the society from the injustice or oppression of every other member of it'; and the third is the provision and maintenance of necessary public institutions and public works, such as roads, bridges, harbours and the like. That such things are necessary, and that most of them cannot be expected to pay for themselves, is evident (although the debate on the ownership of certain utilities, such as railways and other forms of public transport, is unending). The scope of this work excludes any full discussion of Smith's 'third duty', and my comment on it is simply that the provision of public utilities must not be allowed to contribute to inflation: I stick, therefore, to my own third essential. Smith's first two duties are the same as mine.

and leisure? To say nothing of State intervention in commerce and industry. . . .

The answer to such objections is really very simple: some or all of the activities just listed may be desirable, to a greater or lesser extent. But none of them, taken in isolation, is an *essential* requisite of State and government. This applies even to education through all its phases. A government which delivers such items yet neglects security, defence, and the currency, is a bad government. A government which attends to the three essential needs is a good government. Having delivered them, it may turn its attention to other activities, should these be desirable, and should they be consistent with the requirements of the good administration of a country's finances.

Today, we have a plethora of unnecessary laws, a proliferation of the inessentials of government, a bureaucratic invasion of people's privacy, an ever-growing curtailment of individual liberties, and the three essential purposes of government are neglected or even ignored.

It is not difficult to prove the assertion that the major Western countries and Japan are badly governed. Fear stalks the streets of America's major cities. Old-age pensioners, and even younger people, walk the streets of New York at their peril. What has happened to the government's duty to watch after the safety of its citizens? As for security, in the sense of protection against the internal enemies of the State, it has simply been swept away in the wake of the great Watergate scandal. All the law-enforcement agencies are starved of the information and intelligence they need to do their jobs. The Soviet KGB functions with impunity in the United Nations headquarters in Manhattan, and swarms over Capitol Hill. The Federal Bureau of Investigation is banned from both. The police learn of the movements of Mafia gangsters after, not before, they have taken place. The Customs Department and the Internal Revenue tell the same story. Safety and security have collapsed in the world's greatest democracy.

What about defence? While successive American Administrations have fallen for the dangerous delusion of *'détente'*, the Soviet Union, with a global economy not much more than half the size of the American, has caught up and overtaken the United States in strategic capability, while already well ahead in conventional weapons. It is hardly an exaggeration to say that today the US does not protect its citizens adequately, that it neglects the requirements of security, that it is dangerously negligent in the protection of the great republic. For the remarks I have already made about law-enforcement agencies are every bit as true of the Central Intelligence Agency (destroyed as much by 'investigative' journalists and irresponsible Congressmen and Senators as by the KGB), while major decisions on armaments—such as the cancellation of the B1 bomber and suspension of plans to produce a neutron bomb—have played into the hands of the world's greatest expansionist power: the Soviet Union.

One would expect the custodians of the wealthiest economy in the world to present an example of financial and economic management. But the enormous resources of the United States and the prevalence of high skills and technology have served, rather, as inducements for profligacy and mismanagement. Of course inflation at 6 per cent was minute by Latin American standards. But the national cost of living had increased by 75 per cent in the decade from 1966 to 1976, and the country suffered from bureaucratic gigantism and soaring taxes. In June 1978 the fury of over-burdened taxpayers exploded in sunny California, when citizens voted two to one in the referendum in favour of slashing property tax by 57 per cent. The voters had had enough: they were no longer going to put up with the follies of those whom they had put in power.

For three decades the American dollar had provided the strong currency that guaranteed the stability of the gold-exchange standard created by the Bretton Woods Conference. Then in 1971 America devalued the dollar, by allowing gold to find its own price level. Things could never be the same again, and today the US dollar is outstripped in firmness and reliability by the Japanese yen, the Swiss franc and the German D-Mark.

Wherever you look, it is the same story with only minor variations. In Britain, the degree of individual security is not yet anywhere near as low as in the USA, but the crime rate has been soaring for some years and many urban areas have become unsafe. On defence, the British record is pitiful: successive cuts in defence budgets have left the British Isles frighteningly vulnerable to external enemies. As for the pound sterling, once the envy of the world, its purchasing power dwindled by two-thirds between 1938—the year of the Munich surrender—and 1956—the year of the Suez humiliation. Between 1972 and 1977, inflation raised prices by 122 per cent. During the same years, unemployment rose from 3·7 per cent to 6 per cent. Externally, the pound is an object of derision in many countries and a source of humiliation for the British traveller abroad. Nor can the blame be attached to only one of our major political parties. The great British inflation began under the Tories with the self-indulgent folly of the printing press. It was compounded under Labour which borrowed heavily abroad to sustain more legislative follies at home.

In France, although the rise in consumer prices is a constant source of popular grumbling, prices rose by 'only' 69 per cent during the same period of 1972–77. Although there was much to criticise in General de Gaulle's decision to go it alone in defence, by pulling France out of the integrated military command of NATO, the strong medicine of self-reliance had acted as a stimulant, and the French performance in defence was a good deal more impressive than Britain's. But in France, too, crimes of violence were on the increase, and so therefore was insecurity. Gangs of Algerian youths prowled in the technological wasteland of the new Metro lines, which were automated and virtually unmanned.

The efficient West Germans have kept the value of their money higher than most, and perform reasonably well on defence, bearing in mind treaty limitations imposed on them as the price of defeat in the Second World War. Security is another story. One of the worst gangs of terrorists in the world plagues the Federal Republic and boasts among its achievements the murders of a judge, the head of the employers' federation and the president of a bank.

In Japan, the price for defeat in the Second World War was a constitution imposed by the American conquerors, under which the nation renounced nuclear weapons or indeed armed forces other than for self-defence. By the mid-1970s, the Self-Defence Forces had nevertheless grown to impressive proportions, but the habit of reliance upon American power died hard, and it was perhaps unfair to criticise this great and formidable people for failing to provide an adequate defence against potential enemies. Crowded in largely barren islands, and painfully dependent upon imports of steel, oil and other vital raw materials, the Japanese had canalised their energies into economic development with spectacular success. A unique combination of paternalism, self-discipline, ingenuity and hard work, and a risk-taking banking system of great flexibility, had contributed to this success story. But affluence and high technology did not suffice to eliminate the tradition of violence in Japanese politics; and in the United Red Army Japan had one of the most virulent terrorist gangs in the world. For several years, the Japanese authorities were unable to complete and operate a second airport for Tokyo because of the effective violence of protest demonstrations.

By far the worst of our case-examples is of course Italy—where the tradition of central government has never been very strong (even under Mussolini). For years, a large and powerful Communist Party —the biggest outside the Communist bloc—had systematically attacked and undermined the symbols of authority, such as the police, the armed forces and the judiciary. The result, inevitably, was a paralysed economy; defence forces so penetrated by hostile elements that in the event of a crisis they would probably be useless; and surely the world's record in insecurity, with about 1,000 extremist gangs operating with apparent impunity. Where else has a former prime minister been kidnapped and held at the pleasure of political extremists, then contemptuously killed? As these lines were being written, the State had almost ceased to exist.

And yet, turning briefly now to peaceful and prosperous Switzerland, what do we find? An almost negligible inflation rate, probably no more than 0·5 per cent in 1978. A country with a gun in every household, yet virtually without crime. And a defence system so efficient that it has served as a model for beleaguered Israel. And yet, Switzerland too is a pluralist and representative society; and moreover a society of different races and languages cohabiting in peace. Good government, therefore, is still possible in the latter decades of the twentieth century.

Why, then, are we so badly governed? And why at the same time are we so grossly over-governed? I have studied and thought about this problem for many years, and I have come to an inescapable conclusion (which I share incidentally with the late General de Gaulle): that the central cause of bad government everywhere, the cause that dominates over all others, is the party political system.

The party system might perhaps work, as it once did, with a restricted or even weighted franchise; but on the basis of equal and universal suffrage, it is everywhere a disaster. Competing political parties determine their promises on the basis, not of the needs of the people and nation, but of the requirements of sectional popularity at election times. They promise knowing they cannot fulfil. Or, worse still, they attempt to fulfil evil or irresponsible promises, thereby compounding the disease of bad government. Occasionally, the party system throws up a great leader. But very rarely. The constant trend, over the decades, is downward. The prevailing tendency is towards the lowest common denominator. Knaves, incompetents, or even crooks come to the fore. So busy are the politicians with their favourite schemes or absurd prescriptions, that they multiply their unnecessary laws while neglecting the elementary requirements that justify their own existence. Moreover, the party system—far from protecting and guaranteeing the pluralist and representative society—leaves it in the end defenceless against its enemies.

For let nobody suppose that the writer of these lines is against the pluralist or representative society. What is at stake is the survival of the things that make this type of society worth preserving. Manifestly, the party system does not do this: it is a cause of disintegration, not a means for preservation.

The exception which justifies this rule, and to which I devote a chapter of this book, is Switzerland. It is a highly instructive exception, the reason for which resides in one word: decentralisation. The Swiss mitigate the evils of the party system by allowing the citizens to take nearly all decisions affecting their daily lives at the local level. In effect, the Swiss Confederation is a collection of self-governing city-States, which give real meaning to the concept of choice. If the inhabitants of a Swiss commune or canton wish to spend money, say, on a new stretch of road or a new municipal library, they know the cost will have to be met out of local taxes. This admirable system removes a major instrument of tyranny from the hands of central legislators, by ensuring that the taxpayers do not pay for somebody else's consumption but only for the amenities which they themselves consume.

This is real, as distinct from apparent, choice. But the Swiss example does not prove the value of the party system, although it offers a way of reducing its ravages. Many people may object that surely the party system is essential to a pluralist and representative society? My own opinion is that it is not, and that the time has come when it is imperative to explore alternatives to the present and surviving party systems, while preserving the things that make democracy desirable: choice, and the possibility of changing one's government peacefully and periodically at the polls.

There are no fully satisfactory political systems and many Utopias are on offer. But a system that did these things, and provided the chance of good government, would be worth trying.

TWO

POLITICS OF THE TRIVIAL

Some of the best journalism today—readable, witty and consistently funny—is in the work of the parliamentary sketch-writers. And among them perhaps the best in Britain are those irrepressible alternating twins of the *Daily Telegraph*, Frank Johnson* and John O'Sullivan, who compete with each other in style, dexterity and ebullience. This is a symptom of the political *malaise* of the United Kingdom in the 1970s. For the subject matter of the parliamentary sketch-writers is the elected fauna of the House of Commons—the politicians who have become an object of fun and derision. In a way, this is grossly unfair, for Members of Parliament are no worse, by and large, than other sectors of the population. They are hardworking (and indeed have to be, given the absurd hours and schedules they impose upon themselves), no more dishonest than other people, and normally well-intentioned. And they are, by definition, more powerful than the rest of the population. Even MPs in Opposition exert power by the energy and assiduity with which they oppose for the sake of opposing, and try, sometimes successfully, to defeat the majority. The nature of this power, and the legitimacy conferred upon those who exercise it by the processes of the popular vote, might seem to endow their situation with some awe and solemnity. Yet their reward is satire and irreverence.

The decision, taken in 1978, to broadcast in part the proceedings of Parliament has merely deepened the irreverence with which politicians are regarded. Anybody (such as myself, as it happens) who had the misfortune of exposure to the broadcasting of parliamentary proceedings in Australia could have predicted that this would be the outcome. And clearly, it would be infinitely worse if Parliament were televised as well. Observation suggests a trend which is probably by its nature unprovable but will not, I think, be widely disputed: that for years the best young brains have been decreasingly attracted to the prospects of a career in politics, but have opted instead for business, industry, the professions or finance.

I am not an advocate of the utterly open society, as I hold that a State that ceases to have secrets also rapidly ceases to have authority.

* Mr Johnson has now left that newspaper.

We do not live in a Utopia of universal friendship and goodwill, but in a real world in which there is no shortage of enemies: a 'secret' made available to all is available to enemies as well as allies. I believe, however, that the *Sunday Times* (a newspaper with which I am rarely in sympathy) served the cause of freedom when it fought and won its case for the publication of the late R. H. S. Crossman's *Diaries*. It is impossible to read them or even to dip into them, without being struck by the triviality and even the self-seeking tawdriness of politicians at work. Since politics is about power, this is not altogether surprising, but it is still possible to be amazed by the evidence of pettiness and irrelevance in the decision-making process. There is no consistent philosophy of government or consistency of approach. There is no, or hardly any, serious discussion of issues on their merits, or in the light of the national interest as a whole. Speeches are made, points are scored and in the end decisions taken, for party advantage, to discomfit rivals within the party team, or as a sop to the ideological extreme Left. Crossman was of course recording what he saw of the Labour Party in office between 1964 and 1968.* But the irrelevance and essential frivolity of a party in Opposition is perhaps even more striking, as any issue of Hansard will show. The Opposition—so runs the cliché—has a duty to oppose. This means in practice that with very rare exceptions the government's proposals are not considered on their merits. They are opposed merely because the Tories (or Labour as the case may be) happen to be in Opposition. The criterion is not necessarily the national interest. It is more likely to be the standing of the party in the public opinion polls, or the search for support in the next general elections.

I now cull from the Crossman *Diaries* some examples of the system at work. In December 1966 Harold Wilson's alternate attempts to bully and cajole Ian Smith of Rhodesia out of his Unilateral Declaration of Independence had failed.

Harold Wilson's main concern was the picture of Smith we should give the British public. . . . Should we publish all the dirt about him which had come out on the *Tiger* and so try to destroy him, or should we regard him as something worth preserving? I soon discovered that Harold Wilson wasn't interested in planning psychological warfare because he hadn't decided what he wanted to

---

* Richard Crossman, *The Diaries of a Cabinet Minister, Volumes I, II and III* (Hamish Hamilton and Jonathan King, 1975–76). For an account of official attempts to suppress the *Diaries*, see Hugo Young, *The Crossman Affair* (Cape, 1976).

happen in Salisbury. What he was doing was to work himself up for his swing from his attempt to appease Smith on the *Tiger* to an attempt this coming Thursday to appease his anti-Smith back-benchers in the House of Commons [Vol III, 152–53].

The big Rhodesia debate came on 8 December. 'It started,' writes Crossman, 'with a perfectly decent lightweight speech from Douglas-Home.'

Then Harold began. As I suspected from his attitude on Tuesday morning he had swung right back. Having come to the edge of an agreement with Smith for which he had paid with very heavy concessions, he had now swung back to the other extreme and made an ultra-moralist speech addressed in particular to the 40 or 50 left-wingers who'd have refused him their vote if he'd got his agreement with Smith. The central theme was that this was a great moral issue, that anybody who was against Wilson was for Smith, that the Tories were the allies of the rebels in Rhodesia, and he ended with a peroration quoting Abraham Lincoln addressed to the workers of Lancashire and which worked up the Labour Members to such a passion that when he sat down they gave him a standing ovation, waving their Order Papers. I found the Chief Whip was standing beside me and I also rose though I couldn't bring myself to wave my Order Paper [Ibid., p. 154].

Next day, Wilson 'was wild with fury at the badness of the press'.

'The press are contemptible and corrupt. Unbearable! Look at what they have done to my speech.' 'True,' I said, 'but if you lambast the Tory leader you mustn't expect the Tory press to be wildly enthusiastic. And then you have also got to notice that Reg Paget has made the headlines by resigning the Party Whip. I knew it was a mistake to let him resign.' 'What?' he said. 'Yes,' I said, 'I knew Reg Paget wanted to vote against us and John told him he should resign first. I think we shouldn't have let him resign but kept him in, let him vote and then expelled him. Then we wouldn't have had the headlines against you which we've got today.' [Ibid., p. 155.]

Always, the concern of politicians is with their 'image'. Never was this more so than at the beginning of 1967, when Harold Wilson saw his chance of playing the role of a 'man of peace' and helping to bring the Vietnam War to an end. Between 6 and 13 February, the Soviet Premier, Kosygin, paid an official visit to London. The

Prime Minister contrived to give the impression that he and Kosygin might have been able to act as intermediaries between the Americans and North Vietnamese. But it was soon clear that this was pure illusion and, possibly, self-delusion. For Tuesday 14 February, Richard Crossman records that:

> Harold was in his more elevated form, telling us how he had 'the absolute confidence of L.B.J.' and now had 'won the absolute confidence' of Kosygin. Then he told us graphically how on two occasions—first on Friday and then on Saturday—they'd been on the very edge of success and how it had been dashed away and how disappointed they were. But, he added, one must be fair to both sides. We must not be anti-American. On the other hand, we must not be anti-North Vietnam. What we should rejoice at is that the mechanism for peace negotiations has now been established and in the coming months they would succeed [Vol 3, p. 237].

In fact, the Americans had resumed bombing after a brief truce to coincide with the four-day Lunar New Year in Vietnam. Rather waspishly, Crossman contrasts the Cabinet minutes reporting on Harold Wilson's little speech at 10 Downing Street, and what he actually said.

> 'We had taken advantage of the opportunity [as the minutes put it] to try to ascertain whether some contact could be established between the American and North Vietnamese Governments. There had appeared to be some prospect of success in this attempt at one stage but in the end it had failed and the United States' bombing of North Vietnam had now started again.'
> What a contrast there is between those words and what Harold actually said in Cabinet. I vividly remember the PM's claiming that he was twice on the edge of peace—by which he meant prolonging the bombing peace. The cautious record smoothed out the exaggerations [Ibid., pp. 237–38].

Throughout the *Diaries* Richard Crossman revels in his self-cast role as the Cabinet's *enfant terrible*, never resisting the temptation to speak his own mind whatever the consequences. As a result, few of his colleagues come out with any credit. One of those most discredited is in fact Harold Wilson's successor as Prime Minister, James Callaghan. In January 1968 Crossman records a Home Affairs meeting at which Callaghan presented a paper on certain aspects of the Race Relations Bill which he had inherited from Roy Jenkins.

Once again he was his new breezy irresponsible self. In yesterday's Cabinet he had opposed with all his old-fashioned Great Britain jingoism the cuts he had been trying to impose as Chancellor. Now as he sat down beside me at the Committee he said *sotto voce*, 'I haven't got a liberal image to maintain like my predecessor; I am going to be a simple Home Secretary.'

And so on. The characters who people the Crossman *Diaries* emerge as irresponsible players in an elaborate private game, saying one thing one day and the opposite the next according to the 'image' the player wishes to project to his audience—that fiction known as 'public opinion'. Or alternatively, to impress their colleagues or Parliament. It is scarcely a discovery that politicians so behave, nor should one assume that Richard Crossman was overstating the behaviour of his colleagues. The politicians of the French Fourth Republic behaved in much the same way, and so today do the politicians of the Italian republic. The Italians indeed have a word for it: a politician who treats politics as a game is called a *politicante*, with a pejorative flavour absent from the more neutral *politico*. That there are honourable exceptions is not in dispute, nor is it the issue: statesmen are rare and exceptional men (or women). What is a matter of concern is that such politicians are so clearly the rule, not the exception. And one is entitled to ask whether it is the system that is to blame, and if so which aspects of the system. Is universal suffrage the real cause of our political mediocrity? Or is it the party system? I have already suggested that it may be the combination of the two. Both are historically of relatively recent origin, yet both seem deeply anchored in our traditions. Is it possible to rid ourselves of either or both, and yet remain a democracy?

The case for universal suffrage rests upon two propositions, which it has become unfashionable to challenge: the sovereignty of the people, and their supposed equality. Both are again, in historical terms, very recent conceptions. Traditionally, sovereignty was vested in the *sovereign*, who had either inherited it from his father, or had asserted it by force over his rivals. The Greek city-States were of course republics, and the Romans set up a republic of their own in 509 BC, but although these ancient republican experiments were elective, such popular sovereignty as existed was the privilege of a relatively minute number of free men in a teeming population of slaves. It was not until the eighteenth century that the notion of the sovereignty of the people was popularised by such writers as Rousseau, Locke, Mill and Paine.

From the start, the advocates of popular sovereignty and of true democracy faced logical dilemmas that have never been satisfactorily resolved. If the people are indeed sovereign, then logically the franchise must be universal. But universality presupposes equality, and while 'equality' may be a dream, aspiration or theory, the reality of inequality is a pervasive fact. People may be equal in the sight of God (a question I leave to the theologians) and in theory may certainly be equal in the sight of the law. But they are indisputably unequal both in their natural endowments and in their actual attainments. Some people are tall, others are short, and more are medium. Some are fat, others are thin. Some are clever, others are stupid. At the top end are the geniuses, at the lowest level the cretins. Moreover, among people of roughly equal intelligence, some will be prudent in character, and others profligate. Take two men earning the same salaries. One will save and die rich; the other will indulge himself and gamble or spend his potential fortune, dying poor. It has always seemed to be a pity that so much time and emotion should be expended on lamenting such facts or pretending that they are not true. Lenin postulated the perfectibility of Soviet Man and Stalin gave his full backing to a charlatan called Lysenko who thought he had proved that it was possible to inherit acquired characteristics. Human nature obstinately went on as before, and in due course Lysenko was discredited. I may wish I could run as fast as Jesse Owens, or punch as swiftly as Muhammad Ali or lift staggering weights as do the great Soviet weightlifters. But I know that I could never rival such achievements and lose no sleep over it.

In practice, and whatever the words and the theory may say, there is no universal suffrage anywhere on earth, nor could there be. Babies are an obvious exception to the rule of universal franchise (and incidentally, in Britain Church of England clergymen, but not ministers of other religions, are debarred from being candidates for election to Parliament). Although in line with fashionable trends and calculations of electoral popularity, the voting age, in Britain and some other countries, has been reduced from twenty-one to eighteen, this leaves the seventeen-year-olds (for instance) without the vote. In Britain, for that matter, 'universal' suffrage came only in 1928, with the extension of the franchise to women. Yet in Switzerland, by common consent one of the most democratic countries on earth, women only got the vote in 1971; and in some cantons they still do not have it. It remains to be seen whether Swiss women will make as little of their opportunities as English or American women.

Let us note in passing that universal suffrage brought Hitler to power in 1933, and that it regularly sustains the two most monstrous tyrannies on earth—in the USSR and the Chinese People's Republic. Clearly, it offers in itself no guarantee whatever of the preservation of the freedoms we associate with pluralist and representative societies. One is therefore entitled to ask not merely whether it is possible, but also whether it is necessarily desirable.

Democratic theory rests not merely upon the assumption of universal suffrage but upon another assumed condition which is nearly always impossible: the belief that the people can govern themselves, or that Lincoln's government of the people, by the people and for the people, is a possibility. Clearly, except in very small communities, it is simply impossible. What makes Switzerland more democratic than other democracies (whatever the state of feminine suffrage) is the fact that the cantons of the Swiss Confederation are small enough for self-government, while the exercise of power is decentralised. In this, they resemble the ancient Greek city-States.

In the major democracies, the centralisation of power renders universal suffrage ineffectual at all times except general elections or the occasional referendum. True democracy being impossible, the people are supposed to exercise their theoretical power by delegation —normally to political parties. Even at such times, the voter's freedom of choice is rigorously circumscribed. He is supposed to choose between candidates, but he has no say in whether people are candidates or not. This pre-selection is done for him by the party machines. Moreover, he or she chooses between candidates, not as a rule on the basis of their personal qualities, but in the knowledge that each represents a party with a programme.

In practice, the programme is more important than the party, or than the merit of respective candidates. If a candidate has exceptional qualities of intelligence and character, but happens to represent a party whose programme you reject, the choice is unattractive. For the voter who likes certain aspects of the Labour Programme and others in the Tory offering, the element of choice tends to become meaningless. Moreover, under the special absurdities of the British system of simple majority and winner-take-all, anybody who votes for a losing candidate has in effect been disfranchised, and will be represented in Parliament by a candidate not of his choosing.

A particularly objectionable feature of the democratic system is the doctrine of the political mandate. Having won an election, a political party assumes that it has thereby acquired a 'mandate' to apply every detail of its electoral programme. But a party programme, however edited and simplified for the needs of vote-catching, is necessarily a complicated set of propositions, many of which will be unintelligible to the uninitiated—that is, to the great majority of the electorate—either because of inadequate intelligence or lack of expertise, or simply because the average voter has other things to think about and occupy his time. Many voters would be horrified if they realised what they were letting themselves in for by voting for a particular party's programme; and may learn about it when intentions are transformed into bills which become acts and laws.

A fairer and genuinely more democratic procedure is that of the referendum, practised with great frequency and success in Switzerland and to a lesser degree in other countries; and in Britain only once over the controversial and extremely complex issue of membership of the European Economic Community. Yet here again the initiative rests entirely with the government, which will decide on the issue and on the form of the questions to be put to the voters. Some issues are simple enough for universal understanding, and will affect every member of the community. Such issues might be whether to sell liquor or to open the theatres on Sundays, or to ban smoking in all public places. On such issues, it is reasonable and feasible to seek the view of the electorate as a whole, although the view of the majority would not necessarily be the sensible one. Everybody knows that if the issue of restoring the death penalty were put to the test of a referendum in the United Kingdom there would be an overwhelming majority in favour. Yet the House of Commons has long had a built-in majority against. To say this is not to express a value judgement on whether the death penalty is a good thing or a bad one; merely to comment on the absurdity of democratic theory.

Moreover, there are many issues of such complexity that it is unfair to expect the electorate to grasp them in all their detail. One such was surely that of British membership of the EEC, yet this was still at the time of writing the only issue ever put to the British people in the form of a referendum.

A word here about elites. For years, it has been fashionable to denounce 'elitism'; since everybody is held to be equal to everybody else—women and men, blacks and whites, the dull and the bright, the swift and the slow, the rich and the poor—even to admit the existence of an elite is to be considered reactionary. And yet, it is not difficult to demonstrate that every society has an elite, and that the same is necessarily true of all political systems, including the democratic ones. In political terms, the elite does not necessarily consist of men and women of wealth and educational privilege (although it does not necessarily exclude them either). The political elite consists exclusively of those aspiring candidates lucky to be picked as official candidates at general elections. The successful may be poor and possibly dull, although they may also be rich and bright. All that can be said with certainty is that they will reflect the views acceptable to the relatively tiny group of people who sit on the party selection committees. The Marxist–Leninists grasped this important reality some years ago in Great Britain. Invariably rejected and humiliated at the polls, they decided to make good their deficiencies by worming their way into the party machine at the party level. The doubling of the strength of the extreme Left in the Parliamentary Labour Party in the 1974 elections was a tribute to their tactical skill.

Is democracy, then, a fraud? The short answer is yes. But not for the reasons advanced by the Marxist–Leninists, who argue that democracy is necessarily fraudulent because the parties, irrespective of their labels, merely reflect the class structure of society. Every time a Marxist–Leninist, posing under another label, penetrates a selection committee, he disproves the validity of his own propositions. It is a fraud for morally neutral reasons—because universal suffrage and democracy are both practical impossibilities. The fraud lies in the pretence that they are not.

It does not follow that the people who hold such views are themselves necessarily fraudulent. Very few of them are. The great majority no doubt sincerely believe in the things that are self-evidently impossible and would be deeply disturbed at the suggestion that they are not. Their attitude, which involves sincerity and idealism, has nothing whatever to do with the Marxian criticism of 'bourgeois' democracy and of political parties as no more than the representatives of oppressive class interests. This is not to deny the correlation between classes and political parties. But it should be remembered that the Communists regard even Social Democratic parties with contempt—a greater contempt than that reserved for Conservative or Liberal parties. That is why, once in power, they invariably either destroy or absorb existing Social Democratic parties, and when in Opposition seek to penetrate them and control them from within. But in any case, the class/party connection is increasingly blurred by social mobility and the growing affluence of the factory worker. In Britain, the Parliamentary Labour Party increasingly consists of professional people with impeccable middle-class backgrounds. Nor does this prevent many workers voting Conservative at general elections: if they did not, the Conservative Party would never be in power. Similarly, a large and probably growing section of the business community supports the Labour Party in office, and with funds outside, in the belief that a Labour government is better able to deal with the trade unions than a Conservative one.

THREE

WHEN FREEDOM DIES

I have pointed out that there are, broadly speaking, three constitutional options open to peoples and nations. One is the pluralistic and representative system usually known as democracy. The second is the authoritarian type, usually with a military participation. And the third is the totalitarian, which I prefer to call 'totalist', because there is nothing sacrosanct about 'totalitarian' and 'totalist' is shorter. But in political and economic terms (as distinguished from constitutional), there are really only two broad tendencies: collectivism, and individual freedom. In Britain, of course, as in many other countries, there is what is known as a 'mixed economy'; but what really matters is the *tendency*. Is the country moving towards more collectivism, or towards greater individual and economic freedom? These questions lie at the heart of our dilemmas and of this book.

No issue is more widely misunderstood, because it is systematically misrepresented, than the connection between collectivism and tyranny. All collectivist regimes in the world are totalist tyrannies, and the more collectivist they are, the greater the tyranny. Thus, under the Chinese People's Republic, where the individual has lost all rights and nearly all economic activities are collectivised, the tyranny is pretty well total. The only freedom left to the peasant is that of cultivating a small private plot of land, the produce of which he can sell on the open market. Instructively, this contribution is out of all proportion to the size of the holdings, and at times of severe food shortages, the individual farmer has rescued the collectivist empire. The same is true of the private plots in the Soviet Union.

In Cambodia, when the dreadful Khmer Rouges came to power with the collapse of the American military effort, a gigantic effort to collectivise the entire population was initiated with an unprecedented brutality, so that proportionately more people lost their lives in Cambodia than under any other tyrannical regime of the twentieth century, including Nazi Germany and Stalin's Russia. That the rule is a valid one is shown by the fact that in Communist countries that have not pushed collectivism to the ultimate (such as Poland, where agriculture remains predominantly in private hands and where the party has stopped short of ruthless persecution of the Church for fear of the consequences in a deeply Catholic country, or Yugoslavia, where some individual initiative is encouraged), individual freedom has not been totally extinguished.

I deliberately used the words 'collectivism' and 'collectivist' in the preceding paragraph, but it will be noted that in each case the proper synonyms could have been 'Marxism–Leninism and 'Marxist–Leninist'. It is fair, therefore, to assume that there is a connection between Marxism–Leninism and tyranny. At all events, all Marxist–Leninist regimes established anywhere on earth since 1917 have become tyrannies, to a greater or lesser degree, and all are marked by political and ideological control of the judiciary, arbitrary arrest and concentration camps, and the extinguishing of a wide range of normally accepted freedoms, including that of marriage (where it involves a foreign national), internal and external travel, private property and choice of employment.

Would it be fair to go further still, and to equate 'collectivism' and 'socialism'? This is a difficult one, for no political term in current use is vaguer than 'socialism'. The Soviet Union and the Communist countries of Eastern Europe term themselves, collectively, 'the Socialist Commonwealth'. The late President Nasser of Egypt boasted of 'Arab Socialism', and General Ne Win's cult of scarcity in Burma is self-styled 'Burmese Socialism'. The near-totalist regimes in Algeria and Guinea likewise call themselves 'Socialist'. Mr Eric Heffer and other members of the Tribune Group in the Parliamentary Labour Party are in the habit of telling us that what goes on in the Soviet Union is not socialism, and indeed that socialism as they understand it does not exist anywhere on earth. One may perhaps be forgiven, therefore, if one supposes that the 'socialism' they want to impose upon us is a kind of Utopian fantasy.

Perhaps the connection between socialism and tyranny is best illustrated by considering the differences between 'social democracy' and 'socialism'. It is possible for a government to nationalise various industries and increase the range of social services, as the Attlee government did between 1945 and 1951, and preserve the democratic freedoms. This is essentially what social democracy is about, and in the inevitable contest between socialism and democracy, the social democrat (if he is sincere in his beliefs) gives the edge to democracy, not socialism. Latterly, because of the increasing penetration of the British Labour Party by totalist elements, it has become fashionable for people who used to describe themselves as social democrats to say that they are 'democratic socialists'. A case in point is the former Education Minister, Shirley Williams, who has taken to using the term without any apparent awareness of its incongruity.

It is possible to have socialism and it is possible to have democracy; what is impossible is to have both, unless the dose of socialism is relatively small. It is the belated realisation of this painful truth that has caused so many social democrats to desert the Labour Party or even politics in recent years. One needs only to mention Mr Roy Jenkins, lured from Westminster to Brussels by an admittedly enticing salary; Mr Brian Walden, stepping into the shoes of Mr Callaghan's son-in-law as a television personality when the latter was appointed Britain's Ambassador to Washington; Mr Reg Prentice, crossing the floor to the Conservatives; Mr Woodrow Wyatt, who put his disillusionment in book form in *What's Left of the Labour Party?* (Sidgwick & Jackson, 1977); or Mr Paul Johnson, formerly the editor of the *New Statesman* but ready in 1978 to accept the annual Freedom Award presented by Aims for Freedom and Enterprise (formerly Aims of Industry). If I, as a non-party observer of politics, say these things about socialism and democracy, I scarcely expect the converted to listen. But it is surely another matter when social democrats realise the dangers of socialism.

It is worth examining just why socialism and real democracy are incompatible. The political consequences of economic socialism have been extensively analysed, at times with great insight and brilliance, for instance in the works of Professor Hayek, *The Road to Serfdom* (1944) and *The Constitution of Liberty* (1960). If all economic activity is State-owned and centrally planned, then all individual choice about employment and consumer needs is thereby removed. But there is another argument, to which insufficient attention has been paid. In the first of its two manifestos of 1974, the Labour Party called for 'a fundamental and irreversible shift in the balance of power and wealth in favour of working people and their families'. It is the word 'irreversible' that is incompatible with democracy.

It is obvious that if full socialism is to be introduced, whether in Britain or in any other country, it must be 'irreversible' if it is to work. You cannot introduce socialism under one government, and dismantle it in the next; and to continue to play this see-saw game would be frivolous and dangerously irresponsible. In fact, what has happened since the Labour government came to power in 1945 has been that successive Tory administrations were, by and large, content to administer the mixed economy more or less as it stood when they came to power—with the sole exception of the steel industry, which was denationalised, then renationalised. But we are no longer talking about social democracy or a relatively mild dose of socialism. We are told that Labour intends to nationalise all the banks and insurance companies and a wide range of industries, in addition to those already seized by the State. If this happened, it would indeed be hard to reverse.

Supposing a Labour government did these things but clung to the illusion that they were compatible with democracy, and therefore allowed a further free general election. Supposing this election were won by the Conservatives with an overwhelming majority and a mandate in favour of fundamental change. Would the Socialists allow the Tories to reverse the 'irreversible'? Could this be done at all without a grave social crisis, and perhaps a violent confrontation?*

The Communists, Trotskyists and other Marxist–Leninists who for many years have burrowed away within the Labour Party to bring it under their control, have not done so for fun or to pass the time of day. They mean business. Indeed the Communist Party of Great Britain, in its 1977 manifesto, has been candid enough to spell out the exceptions to its professed abandonment of violence. If the wicked bourgeois and capitalists tried to dismantle socialism, they would fight—meaning they would cause their followers in the powerful trade unions to organise major strikes without excluding violent action. For all these reasons, people who call themselves 'democratic socialists' are either unaware of the meaning of the words, or stupid or ill-intentioned. The end result of collectivism, socialism and irreversible change can only be the totalist State.

It is not the least of the structural absurdities of the party system that it paves the way for the enemies of democracy. It is supremely important to understand what freedom means and to grasp that limitations must be imposed on its exercise if it is to survive. Freedom that is not available to the individual and his immediate dependants is not freedom at all. As a free man, I claim the right to change my place of employment or to become self-employed; to marry the person of my choice; to have a choice in education; to travel freely inside my country and out; to hold whatever currency I choose to hold. I claim also the right to hold whatever opinions I wish, and to read and see whatever takes my fancy. I claim the right to join, or not to join, an organisation, and to hold and advocate whatever political or philosophical or religious views I wish to hold and advocate. But I do not claim the right to impose my views on others, to compel them to listen to things they do not wish to hear (such as piped 'music' in public places). Nor do I claim the right to impose 'irreversible' change upon my fellow men and women.

* These lines were written before the general elections of 3 May 1979.

The great paradox of pluralism is its tolerance of the intolerant. We do not permit criminals to advocate the benefits of crime in public print or on radio or television. Yet we permit the avowed enemies of freedom to compete for political power by foul means as well as fair, thus conniving at the destruction of freedom. The distinction between advocacy and power is a vital one. We have allowed it to be blurred. It is entirely right and proper that the advocates of Marxism–Leninism should be able to express their views, and even to propagate them. A similar freedom must be available to Fascists and Nazis, who are no worse and no better. What is intolerable is that groups and parties based on these creeds, which are repugnant to the great majority of the people, should be given the opportunity to come to power. The results of a referendum in any Western country would be a foregone conclusion if the following questions were asked:

—Are you in favour of sending political dissidents to psychiatric hospitals?
—Are you in favour of political control of the judiciary?
—Are you in favour of a regime that restricts internal travel to holders of a passport?
—Are you in favour of concentration camps for 'enemies of the State'?

This dismal list could be indefinitely extended. Each item on it is a characteristic of collectivist or Marxist–Leninist regimes. Each item would be the inevitable consequence of allowing Marxist–Leninists to gain political power in this or any other country. But the questions are not put in this form, or indeed at all. The electorate are merely asked to choose between two parties, the leaders of both being apparently reasonable and moderate people. The Labour Party does not advertise the fact that its party machinery and its National Executive Committee are in the hands of collectivist extremists. It does not advertise its heavy dependence upon the block votes and the funds of trade unions, many of which are in the hands of Marxist–Leninists. The public is therefore deceived, and the deception is intentional. But it is important to remember the reality, and to draw the necessary lessons from the facts.

The Subversion of Labour

The story of the subversion of the British Labour Party has been told, ably and in detail, by Woodrow Wyatt in the book already mentioned, and by Stephen Haseler in *The Death of British Democracy*

(Paul Elek, 1976). I shall not recount it in comparable detail here, but draw attention to relevant points.

The special structure and history of the Labour Party in Britain needs to be remembered. Historically, the party is the emanation of the trade-union movement; and it is still the creature of the trade unions. Every year when the party meets in conference, the trade-union delegations dominate the show. Each delegation is empowered to vote in the name of the entire membership of the union, so that the Transport and General Workers' Union, for instance, carries about 2 million votes, and the Amalgamated Union of Engineering Workers $1\frac{1}{2}$ million. This is known as the block-vote system, and it is strange that a party which has always prided itself on its democratic tradition should tolerate so undemocratic a device. With 90 per cent of the votes at the party conference, the trade unions dictate the party's policy. What is more, they provide at least 80 per cent of the Labour Party's funds. Yet in most cases, the executive committees of the major unions are undemocratically elected, by a tiny portion of the total membership, many of whom are totally out of sympathy with the extremists who vote in their names. To give a typical example, Hugh Scanlon, for many years General Secretary of the AUEW—a Marxist and an ex-member of the British Communist Party—was elected by only 10 per cent of his union's membership. (Now of course, as a casualty or a beneficiary of the hated class system, he sits in the House of Lords.)

For many years, the political apathy of rank-and-file members of trade unions did not matter very much. For the leaders of the principal trade unions were determinedly, and indeed militantly, anti-Communist. Men like Arthur Deakin of the TGWU, George Woodcock, chairman of the Trades Union Congress, Sir Walter (later Lord) Citrine in his earlier day, and Ernest Bevin, understood the challenge of Marxism–Leninism and met it with determined action. The death of Deakin in 1955 was a major loss, not simply for the trade-union movement but also for the Labour Party, and therefore for the people of Britain. Deakin's death, and the death of other anti-Marxist trade-union leaders over the next few years, opened the doors for Marxist penetration. The Communist Party in particular had long planned its strategy. It was simply this: to gain control, or decisive influence, in the executive committees of the major trade unions, and thereby to exert a Marxist influence over the Labour Party itself. There was a time when the Communists kept such ideas to themselves, but in the 1970s they have felt self-confident enough to boast about it, and their approach is now well documented.

Perhaps the best illustration of the change in the Labour Party is provided by the contrasting attitudes of Harold Wilson during his two terms as Prime Minister. In 1966, during his first term, the country was almost paralysed by a prolonged strike of seamen. On 28 June, in a speech that has since been much-quoted, Mr Wilson explained the part played in this damaging affair by the Communist Party:

'The House will be aware,' he explained, 'that the Communist Party, unlike the major political parties, has at its disposal an efficient and disciplined industrial apparatus controlled from Communist Party headquarters. No major strike occurs anywhere in this country in any sector of industry in which that apparatus fails to concern itself.'

During the whole of his second period of high office, however, from 1974 to the late summer of 1976, Mr Wilson never once mentioned the Communist or Marxist threat to his own party. At the end of 1975, Labour's National Agent, Reg Underhill, submitted to the National Executive Committee a report on penetration of the party, mainly by Trotskyists. Mr Wilson personally intervened in favour of publishing the report, but he was outvoted on the NEC, by now controlled by the extremists, and said no more. It was only after he had resigned from the premiership that he began to make a series of speeches about the invasion of his party by the Marxists—which he had done nothing to prevent while in office.

His successor, James Callaghan, was equally impotent, whether by inclination or circumstances is not entirely clear. For instance Mr Callaghan intervened to prevent the appointment of a Trotskyist, Andy Bevan, as National Youth Organiser of the Labour Party; but like Mr Wilson over the Underhill Report he was outvoted by the NEC, and was unable to influence the decision of his own party. In the heyday of the social democratic Party, during the Attlee Government, a secret organisation to provide unattributable documentation about communism was set up within the Foreign Office, under the title of Information Research Department. Under Callaghan, and with Dr David Owen as Foreign Secretary, the IRD was closed down.* In 1939, the Labour Party banned individual membership both of the party and of a large number of Communist or Trotskyist front organisations. Out of office between 1970 and 1974 the party moved sharply Left-ward, in the sense that it was increasingly penetrated by Marxist–Leninists of various shades, and in 1973 this famous list of 'proscribed organisations' was discontinued. This was like opening the flood-gates, and the penetration

* See the *Observer*, 29 January 1978 and the *Guardian*, 27 January 1978.

grew apace. It was during the same period that the Marxist grip on the NEC tightened, but the real breakthrough came in 1975. Today (in mid-1978) the situation is that of the twenty-nine members of the National Executive Committee, seventeen are of the extreme Left. Meanwhile, the Trotskyists and other Marxist–Leninists were burrowing away in the constituency organisations, bringing more and more of them under their control.

In these new circumstances, the fact that so-called 'moderates' outnumber extremists in the Parliamentary Labour Party by about three to one is of relatively little importance. True, when a combination of socialist legislation and the unforeseen calamity of the quadrupling of oil prices had virtually bankrupted the country, the fact that 'moderates' were in power enabled Denis Healey, as Chancellor of the Exchequer, to apply a conservative economic and financial programme in effect dictated by the International Monetary Fund. In electoral terms this was unfortunate, since it gave the public at large the impression that the Labour Party had not changed; an impression which Mr Callaghan's avuncular and reassuring manner powerfully strengthened. To keep the Left happy, however, the government pursued an essentially Marxist foreign policy, especially in Africa.

Not surprisingly, the 'new' Labour Party of the 1970s openly fraternises with the Communists at home and abroad. Joan Maynard, MP, has spoken more than once at rallies organised by the Communist Party newspaper, the *Morning Star*. More than thirty Labour MPs are among the sponsors of an organisation styling itself the Anti-Nazi League and set up by the biggest Trotskyist organisation, Socialist Workers' Party. These examples could be multiplied.

The international links with the Soviet Union and its East European empire are even more striking and disquieting. Here again, past history has to be remembered. In 1949, the TUC took the initiative in the decision of free trade unions to withdraw from the World Federation of Trade Unions (WFTU) because it had passed under Communist domination. At the TUC Congress that year, Arthur Deakin declared: 'It is part of the Communist set-up that the trade unions are part of the State apparatus, answerable to the government, carrying out the policies and the dictates of the government on every occasion.'

As late as 1962, George Woodcock told Congress: 'We have been driven by bitter experience, not by theory, to the conclusion that there is and will be for some time ahead complete incompatibility between organisations known as trade unions on one side of the iron curtain and organisations known as trade unions on the other side.'

Only four years later, however, the TUC sent its first delegation to the Soviet Union, and since then it has sent visitors to all the East European countries, many of which have in turn sent delegations to Britain. The most notorious of these return visits was that paid to Britain in March 1975 by Shelepin, as head of the Soviet All-Union Central Council of Trades Unions (AUCCTU). A former head of the KGB, Shelepin was in no normal sense a trade unionist at all. His visit was curtailed because of hostile demonstrations, and he lost his job shortly after returning to Moscow.

A more profound symbol of the changed character of the Labour Party was, however, the visit, at the invitation of the National Executive Committee of the Labour Party, of Boris Ponomarev, head of the International Department of the Central Committee of the Soviet Communist Party and undoubtedly the grand master of Soviet subversion throughout the world. This visit would have been unthinkable during Harold Wilson's first term of office, or indeed at any previous time.

These trends and developments are of momentous importance for the future of the United Kingdom. In the context of this book, they illustrate the folly of accepting totalist groups and parties as normal contenders for power in the democratic process.

With this background in mind it becomes easier to explain the appearance of three extraordinary documents, one of which was mentioned earlier in this chapter: the Labour Party Manifesto 1974, the Labour Party Manifesto October 1974, and Labour's Programme 1976. All three are Marxist documents, which is hardly surprising since they were drafted by Marxists. What *is* surprising is that they now constitute the official doctrine of the Labour Party. This is the important reality, and not the fact that the moderates outnumber the extremists in the House of Commons. The first was drafted for the February election of 1974, and includes the telling phrase already quoted about 'irreversible' change. The second, drafted for the second election of 1974, at least acknowledges public concern over violence and lawlessness (one of my three prerequisites of good government) in the following passage:

. . . we share the view of those who are alarmed at the growth of violence in our society, particularly among young people. Labour believes that law-abiding citizens are entitled to full protection. We will strengthen and uphold the police in the exercise of their proper function.

But this praiseworthy intent was vitiated by the addition of verbiage about the undesirability of private armies, eliminating 'areas of deprivation', and making it easier for the public to complain against the police.

On money (the third of my requisites), the manifesto blamed the Heath Government (not entirely unfairly) for allowing a huge deficit to accumulate in the balance of payments; for printing hundreds of millions of pounds; and for allowing scarce resources to go into office blocks, luxury flats and property speculation. But it went on to pledge an irrelevant and envy-ridden tax on wealth exceeding £100,000 (later fulfilled) and to propose a wide range of necessarily inflationary subsidies.

Interestingly, the far more detailed 1976 Programme deleted even the previous passing reference to the need for strengthening the police. In other respects, it merely reiterated and elaborated its previous proposals.

The general elections of 3 May 1979 fortunately went the right way. Had Labour won, the party system would have delivered the country, bound hands and feet, to its external and internal enemies. Fortunately, the Tories won decisively, and the people of Britain were at least given a chance—doubtless the last if it were misused—to undo the past follies of its rulers. In office, Mrs Margaret Thatcher's government immediately acted to improve the pay of the police and armed services, and abolished the Price Commission. The Queen's Speech, delivered in Parliament on 14 May, pledged steps to improve the nation's security and strengthen its contribution to NATO; legislation to amend the law on picketing (which had degenerated into an unpleasant form of mass intimidation) and the closed shop; and proposals to restrict the activities of the National Enterprise Board (which had been used extensively by the Labour governments to 'save jobs' by using taxpayers' money to keep unprofitable industries alive). On two at any rate of the criteria of the State (safety/security and defence), here was a welcome demonstration that the new government was aware, as preceding governments were apparently not, of its irreducible duty as the custodian of power. It remained to be seen whether the conservative fiscal and budgetary measures foreshadowed in the Queen's Speech would rectify the dismal economic situation inherited from Labour.

At least it could be seen that the Conservative Party, for all its past failures of courage and judgement, now seemed to understand, or to have relearned, the principles of good government. But even if the headlong drop to perdition could be halted and indeed reversed, there could be no guarantee, under the political party system, that the threat of collectivism could be defeated and eliminated. This is the fundamental problem, which has not until now been expressed in these terms because of the general reluctance to question inherited doctrines. For have we not been told since infancy that democracy is the best of all possible systems? Nor do I, indeed, question the assumption as such. But I ask: what democracy? Is it not possible to envisage a democratic system in which political parties are no longer allowed to contend for power?

FOUR

VARIATIONS OF THE VOTE

True democracy is impossible. It is necessary to restate this basic fact from time to time because the prevailing wisdom is that democracy, in certain countries at any rate, is a going concern. Twenty people may govern themselves democratically. One hundred may do likewise. One thousand may find it impossible, or at any rate very difficult. A population of millions cannot possibly do so, and since the impossibility is manifest, some way round it has to be found.

The student of politics is bound to give some of his attention to voting arrangements in different countries. The variations are both fascinating and bewildering. But in the end, there are in practice only three basic systems: the simple majority vote ('first-past-the-post'); party lists with proportional representation (PR); and the single transferable vote (STV). In effect, each of the three is an attempt to square the circle—that is, to make the impossible seem possible by a more or less unsatisfactory system of representation and delegation. Another way of putting it is that alternative voting systems are so many attempts to reduce the natural imperfections of democratic theory.

Although the United Kingdom possesses the generally acknowledged 'Mother of Parliaments', and has exported democratic systems to, or inspired them in many countries, its voting system is the most primitive and unsophisticated of all. The country is divided into 635 single-member constituencies. These electoral divisions are supposed to be as nearly of equal size as possible, but natural boundaries cannot be ignored. In general, the Scottish and Welsh constituencies are smaller than the English, while those in Northern Ireland are particularly large. This last anomaly is normally ascribed to the fact that the province enjoyed its own parliament (Stormont), until the terrorist challenge forced the government in Westminster to impose direct rule upon it. At the time of writing there was much talk of the need for the province to be given greater representation in the near future. Candidates for election in the UK must be nominated by at least ten electors living in the same constituency.

The winning candidate is not required to attract more votes than all the others put together, but merely to beat the next down the line.

Except from the point of view of the winning candidates, and more particularly of the candidates of the winning party, the system is anomalous to the point of absurdity, and even iniquity. In recent years one of the most striking illustrations of this strong statement was the February election of 1974, when the Conservative Party gained 300,000 votes more than Labour but lost the election, the Labour Party having gained a majority of four, as measured by seats in the House of Commons. The Liberal Party polled 6 million votes, but was awarded a mere 14 seats.

Under the British system, those who vote for losing candidates are in effect disfranchised. In any constituency where one of the major parties is clearly in the ascendant, most voters will feel that their votes are irrelevant to the outcome of the elections. Those voting for the dominant party often feel their votes are not needed, since so many others will be doing the same anyway; and those who would prefer an alternative are seized with the futility of voting at all. Moreover, as many constituencies are unlikely to change hands, the voting system inevitably exacerbates differences between different parts of the country.

For example, no fewer than twenty-five of the twenty-nine MPs in north-eastern England are Labour. That this reflects Labour dominance of the region is not in question, but the return of twenty-five out of twenty-nine seats to Labour does not reflect the true voting patterns. In local elections, the same area (at the time of writing) yielded 151 Labour councillors but also 142 Tories, eleven Liberals and twenty-three others. In percentage terms, in the local elections—which are more likely to be accurate because of the fragmentation of wards—the Tory party therefore emerges with 49 per cent of the total vote; in the general election, the proportion of Tory representation is down to about 17 per cent. This may be practicable, if a strong ruling party is desired, but it is scarcely equitable. Similarly, Surrey returns only Conservative MPs although the party scores only just over 50 per cent of the vote.

In his book *The Dilemma of Democracy* (Collins, 1978), Lord Hailsham defends the first-past-the-post system, no doubt bearing in mind the advantage his party derives from it when in office. But he is unquestionably on weak ground, and the 'elective dictatorship' of which he complains, would never have developed under a fairer voting system.

Holland

Here we are at the opposite extreme to Britain—the ultimate proportional representation system. The country is divided into eighteen voting districts. Within any of them a group of electors, at least twenty-five strong, may nominate a list of candidates. The candidates may then choose to stand for election in that district only. A national party, however, will submit a list in every district but may vary the order, according to which candidate may do better in a given district.

The voters then vote for a candidate on the list. The total number of votes cast for a particular party is added up at the national level. Each party is thereupon allotted seats in accordance with its proportion of the national vote. The total number of votes secured by any party is then divided by the number of seats it has been awarded. In this way, a 'list quota' is devised. Any individual candidate who has gained sufficient votes to take him up to the level of the 'list quota' is elected. But if a candidate has more than the required quota of votes, his surplus votes are transferred to other candidates on the party lists to bring them up to the required quota. Each elected candidate must, however, receive at least 50 per cent of the votes required by the quota *by his own efforts* before the surplus votes have been reallocated.

It is worth pointing out that this system, which is as near to perfection as human ingenuity can make it, is less practical than the far less democratic British system, in that it encourages a multiplicity of parties and has often left the Netherlands without a government for weeks or even months on end.

Belgium

Holland's neighbour offers a rather similar variety of PR. The Chamber of Representatives is composed of 212 members. These are elected from thirty constituencies, each of which coincides with local government administrative units. The number of representatives in each constituency varies from two to thirty-two.

All candidates are nominated by political parties, and the list supplied by a party may contain as many candidates as there are representatives for that constituency. The party lists are placed in a column on the ballot paper. The voter can mark the beginning of the list indicating that he supports the list of the party as given, or he may choose to vote for an individual, indicating his preference for a particular candidate.

All votes, whether personal or on the list, are counted as part of the party's total. Seats are awarded to the parties on the basis of making the number of votes per elected member as nearly as possible equal for all members. The candidate placed first on a party list has first claim on a vote for his own party's list. If these and any personal votes together amount to the required total or above, he is then elected. The list-votes left over go to the second candidate on the list but if they, plus any personal votes for the second candidate, are insufficient to elect him and if a candidate further down the list has sufficient personal votes to bring him up to the quota, this candidate is elected.

It must be admitted that this system offers special advantages for Belgium in that it caters for the country's cultural bilingualism by giving the voter a chance to vote for difference tendencies within one party. Having said this, PR subjects Belgium as well as Holland to built-in ministerial instability because of the need for shifting party coalitions and the absence of a ruling party with a clear majority.

Italy

The Chamber of Deputies contains 630 deputies elected from thirty-two constituencies. In principle, one member is returned for every 80,000 voters. The number of members for each constituency thus varies from five to thirty-six.

All candidates are nominated by parties, and there are no independents. Each party presents a list which is reproduced on the ballot paper complete with a symbol. The elector marks the symbol of the party he prefers, thus casting his vote. He may also record personal votes for up to three candidates on the list if there are fifteen or fewer seats to be filled; or four if there are more than fifteen. In each constituency the total number of votes for a party is divided by the number of seats plus two. Each party is then awarded a seat for every quota it fulfils.

In the end, candidates are elected according to the number of personal voters they attract. One would expect, therefore, that the preferences of voters for individual candidates would have a powerful influence on the composition of the Chamber of Deputies. In reality it does not, because most Italians cannot be bothered to put down any preferences. When this happens, voters are deemed to have accepted the order of candidates approved by the party list.

I have dealt with the Italian situation in a separate chapter. All that needs to be said at this point, of a country that shares with Britain the regrettable honour of being the sickest man in Europe, is that party democracy has not prevented the rapid decline of Italy from the pinnacle it reached briefly some years ago. Free enterprise delivered the goods; the political system and the irresponsibility of the politicians, together with the organised ill-will of the Communist Party, denied the Italian people the fruit of their labour.

France

The French system has the originality that it offers the voters a chance to change their minds. If a candidate obtains an absolute majority over all his competitors and polls at least 25 per cent of the electorate's votes he is declared elected on the first ballot. If, however, the leading candidate has not secured a decisive lead over his combined rivals, a second ballot is held the following week. Any candidate failing to secure 10 per cent of the votes on the first ballot is excluded. It is also customary for defeated candidates from the first ballot to drop out in favour of the candidate most likely to topple the leader. In any event, the second ballot is decisive. Whether or not the leading candidate secures 51 per cent of the votes he is still elected. Each candidate names a second person to act as his substitute; the same vote automatically elects both. If the elected candidate is subsequently made a minister or dies, the substitute takes over. However, if he is subsequently elected to the Senate, then a new election must be held.

The Senate is elected by the National Assembly on the basis of a list of nominations prepared by the latter. One-third of the Senate is elected every three years, which means that the entire Senate is replenished over nine years.

Under General de Gaulle's Fifth Republic, the President enjoys extensive reserve powers which make him the ultimate boss. He appoints the Prime Minister and he alone decides on dissolution or a referendum. The Prime Minister is so-called (*Premier Ministre*) whereas under previous republics he was known as the President of the Council. In fact, the President now takes the chair at meetings of the Council of Ministers or Cabinet.

Presidential elections are based on the same procedure as elections to the National Assembly, but the period of office is seven years— two years longer than the legislature. In theory, this could lead to a difficult situation. For instance, if the Socialist–Communist combination had won in the legislative elections of March 1978, President Giscard d'Estaing would have found himself politically paralysed during the last two years of his term of office. Instead, they lost—to the benefit of the President, of France and of the whole world.

Instead of being paralysed, the President found himself with a freer hand than his predecessors since the death of de Gaulle.

The two-ballot principle offers an advantage over the British system in that the electorate need not fear to split the vote. In the first ballot, the voter may feel free to indulge his or her particular whims. It has been well said that the French vote with their hearts in the first ballot and with their heads in the second.

This elaborate system may still, however, yield imbalances in representation. In the 1978 elections, for instance, the government ended up with a majority of eighty-nine seats, although its numerical lead was not much more than 1 per cent (50·49 to 49·29 per cent).

Switzerland

I have given Switzerland a special chapter as a model of good government. Appropriately, its system of government is unique. There are two assemblies—the National Council and the Council of State—but neither has precedence over the other. Their powers are precisely equal.

The National Council has 200 members and is elected every four years by PR, with the canton as the basic electoral unit. A canton elects representatives on the basis of its population. Berne, for example, has a much larger representation than some of the very small cantons.

The political parties submit lists of candidates at the election, and the voter votes for the number of seats allotted to his canton. It is not, however, just a question of voting for a party list. If the voter wishes to vote for a candidate belonging to different parties on the same ballot sheet, he is free to do so.

The Council of State is composed of two members per canton regardless of the size or population. True to this federal principle, each canton has a choice in the method of selecting its representatives, according to local traditions. Some are nominated; others are elected.

The Government itself is elected by a joint vote of the National Council and the Council of State. There are only seven ministers and as they are appointed in this way it is unusual for them to come from any single party. Elections to the government take place every four years—the year after election to the National Council.

Australia

The Australian system is an elaborate variant of the Single Transferable Vote system. It is based on the preferential marking of ballot papers, and is therefore known as Preferential Voting. If the number of first-preference votes given in favour of a candidate for election to the House of Representatives is greater than half of the total vote, that candidate is elected. If no candidate has received an absolute majority of votes, the one who has received the fewest first-preference votes is excluded from the count, and each ballot paper counted to him is transferred to the voters' second preferences. Candidates are excluded one by one until a candidate finally receives more than 50 per cent of the votes and is then duly elected.

As in the United States, there is a Senate to represent the interests of each State: in Australia's case, there are only six States (plus the Northern Territory and the Capital Territory of Canberra, each of which has a member in the House of Representatives) but each State is entitled to ten Senators, as compared with only two in the greatly more populous USA.

The Australians, as I discovered when I lived there and exercised my right to vote, regard their system as fairer than others. This is debatable: at least it has the merit of originality. It should be noted that voting is compulsory, on penalty of a small fine. Compulsion has done what was expected of it by enticing a high proportion of voters away from the competing attractions of beer and horses on election days. Whether it is compatible with freedom is another matter.

The Republic of Ireland

The Republic has forty-two constituencies, each with three, four, or five seats. In an unusual tribute to Irish egos, candidates may nominate themselves. The parties, however, have to prove that they have a significant and visible organisation before being officially recognised. When recognition is achieved, the name of the party may be added to the ballot paper. The Communist Party of Ireland, for instance, was not officially recognised until 1975.

A substantial percentage of the vote is required to secure election, according to the following percentages. If a constituency has three seats, then the candidate needs one vote more than a quarter of the votes cast; in a four-seat constituency, the requirement is one more than one-fifth; and it is one more than one-sixth in a five-seat constituency.

Voting is by numbering—in a preferential system not unlike the Australian. The voter marks the ballot sheet by preference as many times as he wishes. If the candidate marked '1' has already been elected, then preference '2' is taken into consideration. The second preferences may then be transferred to number 3 and the process goes on until all the seats in the constituency have been filled. In practice, it is very unusual for more than two preferences to be required. It is customary for voters to place all their preferences for the same party (remembering that there are several seats in each constituency), but the system does allow for some flexibility in choice. As under the Belgian system, a voter can indicate a preference for particular groups within a party.

West Germany

The Federal Republic of Germany (FRG) has an exceedingly compli-cated PR system, with an ingenious device to rule out the main drawback of PR which is the proliferation of small groups.

There are two assemblies: the Bundestag and the Bundesrat. Delegates to the Upper House, the Bundesrat, represent each of the Länder. The number of delegates for each Land varies according to the size of the population, but is modified by the size of weighting. This simply means that while each Land has a minimum of three delegates, those with more than 2 million inhabitants have four, and those with more than 6 million have five.

The Bundesrat serves as a check on the Lower House, which otherwise might be excessively powerful, and as in other federal systems maintains the country's diversity.

For the electoral purposes of the Bundestag, the country is divided into 248 single-member constituencies, all of considerable size. They vary from 110,000 to about 230,000 people. The Federal Republic is also divided according to the ten Länder. At one end of the scale, Bremen returns one member, and at the other, North Rhine–Westphalia no fewer than seventy-five. The representatives of the Länder also total 248, so that the total membership of the Bundestag is 496. The Germans go to great trouble to ensure that the total representation of each Land is kept proportional to the size of the electorate. Constituency boundaries are occasionally redrawn, but the number of list seats is increased or decreased according to changes in local populations. In any one Land, the number of list seats may differ from the number of constituency seats because of this process.

The ballot paper is in two halves. On the right-hand side is a list of the parties contesting the elections in a particular Land, together with the names of the first few candidates on each party's list. On the left-hand side are the names of the parties together with candi-dates contesting the individual constituency. The voter marks one of the candidates on the left and these votes are counted exactly as in Britain: a candidate who attracts more votes than his nearest rival is elected.

On the right-hand side, the voter marks one of the party names. These second votes for each party are totalled over the entire Land. From the Land totals, the total number of seats to which each party is entitled is calculated. The guiding principle is the d'Hondt rule,* a method of calculation designed to make the number of seats per elected member as nearly as possible equal for all parties. From this total of list seats which the party has won is subtracted the number of constituency seats which the party has won in the Land—the remaining difference being the number of list seats which are finally allotted in addition to the number of constituency seats. These seats are filled by candidates in the order in which they stand on the party's list. It sometimes happens that the party wins more constituency seats than its list entitlement. In that event, the party is allowed to keep the extra seats and the Bundestag is increased beyond its usual membership of 496.

List votes are also calculated on a national level, with two purposes in mind. First, small parties are eliminated. To win any representation on the distribution of list seats, a party must poll at least 5 per cent of the votes over the entire country or win at least three seats on the constituency basis. Secondly, a party having a substantial remainder of Land votes may utilise them in another Land. In practice, this hardly ever happens.

Japan

It seems logical to switch now to the other big, bustling democracy that arose from the ruins and ashes of militarism. Japan has a Diet of two Houses: the House of Representatives and the House of Councillors. The latter has replaced the old House of Peers of the Meiji Constitution of 1889. The new Constitution of 1947, sometimes known as the MacArthur Constitution after the American conqueror of imperial Nippon, brought the theoretical delights of democracy to a people with absolutely no democratic tradition. I say 'theoretical' because ever since 1947 Japan has been ruled by the same Liberal-Democratic group which has on occasion changed its

---

* The d'Hondt rule, after its inventor, Victor d'Hondt of the University of Ghent, is also known by its French name: la règle de la plus forte moyenne (the law of the highest average). The idea is to make sure that when all seats have been allotted, the average number of votes required to win one seat shall be as nearly as possible the same for each party. (Lakeman and Lambert, How Democracies Vote: see Short Reading List.)

name but never its commitment to an extraordinary system of free enterprise closely overseen by a largely State-dominated banking system: never having given another party or group of parties the chance to provide an alternative government, it is fair to say that democracy has never really been put to the test in contemporary Japan. (This is not a criticism, but a statement of fact.)

Both Houses are elected by the single non-transferable vote, and the country is divided into constituencies on the English model. There the resemblance ends, however. For although the voter has only one vote, each constituency may return several representatives. The system was, in fact, specifically designed to ensure that minority opinions could be represented in the Diet. It is distasteful to a Japanese to vote for a losing candidate, and the favourite usually gets a massive vote. But since several representatives are elected at once, the Japanese voters are less likely than, say, the British, to feel they have wasted their votes.

Unless there is a parliamentary crisis and a dissolution, Representatives serve for four years: there are 491 of them, representing 124 constituencies. The Councillors have a longer life of six years, but half of them are re-elected every three years, much as for the American Senate. The House of Councillors is a compromise between the usual regional requirements of a second chamber and national representation: 100 of them are elected by a nation-wide electorate; the remaining 152 are elected from forty-seven prefectural constituencies. The Councillors have a revisionary and advisory role, but do not in the true sense constitute an upper chamber: the Representatives rule.

'Universal' suffrage is interpreted in Japan to mean all men and women aged twenty or older.

The United States

I have left the greatest democracy till the end. The most distinctive feature of the American electoral scene is the 'primary', but there is no consistency about the way primaries are run. One State may run closed or partisan primaries, in which only registered members of a given party may vote; another may favour open or non-partisan primaries in which anybody may vote, and the candidates, in theory at least, are not supposed to compete on party lines.

Most governors and other State officials are eliminated or chosen at primaries, but there again there is no consistency: in most States primaries for such offices are obligatory, but in several Southern States they are optional. Both nationally and internationally, the greatest interest is naturally concentrated on the presidential primaries, which are held in some States, but only in some, to elect delegates to national party conventions, which in turn nominate candidates for the presidency and vice-presidency of the USA. At that level, the primary is certainly a useful device in that it quickly exposes the weaknesses and inadequacies of the less satisfactory candidates.

Are primaries in all aspects a good thing? That is another matter, and it is hardly possible to give a straight answer, since the practice of the primary varies from State to State. In open primaries, for instance, it is open to members of one party to vote for the opposing party's weakest candidate, thus favouring their own man in a national poll. On the other hand, the open primary can be said to help prevent the intimidation of voters.

The legislature reflects the federal origins of this vast and varied country. The House of Representatives is a larger version of the House of Commons, with delegates elected to represent constituencies and on a simple majority vote (with the same obvious disadvantages as in the United Kingdom). As far as possible, constituencies reflect the distribution of population, although in a land of massive internal migrations, the reflection tends to be less than faithful. The most populous States, however, can count on having more Representatives (usually called Congressmen) than the more sparsely inhabited ones.

The Senate, however, is federalism at its purest. Whether a State has about 300,000 inhabitants (as Alaska does) or nearly 20 million (California) matters not at all: each and every one of the fifty States of the Union returns exactly two Senators to the upper house. (And it really is an *upper* house, with formidable powers of veto over the work of the House of Representatives.)

The President of the United States, holder of what is generally regarded as the most powerful elective office in the world (a view that has perhaps been rendered obsolete in the wake of the Vietnam war and Watergate), is chosen by a curiously archaic procedure—not by the voters themselves (not, then, by the people as such) but by an electoral college. True, the voters vote for delegates to represent them on the electoral college; and true again, the delegates normally vote as expected of them (although theoretically they might change their minds). Another curious feature is that the names of the presidential candidates do not actually appear on the ballot sheet.

It is interesting to recall the origins of the electoral college, for they show the formidable distance covered by the American people since the Founding Fathers met in Philadelphia a couple of centuries ago to work out a constitution fit for gentlemen freed from the burden of taxes paid to a distant motherland. In those distant days communications were bad, and a need was felt for a consultative body. Today the need has gone, but the body has remained, and has resisted attempts to abolish it.

The right of an American to become a Congressman or Senator is not unlimited. To be a candidate for the House he or she will have to be at least twenty-five years old, to have been a US citizen for at least seven years, and to live in the State which he or she hopes to represent: a New Yorker may not represent a Californian constituency—a marked contrast to Britain, where the residential qualification is much slacker.

To be a Senator, an additional *gravitas* of five years is required: nobody under thirty need apply. Nor is the newly naturalised American welcome to the club; he will have to contain his soul in patience for fully nine years before yielding to Senatorial ambitions. It is after all a rather exclusive Club: only 100 members (compared to 435 Representatives).

These, then, are America's choice of imperfections in the world's greatest (but not, by my criteria, its most successful) democracy.

Some observations

I repeat, true democracy is impossible, and any country that attempted it would collapse under the weight of its anarchical absurdity. All election systems, of which I have examined a few samples, are designed to disprove this self-evident proposition, or at least to convince the people that democracy can work. I have called this process the 'choice of imperfections'. I have still not exhausted the list of idiosyncrasies. There are, for instance, wide variations in the qualifications required of potential candidates for election. Usually, the minimum requirement is that he or she should be a voter. But, as mentioned here and there, a certain experience of life is sometimes required. A candidate of thirty may become a Senator of the United States, but for reasons that are unlikely to be biological a Belgian has to wait until his fortieth birthday before entertaining a corresponding ambition.

Alarmingly (from the standpoint of observers, including myself, who seek to rationalise and raise the standard of government) candidates are scarcely ever required to demonstrate either intelligence or special capacity. However, Turkey, the Sudan and Egypt debar illiterates from election.

Understandably, there is a nationality qualification in most countries, although the variations are wide. In France, a naturalised citizen may stand for election, but only if he has held his French citizenship for ten years. In the United States the lower limit is seven years, but in West Germany only one. In some countries, such as Australia, the nationality qualification is supplemented by a residential one.

Britain is doubtless alone in barring Peers and Church of England clergymen from standing for election. It is more normal to rule out civil servants, members of the armed forces, and judges. The FRG, France, Israel and Holland permit civil servants to suspend their career on election to parliament, and to re-enter the civil service on vacating their parliamentary seat, retaining all their accrued privileges, promotion and superannuation. This kindness from one arm of the State to another is by no means universal.

FIVE

DEMOCRATIC FALLACIES

The assumption that democracy is always and necessarily a good thing has bitten deep into our collective unconscious. The term is not necessarily defined but is invariably taken to mean 'party democracy'. It has become a criterion of moral acceptability, not to be questioned or even defined but simply taken for granted. Open almost any newspaper on almost any day of the week and you will find the assumption made in a leader or in a report of a speech.

I put this assertion to the test the day I started writing this chapter, which happened to be 13 July 1978. Sure enough, *The Times* carried a leader headed 'Two Political Setbacks in South America'—a reference to general elections in Bolivia and Guyana which had been marred by alleged irregularities. I should not wish to be misunderstood: I am not in favour of electoral irregularities. Elections may or may not be useful, but if they are held they should be honest, and seen to be honest—or they would be a good deal worse than useless.

No, what I question is the assumption that in assessing a country's progress, the criterion which takes precedence over all others is whether it is moving towards or away from the thing called 'democracy'. It never seems to occur to the leader writers to ask themselves whether a country is moving towards, or away from, good government. Democracy is equated with moral good.

This sole criterion was applied to Spain throughout the long years of General Franco's dictatorship (although not to anything like the same degree to Salazar's Portugal, a far more repressive regime than Franco's, but admitted to the NATO club because unsoiled by the emotional legacy of a civil war). From about 1958 (when the General decided to free the Spanish economy) until the early 1970s (when his grasp of affairs was weakening in the face of organised terrorism) Spain was a remarkably free country, despite restrictions on freedom of the press and political organisation. Certainly it was a relatively much better governed country than the democratic Spain which followed—a country which offered a high degree of safety and security for ordinary people, a solid defence system and economic expansion with a strong peseta. Within a year of the dictator's death, violent crime was soaring and inflation was raging—although defence prospects remained good. But this, apparently, did not matter: the well-governed country under Franco was not 'clubbable'; the increasingly anarchic multi-party regime that followed was. The criterion was 'democracy' and there was none other.

The Spaniards, whose previous experiments with democracy were disastrous, took the concept rather literally at first. Ideally, they would have liked 30 million parties—one for each Spaniard. But they contented themselves during the first year with more than 500 registered parties. Faced with the likely consequences of fragmentation, the groups started combining, but the impulse was there, and I found it rather touching, as though the Spaniards knew by instinct that government of the people by the people logically implies a multiplicity of parties, before very quickly discovering that since democracy is impossible there was no way out but to break with logic and join the party game.

Party democracy, as such, has no moral content. It is merely a mechanism, a device for delivering certain conditions and results. By far the most important of these are *freedom* and *order*. The two are inseparable but must be stated in proper sequence.

If party democracy ceases to deliver freedom, it does not follow that freedom has ceased to be important—but that party democracy must be replaced by something else. If the great mental block represented by party democracy is overcome, the road to fresh thinking is then open. We should start thinking in terms of desirable results and lose our collective obsession with the mechanism.

What then, do we have a *right* to expect of a government as the temporary embodiment of the State? We are back to the principles of the Minimum State, plus some others. The draft Charter of Rights that follows embodies both elementary 'human' rights, and rightful expectations from a government:

1. To be protected, at home and abroad (a right which condenses the first two principles of the Minimum State).
2. To a stable money, so that our pound, or franc, or dollar, buys about the same this year as last, and either the same or better when we travel abroad.
3. To own, buy or sell property.
4. To keep what we earn, subject only to that portion of our income that may be required to finance the needs of the Minimum State.
5. To keep the entirety of our savings and to dispose of our estate as we see fit.

6. To marry the person of our choice, subject only to mutual free will.

7. To be given a minimum education in the elementary disciplines; and access to a choice of secondary and higher education as available.

8. To travel freely, at home or abroad, subject only to the limitations of our means and to limitations imposed by governments other than our own.

9. To choose whatever job may be on offer; to leave when we choose.

10. If an employer, to dismiss employees either for unsatisfactory performance or redundancy, with suitable severance provisions under the law.

11. If an employee, to withdraw one's labour peacefully in the furtherance of industrial claims, and subject to constitutional limitations on non-industrial strikes, strikes in vital occupations, sympathy strikes, and on condition that fellow-citizens not on strike do not foot the bill.

12. To freedom from intimidation by unions, fellow-workers and employers.

13. To attend a church, temple, synagogue or mosque of our own choosing, or not to attend a place of worship.

14. To free inquiry and advocacy, except in the incitement of crimes, felonies and misdemeanours.

15. To freedom from arbitrary deprivation of liberty.

16. To equal treatment under the law, and to freedom from retrospective legislation.

17. To assemble for peaceful purposes and to join or not to join an organisation.

18. If poor and sick, or old and poor, to the satisfaction of reasonable needs.

A State that provided all these rights would be the Minimum State and would offer a free society. We must therefore ask ourselves: what kind of polity would provide and guarantee these rights —and the free society? It will be seen that (with the exception of Switzerland), existing polities do not offer all these rights. In most places, 1 and 2 have either gone or are inadequately provided for. The property rights—3, 4 and 5—are more or less severely restricted even in countries that call themselves 'free', such as the United Kingdom. Confiscatory levels of income tax are immoral as well as self-defeating. Severe inheritance laws are an iniquitous infringement of personal liberty. The freedom of marriage (6) is normally available in 'capitalist' and Protestant countries, but may be, in fact, restricted in strict Catholic or Jewish communities; if not in law then by the force of custom. In Communist countries, it does not exist: it is extremely difficult for a Soviet or a Chinese citizen, for instance, to marry a foreigner.

The right to minimum (and secondary and higher) education (7) is supposedly available in Britain and other advanced countries, but the growing number of illiterates and innumerates in the UK amounts to a serious curtailment of the right of children to be taught how to read, write and do sums. It may be added that the determination of the Welfare State to make higher education available for vastly greater numbers has placed a serious strain on the educational system as a whole, to the detriment of those whose minimum needs constitute a right rather than a privilege: yet another typical example of the bad/over-government syndrome.

The right to travel freely at home and abroad is nominally available in the democratic countries (as it was in Spain under Franco), except when currency-exchange restrictions hamper our wanderlust. This very important right, incidentally, does not exist in Communist countries: the Soviet Union requires an internal passport for travel in the USSR and virtually bars individual travel abroad.

The labour/employer rights I have listed (9, 10, 11 and 12) are of course non-existent in Communist countries, and unfortunately seriously restricted in a number of democratic countries. In Britain, for instance, we have lost 9, since men and women can be and have been dismissed, sometimes after many years' service, for refusing to join a trade union, or have been denied employment unless they join one. The closed shop, given the force of law under the Wilson government in 1974, is an abomination and a disgrace to a country that claims to be civilised. The employer's right of dismissal (10) is severely restricted, not only in Britain, but in France, Italy and other countries. The right to strike (non-existent in Communist countries, and usually restricted in authoritarian ones) is virtually unlimited in countries such as Britain and Australia, in which governments have found it expedient to yield to the massive pressure group constituted by organised labour. In such countries what should be a right has become a licence by one section of the community to damage the interests of another or of society as a whole, even to the extent of inflicting severe hardship on the weakest members of society: the sick in hospitals or the old at home, who suffer most from lack of electricity, nursing or heat. This is a 'right' which must be curtailed, not extended.

As for freedom from intimidation, it can no longer be said to exist in Britain: the mass demonstrations by thousands of hired pickets in front of the small photo-processing plant, Grunwick, in London, constituted intimidation of a severe order, directed at the majority of employees who refused to join a trade union.

Freedom of worship (13) exists normally in Britain and other democratic countries; and is very severely restricted in Communist countries. As for the freedom of inquiry and advocacy (14), we may think we have it (in Britain), but nowadays only subject to the intimidatory pressures of those who think it wrong to inquire into the possibility that some races may be 'less equal' than others in inherited ability; while our right of advocacy, for example in newspaper advertisements, may find itself curtailed with no notice by trade-union disapproval. This right, again, is non-existent in Communist countries, except in certain areas of science; but in genetics and biology, as the critics of the egregious charlatan Lysenko— favoured by Stalin for his theory that acquired characteristics could be transmitted genetically—discovered to their cost, it does not necessarily apply. The notion that communism would create a new man, *homo sovieticus*, dies hard in the USSR.

It is worth noting, incidentally, that in our societies the right of free inquiry (which is of relatively recent historical origin, as Galileo would confirm if we could ask him), is usually taken for granted, while the right of advocacy is usually expressed in terms of freedom of expression and the press. In Western societies, this right is given a disproportionate importance, as if it were a right transcending all others (not surprisingly, since those who exercise it are predominantly the voluble and the articulate, 'intellectuals' now ready to welcome Spain and Portugal into the Western community because pornography has become freely available in both countries. As a writer and communicator myself, I too hold this right to be very important, but I recognise that it is far less fundamental than some of the other rights I have listed, the denial of which usually provokes less intellectual indignation.

Freedom from arbitrary arrest and detention (15) is again taken for granted in democratic countries. It is worth pointing out, however, that it may, in emergencies, prove at least temporarily incompatible with the more fundamental right (under the Minimum State) to be protected against internal and external enemies. During World War II, persons regarded as security risks were detained without trial under Regulation 18B. Nearly all States are prepared to suspend this right in an emergency: there was, for instance, detention without trial in Northern Ireland at the height of the terrorist violence in the province, and it could fairly be argued that the decision by the Labour government to lift it and allow known terrorists to go free was an abdication of the State's duty to protect its citizens. In other words, the rights of the terrorists were given precedence over the rights of law-abiding citizens.

The right to equal treatment under the law (16) should normally be an absolute and is one of the very few spheres of State policy where an egalitarian approach is morally justified. Where national security is at stake, however, circumstances may justify exceptions, which will be more, or less, tolerated by the law-abiders to the extent that the country concerned has a well-established reputation for fairness and concern for justice. The freedom from retrospective legislation ought to be no less absolute, but is sometimes infringed even under democratically elected governments (yet another proof that party democracy, as such, does not guarantee freedom). Under Labour rule in Britain, it was notoriously infringed in reverse by the 1974 Labour government to give retrospective absolution to the Clay Cross councillors who had been fined for refusing to carry out the provisions of an Act on the ground that it had been passed by a Tory government.

Later, under the 1978 Budget, the Chancellor of the Exchequer legislated in retrospect against a legitimate tax-avoidance scheme under which some individuals and companies had managed not to pay 98 per cent of their earnings to the State. Whatever the objective, such a practice is morally repugnant.

The freedom to assemble for peaceful purposes is another right to which intellectuals attach much importance, sometimes to the extent of stretching the definition of 'peaceful' further than is justified. As for joining or not joining organisations, the right no longer fully exists in Britain (with the closed shop in industry and obligatory membership of the Students' Union). In other words, we enjoyed both halves of Right 17 (to join or *not* to join) until an incipiently totalitarian government tried to force people to join a union if they wished to work.

My last 'right' (18) under the Minimum State amounts to limited access to Welfare. Instead of equal benefits for everybody, whatever their widely different circumstances and needs, State welfare would be available only to those who really needed it, as a generous dole from society. Enormous savings in money and resources could be made if this simple and equitable principle were in force. I have not included as a 'right' the provision of unemployment benefit, not because I oppose it but because the problem is one that is best dealt with under detailed proposals for the partial dismantling of the Welfare State (which is considered in a separate chapter).

The trouble with the Welfare State is that a number of Western

countries have No. 18 on my list, but in a manner that provides
Welfare for millions who do not need it—a gigantic and unnecessary
burden on the resources of the State, which are the people's. This
alone virtually guarantees bad, excessive, and growing, government
to the neglect of essentials. In the Minimum State, those really in
need would get twice or several times the present miserly allocations;
and those who scrounged, or merely took what was their legal due
because it was on offer, would do without.

It is a useful and interesting exercise to look at the list of 18 rights
and allocate three points for each right. The idea is not entirely
original. Many years ago, when I was working in Sydney, a distinguished 'New Australian', Dr Emery Barcs, writing in the Sydney
Daily Telegraph, drew a wide-ranging chart of liberties and allocated
points to leading countries: France, at that time, came top of the
list. Dr Barcs kindly found his chart and sent it to me when I started
writing this book. Our approach is not, however, identical, and my
purpose in the following scoreboard is to compare the performance
of a totalist country (the USSR), an authoritarian one (Franco
Spain in its latter years) and a democratic one (Britain) in respect
of my own Charter of Rights in the Minimum State:

Item	Optimum score	USSR	Franco Spain	Britain
1	3	3	2	1
2	3	3	2	1
3	3	1	3	3
4	3	1*	2	1
5	3	1	2	1
6	3	0	2	3
7	3	3	2	2
8	3	0	3	3
9	3	0	3	2
10	3	0	2	1
11	3	0	1	2*
12	3	2*	3	2
13	3	1	2	3
14	3	0	1	2
15	3	0	1	3
16	3	0	2	2·5
17	3	1	1	2
18	3	3	2	2·5
Totals	54	19	36	37

* Clearly these propositions lend themselves only imperfectly to numerical
analysis and these scores can only be a rough guide. Under 4, the Soviet Union
gets a point for low income tax, but of course the regime is a monster State, a
Leviathan, not a Minimum State. Under 11, Britain is penalised by 1 point for
the *excessive* freedom strikers enjoy. Under 12, the Soviet Union is rather
generously given 2 points, losing one because the only employer is the State
which permanently intimidates everybody.

It is possible (although I don't think so) that I have been slightly too kind to Franco Spain, and too critical of contemporary Britain, but the relative scores are close enough (with in my view a slight edge in favour of Great Britain) to underline the fact that a wide range of liberties may be available under an authoritarian State, whereas very few survive under a totalist one. In items 1 and 2, embodying the principles of the Minimum State, Franco Spain gets 2 and 2, and Britain only 1 and 1. This is partly a matter of period. During the year I spent in Spain (1966–67), safety in the streets (freedom from violent crime) was substantially better in Britain and Spain should have earned high marks for security (against subversion and terrorism) and defence. However, I penalised the Franco dictatorship on both scores, because of the rapid deterioration in the early 1970s.

Two conclusions suggest themselves:

1. Authority is not incompatible with liberty, indeed it is a precondition of liberty. The only points at issue are, *who* exercises the authority and *how*?
2. The existence of political parties is unconnected with the prevalence of liberties—except in certain specific areas, including most obviously the right to form and join such parties.

In 1959 a 'Manifesto for a Free Society' was drafted by a committee meeting in Paris with Professor M. Maurice Allais as *rapporteur*. It was never published in printed form, such is the tyranny exerted by the Marxist Left on French publishing. It is a remarkable document, although the drafting committee allowed itself to be side-tracked into an irrelevant consideration of the Algerian problem, at that time dominant in French minds. It is of passing interest that at no point does it specifically stipulate the existence of political parties, although the context several times suggests that the authors took it for granted. The Manifesto does, however, make a point of fundamental importance in the following passage which I have translated from the French:

Necessity of a Strong Government for a Free Society

23. Not only is the existence of a strong State not incompatible with the working of a free society, but it must be considered as an essential condition of it.

In the absence of a strong government it is absolutely Utopian to attempt to achieve the objectives of a free society; nor can such a society be made to work properly.

There can be no free society without a power capable of taking the necessary conditions quickly and effectively and based upon institutions that will guarantee its proper duration, under the control of a democratic authority determinedly devoted to the service of freedom. A weak government can lead only to anarchy or dictatorship and in either case to the disappearance of any free society.

A moment's thought will demonstrate the truth of these propositions. The State must be small (the 'Minimum State') but it must be strong, for how can a weak State guarantee the safety, security and defence of its people and have the nerve to resist the unnecessary expenditures that ruin the value of money?

I deal later with the kind of polity that will best serve the cause of the freedoms I have listed, and the kind of State structure most compatible with them.

Somary's Inverse Ratio Laws

The late Felix Somary was a man of ripe political and financial wisdom. A Swiss and a banker, he is pretty well unknown in the English-speaking world but held in some reverence where German is spoken. During the Second World War he represented his country in the United States, officially but without visible status, living in hotels and without an official car, with a brief to watch over political and financial developments that might affect Swiss neutrality and the value of Swiss money. In 1952 he offered the distilled product of his experience and wisdom in a short book entitled *Krise und Zukunft der Demokratie** (Europa, Zürich: *Crisis and Future of Democracy*). It is a work of striking originality, written in a clear but highly concentrated prose. Part D, entitled 'The Social Laws of the Inverse Ratio' (*Die Sozialgesetze der verkehrten Proportion*) and is worth summarising here for its relevant contribution to the problems under review. These, then are Somary's 20 'laws':

1. The stronger the concentration of force, the weaker the accountability (*Je stärker die Gewalt konzentriert ist, desto geringer ist die Verantwortung*). As Somary puts it, in every large army there are thousands of corporals who are perfectly capable of doing their jobs, but a real military leader emerges at most once in a generation. The principle of equality is all very well, but at a critical time only the top ranks can take decisions. He goes on to ask who can really

* An English translation was published in the U.S. (Knopf, 1952) under the title *Democracy at Bay*.

be made to account for starting a war or for conducting it once it has begun. If a genius at the top makes a mistake, how is revenge to be taken against him, and what good would revenge be anyway? This 'first law' is closely linked with the second and third:

2. In public life, the greater the guilt, the less the atonement. (*Je grösser [im öffentlichen Leben] die Schuld, desto geringer die Sühne.*) For as Somary says, the penalty for causing the death of millions is no greater than for individual murder. Although a government's capacity for mischief-making is unlimited, any atonement is strictly limited. The infamy of dictators lies in their awareness that only the first murder can be punished, not the rest.

3. The more rights a person has, the less he is aware of them. (*Je mehr Rechte jemandem zustehen, desto weniger werden sie wahrgenommen.*) For instance, the beggars of Southern Italy will defend their pitch tenaciously, but the German worker will neglect to assert his rights because there are too many of them to keep in his head. Similarly, a good many American voters cannot be bothered to exercise their right to vote in a presidential election—one of the rare occasions when this particular right matters.

The fourth of Somary's 'laws' is linked with the first and third:

4. The more powers the State assumes, the more difficult (the less easy) it is to control their administration. (*Je mehr Funktionen ein Staat übernimmt, desto weniger ist seine Verwaltung zu kontrollieren.*) How many Russians, for example, have a say in the Five-Year Plan, or for that matter how many Americans have a say in the Budget? Hence the fifth 'law':

5. The greater and the more many-sided the State, the less influence the people are able to exert. (*Je grösser und je vielseitiger der Staat, desto einflussloser das Volk.*) Appropriately in a Swiss writer (and sensibly by any standard), Somary points out that his country-men in any given canton can take decisions at the community level, whereas nearly all decisions are imposed nationally on Soviet citizens, and even on Americans.

6. The stronger the pressure from the government, the weaker the resistance of the masses. (*Je grösser der Druck der Regierung, desto geringer der Widerstand der Massen.*) The English rose in rebellion against their civilised monarch, Charles I, not against the brutal Henry VIII. Similarly, the French rose not against the warlike tyrant Louis XIV, but against the nice and ineffectual Louis XVI.

7. The greater the hunger, the weaker political resistance becomes. (*Je grösser der Hunger, desto geringer der politische Widerstand.*) The hungry Indians don't make revolutions, but the relatively well-fed English, French and Americans do. The Russian Revolution

was a consequence of defeat in war, not of hunger. Similarly, writes Somary, the Chinese revolution was the work of Europeanised intellectuals, not of the hungry millions—an interesting but debatable example, for while Chou En-lai, Liu Shao-ch'i and other Communist leaders qualify as 'Europeanised intellectuals', the real leader of the Chinese revolution, Mao Tse-tung, was Chinese-educated and aroused the peasant masses into revolt.

8. The greater the degree of civilisation, the less freedom there is. (*Je grösser die Zivilisation, desto geringer die Freiheit.*) The nomads of the desert, for instance, are freer than the sedentary city-dwellers, just as the North American Indians were freer than the Europeans who conquered them. Three further 'laws' flow from the eighth:

9. The more laws or legal decisions there are, the less justice. (*Je mehr Gesetze oder richterliche Entscheidungen, desto weniger Recht.*) Another way of putting it, as Somary does, is that everybody could remember the Ten Commandments, but who can be expected to remember the entire Statute Book?

10. The better the means of communication, the easier it is to cut them off and the less they can be used when they are most needed. (*Je besser die Verkehrsmittel, desto leichter können sie abgesperrt und desto weniger können sie benutzt werden, wenn man sie am meisten benötigt.*) The man on foot or in a small boat is the freest, whereas the pilot and the man in the steamer are the least free. The authorities can immobilise motorists by closing down the petrol stations, halt shipping by denying the use of harbours and ground pilots by seizing airfields. Indeed, the paralysis of an entire country can be accomplished within minutes. (It is perhaps worth adding that the Goulart government in Brazil sought to preserve itself in 1964 by seizing all supplies of petrol; a move which was defeated when a technically-minded sympathiser of the military taught the soldiers how to convert solid fuel into a viable agent for land vehicles.)

11. The better the news services, the less is tyranny able to disseminate false information to the outside world. (*Je besser der Nachrichtendienst, desto weniger die Tyrannis dringt ungünstige Meldungen an die Aussenwelt.*) In other words, the better the public is informed, the less can tyrants put over their version of the facts. The message of the Gospels got around, although there were no news agencies or wire services to spread the news; but few Germans knew about Hitler's concentration camps.

12. Sympathy decreases with the frequency of wrongs or ills. (*Das Mitgefühl sinkt mit der Haüfigkeit des Leides.*) This, in Somary's view, is the 'law' that makes war and tyranny possible. A death in

a family causes shock and grief: daily death rolls in the thousands numb the responses: 'a fearful law with fearful consequences' (says Somary on p. 136 of his short masterpiece).

13. The more tyrants there are, the less opposition there is. (*Je mehr Tyrannen, desto weniger Opposition.*) 'One tyrant stirs resistance; several stimulate imitators.'

14. The less well-founded something is, the more passionately will it be defended. (*Je weniger eine Sache begründet ist, desto mehr leiderschaftlicher wird es verteidigt.*) As Renan said, one does not die for truths but for beliefs. Fanatics, however, believe themselves alone to be in possession of the ultimate truth, for which they will suffer and die, torture and cause others to die.

15. The less the State protects its citizens, the more it charges for the job. (*Je weniger der Staat seiner Bürger schützt, desto mehr verlangt es für diese Funktion.*) Somary's example is one of which the Parkinson of Parkinson's Law would have approved: when Britain ruled the seven seas and relieved its citizens of the fear of war, the country was virtually tax-free. Now that it can no longer protect the British people, taxes are at their highest.

16. The weaker the State, the greater the claims made upon it. (*Je schwächer der Staat, desto höhere Forderungen werden an ihn gestellt.*) This 'law' of Somary's might have been written with the Labour governments of the 1970s in mind, although he wrote twenty years before the second coming of Harold Wilson. No more was expected of Washington than that he should relieve his fellow-countrymen of overseas taxes, but the guilt-ridden governments of today are expected to solve all social problems: a costly process, which carries a consequence embodied in Somary's next 'law':

17. The more money is paid out, the less is the intrinsic value of money. (*Je mehr Geld ausgegeben wird, desto geringer ist der gesamte Geldwert.*) This seems to be a matter of common observation, and it is simply the observable basis for the monetarist theory, which (rightly) ascribes inflation to an excessive supply of money: if you print the stuff in large enough quantities, the one certain thing is that it will become worthless. Hence two more consequential 'laws':

18. The more the economy requires tax increases, the more politics will be devalued. (*Je mehr die Ökonomie Erhöhung des Zinses verlangt, desto mehr senkt ihn die Politik herunter.*) And:

19. The weaker the State's finances, the higher the expenditures. (*Je schwächer die Staatsfinanzen, desto höher die Ausgaben.*) As an observer of the great inflation of the Weimar Republic, Somary noticed that never were such luxurious buildings put up as during that bankrupt period.

20. The greater the wealth and power, the smaller the satisfaction and the greater the drive towards still more of both. (*Je grösser das Reichtum und die Macht, desto geringer die Sättigung, desto stärker der Drang nach weiteren Vermehrung.*) In other words, the more you have, the more you want: wealth accumulates in private hands, and power in mass business enterprises.

Let us now drop the quotation marks: Somary's laws are indeed *laws*. All of them are confirmed by daily experience and some are so commonplace as to seem almost trite, were it not that our political parties (and therefore our governments) ignore them, brush them aside, or pretend that those in power, by virtue of this fact, have a wisdom that transcends universal experience. These laws, which are also maxims, constitute individually and in sum the common-sense foundation of the Minimum State. For what they mean, one and all, is that freedom diminishes in direct ratio with the growth of government. The nanny State, the government that tries to solve all social problems and attend to everybody's needs, real or imaginary, is therefore a tyrannical State or government. The only way out of the slavery we have allowed our political parties to impose on us is to reduce government; and at the same time, to reduce the preposterous powers of the parties, and if possible do away with them altogether.

The Horrors of 'Participation'

What is it? 'Participation' means different things to different people and needs to be carefully defined in its different meanings. It became a vogue word in the 1960s, and is still with us. It has undoubted pulling power, and therein lies its danger.

General de Gaulle was much interested in 'participation', although it was only right at the end of his reign in 1969 that he got around to defining it with any precision. There were at least two quite distinct notions competing for recognition: profit-sharing in industry and a share in decision-making for the workers. A French technocrat called François Bloch-Lainé wrote a short book entitled *Pour une Réforme de l'Entreprise* ('Towards a Reform of [private] Enterprise', 1963), in which he advocated giving the workers a financial interest in the companies that employed them. The French word *intéressement* condenses this idea neatly. De Gaulle was fascinated by Bloch-Lainé's book and publicly congratulated the author on it.

The General saw 'participation' as his way of taking the wind out of the sails of the Communists and other Marxists, who together constituted the only serious rival political force in France. The Gaullist movement had always included Leftists, who had flocked to the General's banner both because of his indirect leadership of the Resistance (against the Germans) and of the ideas for social reform he occasionally expressed. Among them were the philosopher David Rousset and the politician René Capitant, both of whom urged him, in the name of 'true' Gaullism, to go ahead and institutionalise some form of participation.

This was indeed the General's intention towards the end of his reign. After narrowly surviving the great Left-wing riots of May and June 1968, de Gaulle became obsessed with the idea of 'participation', which he mentioned frequently at Cabinet meetings. Few of his ministers, however, shared his enthusiasm. In an interview with his favourite television journalist, Michel Droit, he defined participation, at last, as involving both profit-sharing and a share in management for the workers, while students as well as teachers were to 'participate' in running the universities.

He had a grandiose scheme for two referenda: the first on the reform of regional administration and of the Senate, and the second on participation. Unfortunately for his vision of a new France, he lost the first referendum in April 1969 and promptly retired: so that participation was never formally offered to the French nation.

Perhaps this was just as well.

In Britain, participation has been given a more sinister twist by the concealed Marxist party that lives within and feeds upon the Labour Party. Its presumptive Parliamentary leader, Anthony Wedgwood-Benn (formerly Lord Stansgate, but wishing, for reasons of matiness, to be known as Tony Benn) supports a form of participation that would reserve industrial directorships not for workers actually employed in given factories, but for centrally appointed nominees of the Trades Union Congress. This intolerable proposal, which would considerably extend the already excessive power of the trade unions in an arbitrary and undemocratic manner, was embodied in the report of a Royal Commission headed by Professor Alan Bullock (Lord Bullock), the author of a well-known biography of Hitler.

The only form of participation which I find acceptable—within limits—is in its meaning of profit-sharing. There is no very obvious moral objection to giving the work-force a share in the profits generated in part by their labour. Indeed, to do so would in itself be a practical lesson in the absolute necessity of profits in private enterprise. As a device for reducing unnecessary envy and hostility, it could hardly be bettered. The necessary limits are of two kinds:

financial and political. Those who have risked their capital—the normal shareholders—should at all times have precedence in the distribution of profits over those whose contribution is a function of their employment.

In a successful enterprise, however, there is no reason why employees should not have a reasonable share of total profits. But this reward should take the form of cash grants, not shares in the company. If the recipients wish to invest their grants and other savings, let them do so, thus qualifying for first call on profits along with ordinary outside shareholders.

The political limit is of a more serious character. Participation—in whatever sense of the word—must in no circumstances be reserved for trade unionists only: non-unionised workers, whether they belong to groups that have no part in the trade-union movement, or are individual objectors to compulsory trade-union membership, must qualify as a matter of course. In this sense, the un-unionised typist or secretary should have equal rights with the fitter and turner at the factory bench. The objection to centrally appointed trade union nominees is absolute.

As regards worker participation in management, it is fundamentally a misconceived idea, born of envy and political malice. Management is a skill; so is tool-making. But they are not identical skills. A skilled tool-maker is not necessarily a good manager, nor is a skilled manager necessarily going to make high-precision tools if so required. (I speak in the light of wartime experience of factory work which revealed a total unfitness to be a fitter and an un-suspected gift for management.)

Consultation is another matter. Good managements should consult the workers as a matter of course, especially in decisions likely to affect their working environment, but also in major departures in manufacturing policy. The company that ignores this requirement is courting industrial trouble for which it will have only its management to blame. In the course of regular consultation, the worker of exceptional intelligence, ideas and initiative will be spotted and should be offered managerial promotion, if that is what he or she wishes to do. There should be no social or racial barriers to industrial mobility of this kind.

I have left to the end my general objections to participation. During the 1960s, the term 'participatory democracy' was heard quite often. It is a contradiction in terms, and in 1969 I wrote an article in the American magazine *Interplay* (now unhappily defunct) to prove the point. For emphasis, I called it 'Participatory Anarchy'. The danger lies in the distinction between the right to participate and the right to opt out. It is the right to opt out that ultimately distinguishes the libertarian State from the totalist experiments of the twentieth century and earlier. In the ultimate totalist States—especially China, Guinea and Cambodia—opting out is impossible: that is why they are the worst tyrannies currently on offer.

These contemporary examples, along with others from the past, strongly suggest that the right to participate normally turns rapidly into an absolute obligation to do so. Interestingly, this has been true not only of the highly organised and centralised Communist experiments of our time, but equally of the relatively few anarchist experiments of the recent or more distant past. The paradox deserves a pause.

In theory, anarchists (with or without a capital initial) are 'libertarian'. This at least is how they think of themselves. The Spanish Anarchists, who achieved *de facto* power in many places during the Civil War, called themselves 'libertarian communists'. They abolished the institutional signs of authority, and took over factories and courts of law, emptying the gaols, burning criminal records and land registers, and seizing properties. They also tortured and killed on a sickening scale. Nor did 'liberty' come as promised. Since money had been abolished, food and other necessities of life could be 'bought' only in exchange for work coupons stamped by the revolutionary committees, or by black-market barter. No gentle absenteeism as under 'capitalism'. Nor was travel freely available. Before a train could be taken to another area, the revolutionary committee would want to know why the applicant thought his or her journey necessary.

It was the same, and probably worse, with the experiments in theocratic communism of John of Leyden and Thomas Münzer in the sixteenth century: force, libertarian communism, terror and tyranny, execution, all in sequence. In the end, it was total repression, not freedom, that reigned.

Nor is any of this surprising. As I have noted, the State is necessary for the protection of the weak. If there is no State, the bullies and fanatics will take over. That is the end-result of anarchism. But it may be worse still if the bullies and fanatics take over the State itself, as in Cambodia: then there is no escape. And that, alas, is participatory democracy: forced participation, and no democracy.

In the final analysis, 'participation' is a stage on the road to forced collectivism, that is to the denial of liberty. In this sense, it is the antithesis of the Minimum State. Most men and women have no wish to participate in the workings of the State, although the impulse to do so may be stronger at the local level. If some of them really want to participate, by joining the appropriate organisations, they should have the right to do so. But this right should never be allowed to turn into an obligation. The right *not* to participate should be an absolute.

PART II

CASE STUDIES

ONE

THIS IS THE WAY YOUR MONEY GOES

I have performed an instructive private exercise. Taking a three-month period of Parliamentary time at random, I have worked out just what proportions of this time our legislators devoted to the three criteria of the Minimum State.

The period selected ran from 3 November 1977 to 26 January 1978 (I had intended to pick the first three months of 1978, but desisted on remembering that 'industrial strife' during that period had deprived the nation for a week or two of its daily record of the deliberations of its paid politicians). The broad results had better be presented in table form:

Total debating time	344 hours 48 minutes	100%
Defence	6 hours	1·74%
Safety (law and order; crime)	6 hours 45 minutes	1·96%
Money (fiscal policy)	27 hours 30 minutes	8·05%

To be fair, it should be noted that no fewer than 111 hours and 15 minutes were devoted to the admittedly important but exceptional subject of constitutional devolution for Scotland, and 10 hours 15 minutes to the same for Wales. If this lengthy period is deducted from the previous total, we get the following (improved) results:

Total	233·05 hours	100%
Defence	6 hours	2·69%
Safety	6 hours 45 minutes	3·02%
Money	27 hours 30 minutes	12·3%

Against this, it is worth mentioning that *no time at all* was specifically allocated to the internal security of the nation, as distinct from the safety of its citizens. The point may be obscure to laymen, and deserves some explanation. The safety of citizens may be said to be furthered if fewer crimes are committed or more criminals made to pay the penalty for their crimes. *Security* is more intangible. We are concerned here with the defence of a way of life, which is threatened not only by foreign agents, including both spies and 'agents of influence' (spreading ideas helpful, for example, to the Soviet Union and undermining the will to resist Soviet or Communist pressures); but also by subversive groups or parties whose membership is mostly British but whose efforts in the furtherance of totalist creeds is

subversive of British traditions and institutions. This vitally important subject was debated at some length in the House of Lords
on 30 April 1975, but no comparable debating time was allocated
in the House of Commons—in itself a commentary on the degree of
subversion already reached within the ruling Labour Party.

The House did, however, find itself discussing an important
security matter, but only because of the ingenuity and patriotism of
an able Conservative backbencher, Mr Stephen Hastings, who raised
it in the Debate on the Adjournment on 14 December 1977. What
Mr Hastings had to say concerned the information allegedly provided
by a Czech defector, Joseph Frolik, who reached the United States
in 1969. The sweeping and unpredictable nature of Britain's libel
laws makes it difficult for me to summarise the remarks which Mr
Hastings made under Parliamentary privilege: the newspapers of
15 December gave extensive quotations from his speech. It may be
enough for me to say that, according to the information in Mr
Hasting's possession, Frolik, under instructions from his former
employers, the Czech intelligence service, had attempted to recruit
certain leading British trade-union figures. On each occasion, however, having cultivated the necessary contacts, he was suddenly
ordered to drop the matter, but in a cryptic form which the speaker
did not attempt to explain (and neither shall I). Let me now quote
directly from Hansard for 14 December 1977, column 510:

> Next he started to cultivate Mr Jack Jones with whom, he says,
> he liked to think he got on very well.
> 'But—'
> as he puts it in his book—
> 'such things cost money. My expenses started to mount. They
> were forwarded to Prague whence, a little later, I got the brisk
> order "drop the Jones project, he's a horse of friends".
> Again,—'
> he writes—
> 'unwittingly I had bumped into one of the Russian colonel's
> contacts.'

Mr Hastings went on to offer three conclusions (Hansard, 14
December 1977, column 514):

> First, in the national interest, Frolik's evidence should not be
> discounted without further detailed and, so far as possible, public
> examination.
> Secondly, perhaps the best medium for his examination would
> be a Select Committee of the House, charged with duties com-

parable to those of the Senate sub-committee to which I have alluded [to investigate Communist bloc intelligence activities in the US].

Thirdly, our trade-union leaders should at the very least be warned of the consequences of fraternising too frequently or imbibing too deep with foreign Communist so-called diplomats. They are virtually all intelligence officers under cover, as such they are all under direct or indirect KGB control and they are all engaged in subverting parliamentary democracy in this country.

Not surprisingly, given the composition of the Labour side of the House, and despite the glare of press coverage which Mr Hastings's speech temporarily attracted, no action was taken. When it comes to the security of the realm, here was a government that would prefer not to know.

Of course the figures and percentages of Parliamentary time I gave earlier inevitably oversimplify complex issues. This I readily concede. It might, for instance, be argued that if little time is devoted to discussing a subject, it could simply mean that everything in that particular garden was lovely. After all, if we have all the defence we need and if there is no public concern over the level of crime, and if we are all happy with the gross national product, productivity and the sustained purchasing power of our money, there is not much point in talking about them. Instead, why not turn our attention to more fascinating topics such as industry and commerce (18 hours during the period under review), education (10½) transport (9¾), energy (10½), employment (12¾) not to mention such exotica as acupuncture (half an hour) or aid to Mozambique (half an hour).

It is disillusioning, therefore, to turn to the actual record of the debates on the vital issues. On crime (safety), we find Mr Cyril D. Townsend (Conservative, Bexleyheath) saying on 19 January:

> Crime, especially violent crime, is an increasing affliction on Londoners. The latest available report of the [Metropolitan Police] Commissioner—for 1976—records that nearly 500,000 indictable crimes became known to the Metropolitan Police—a rise of nearly 20,000 on 1975. Offences against the person increased to 12,613 and robbery and violent thefts increased to 10,219, including no less than 1,020 attacks on the police.

Mr Townsend was describing the situation in 1976, but six months later came the Report of the Commissioner of Police for the Metropolis, Sir David McNee, for 1977, which made it clear that the situation was continuing to get worse. Sir David's Report, published on 14 June 1978, recorded a 12 per cent increase in indictable crime and the worst wastage of manpower since 1946, with an overall loss of 355 male officers: fewer policemen chasing more criminals.

Back now to our Parliamentary sample, and to defence. The statistics of defence are notoriously misleading to the uninitiated, because of the number of ways in which they may be expressed. One may, for instance, be given a figure for the overall defence budget, but a comparison with a previous figure may turn out to be unilluminating because, in the meantime, inflation has distorted the picture. If one resorts to percentages, one has to be careful to check the basis for comparison. Is it a percentage of the gross national (or domestic) product, or of national income? Or a percentage of a country's total government expenditure? When comparing the defence efforts of, say, two or more members of NATO, do you use percentages (and if so, of what), or absolute figures? Or again, do you calculate in terms of spending *per capita*? All the methods have their points and their protagonists and opponents. The important thing is to know what you are doing, and what you are trying to prove (or disprove).

If you are a Left-wing Labour MP (I am allowing for the possibility that one such, or more than one, may read this book), you will be trying to prove that we contribute proportionately more than our share to the common defence and you will therefore express your figures as percentages of the GNP: you will, accordingly, forbear to mention that our British GNP has been stagnant, or has grown minimally, while the GNP of certain European allies, notably France and Germany, has shot ahead. But if you are a 'moderate' or sensible Commons man or woman, you will not resist the temptation to quote absolute figures (which are damaging to the Left-wing case), or even expenditure *per capita* (a devastating weapon).

The background to my Parliamentary sample on defence is as follows. The Labour Party returned to power in the disastrous circumstances of February 1974 (after the national coal-miners' strike during a three-day week), pledged to massive cuts in the defence budget. In his budget for 1975–76, the Chancellor of the Exchequer, Mr Denis Healey, announced a cut of £110 million or about 3 per cent in the defence allocation. The following year (April 1976), the Chancellor announced a further cut of £100 million; and in December 1976, he announced further cuts of £100 million and £200 million respectively for the years 1977–78 and 1978–79.

Now read on. Rising on 3 November 1977, during the Debate on the Address (that is, the Queen's Speech), the Leader of the

Opposition, Mrs Margaret Thatcher, drew the Prime Minister's attention to an (unprecedented) letter to the government from NATO'S Secretary-General, Dr Luns, complaining of our successive defence cuts. 'It is therefore', wrote Dr Luns, 'a cause for disappointment that the United Kingdom Authorities felt obliged to take steps which will have a direct or indirect adverse impact on the United Kingdom front-line forces.'

Mrs Thatcher was puzzled, however, for had the government not committed itself, in communiqués signed by the North Atlantic Council, to spending 3 per cent *more* on defence in coming years? Replying, Mr Callaghan evaded the issue in this fairly typical way (instantly intelligible to those who read my statistical explanations earlier in this chapter):

On the question of defence, I would only say to the Right Hon Lady that if every other NATO country spent the same proportion of its gross national product as we spend on defence, the troubles of NATO would have been over long since. . . . I believe that if every other country spent the same proportion as we do, it would be worth about $21 billion to NATO. Therefore, let some other people also consider where their responsibilities lie.

Clearly, this Prime Ministerial obliqueness did not exhaust the subject, and on 24 January 1978 no fewer than seven MPs tabled questions on the proposed increase of 3 per cent. They bore familiar names, including Maynard, Allaun, Atkinson and Litterick: all were of the extreme Left, and all wanted to know how the Defence Secretary reconciled the proposal to spend 3 per cent more on defence with the government's avowed intention to reduce the proportion of GNP devoted to defence to the level of our European allies.

The Defence Secretary, Mr Frederick Mulley, decided to deal with six of the questioners together. He confirmed that defence expenditure would rise by 3 per cent in 1978–79, and again by that amount the following year, but only if economic circumstances made it possible. This was made necessary by 'the marked and continuing growth of Warsaw Pact military power'. Pressed on the GNP issue, he pointed out that a 3 per cent increase in the defence budget was not equivalent to 3 per cent of the gross domestic product; moreover, since the GDP was rising, in the end we would be devoting only $4\frac{3}{4}$ per cent of our resources to defence, much as before.

Let us now step away from the Parliamentary sample and look at defence from another angle. I have thought it instructive to study the defence statistics issued yearly by the International Institute for

Strategic Studies in its *Military Balance*. To get an idea of the *trend*, I selected three editions: 1977–78, 1973–74 and 1962–63. One should compare like with like: it is not very illuminating to compare Britain's performance with America's. It makes sense to compare Britain with France, however: both are great (but not 'super') powers in defence terms, and both have been rivals throughout their recorded histories. The most significant facts are set out in the following tables:

1962/63

Britain		*France*
Total armed forces	415,000	705,000
Army	170,000	500,000
Navy	100,000	68,000
Air Force	145,000	137,000
Defence Budget	$4,180m	$3,786m
As percentage of GNP	6·67	7·2

1973/74

Britain		*France*
Total armed forces	361,000	503,600
Army	177,000	332,400
Navy	81,000	69,000
Air Force	103,000	102,000
Defence Budget	$8,673	$8,488m
As percentage of GNP	4·6	3·1

1977/78

Britain		*France*
Total armed forces	339,150	502,100
Army	175,250	330,000
Navy	76,700	68,500
Air Force	87,000	103,600
Defence Budget	$11,214m	$13,740m
As percentage of GNP	5·1	3·7

A few words of explanation. In 1962–63, the French land army was still swollen with the needs of the Algerian war, and the British also, to a lesser extent, through traditional involvements 'east of Suez'. A decade later, total French manpower had been slashed by more than 200,000, yet the defence budget had soared from less than $4,000 million to nearly $8·5 million, to pay for General de Gaulle's nuclear striking force. During the same period, Britain's military manpower had also been heavily cut, but the cuts had fallen mainly on the navy and air force. The defence budget had, however, doubled from $4·2 million to $8·7 million (in round figures), partly owing to the soaring cost of high technology, but also (and this was true of France too) because of inflation. But by far the most striking point about the comparison so far is that during the decade the two budgets, expressed as a percentage of GNP, had declined from 6·67 per cent to 4·6 per cent in Britain, but far more drastically in France, from 7·2 per cent to only 3·1 per cent. In effect, Britain was devoting to defence a percentage of its GNP 1½ times higher than France. The reason for this was simply that the French economy had grown so much faster than the British during the ten years— from $52,583 million to $273,806 million. In comparison the British economy had grown from $62,668 million to no more than $188,543 million. In other words, the French, starting from a much lower total figure, had caught up and overtaken the British during a decade which included the end of the Algerian war and the years of relative political stability and containment of the evils of party rule under the Fifth Republic.

The trend continues, until in 1977–78 we find the British spending 5·1 per cent of a GNP of $224 billion on defence, whereas the French, with a GNP of $353 billion, need to devote only 3·7 per cent to defence. And even at this relatively low percentage, they are spending more, in absolute terms, than the British ($13·7 billion to $11·2 billion). These figures demonstrate the absurdity of Labour's habit of making comparisons in terms of percentages of GNP. In terms of individual sacrifice, the figures are still more to Britain's disadvantage, for in 1977 the average Frenchman or woman was spending $256 a year on defence, and the British only $201. Understandably, these are not the statistics habitually quoted by Labour Ministers at Question Time.

What about the value of money, the third of our criteria? On that score, my Parliamentary sample tells us everything and nothing. The subject permeates every page of Hansard, but few Parliamentarians ever come to grips with it: among the few are the new Tory leaders—Thatcher, Joseph, Howe and others—who have grasped the hard fact that it is not going to be enough, in the future, for Conservatives to administer the legacy of socialism they inherit upon taking office, as Heath and Macmillan did, if the headlong drop into poverty is to be reversed and not merely delayed or slowed down.

A wise saying by a witty American diplomat and scholar, Dr Strauss-Hupé, is worth quoting. Asked at a conference in Brighton, which I also attended, to name the reasons why the defence budgets of the Western allies were inadequate, he replied: 'There are ten reasons. The first is Welfare, and the rest aren't worth mentioning.'

Indiscriminate Welfare in the name of 'equality' is indeed a major, perhaps *the* major, cause of bad government in Britain; and elsewhere too, to the extent that other countries fail to discriminate between those in need and those who can fend for themselves. The subject is important enough to warrant a chapter to itself. At this point, let me simply say that once governments commit themselves to the proposition that every one of their citizens is entitled to be looked after from the cradle to the grave, they have embarked on the road that leads to deepening poverty and even to bankruptcy. For what does 'looked after' mean in practice? It means unlimited health provisions, unlimited housing, unlimited schools, unlimited jobs, and if the jobs are not forthcoming, enough money to live on, so that it makes little difference whether a person has a job or not; in some cases, a person is better off without one.

For appetite, as the French say, grows with eating, and the human appetite for 'free' benefits is infinite. But unfortunately, resources are not: especially in small and crowded islands, poor in natural endowments, resources (including the bonanza of North Sea oil) are sadly finite. If the energies and intelligence of the people are not released for the competitive production of wealth; if the economy is shackled with mounting taxes to pay for non-finite welfare; if more and more of the work force is absorbed into a non-productive bureaucracy to administer the expanding State sector, the results include:

—An ever-growing 'public sector borrowing requirement'—that tasty morsel of euphemistic officialese for a State that can't balance its accounts.

—Inflation, caused either by printing money (which is what the Tories did under Heath), or by borrowing from abroad (Labour's favourite method); or both.

—Discouragement of investment, so that capital takes refuge abroad, or lies idle or involves itself in sterile speculation; all of which are stimulated by such envy-ridden follies as Capital Gains Tax and a wealth tax.

—High production costs and low productivity, so that exports are penalised and imports thrive, causing further imbalance. (If three men are on the payroll where one would suffice with new technology, productivity is three times as low as it need be.)

—Because things are getting worse, they get worse still: in other words, a socialist government (whatever its formal label), once caught in the downward spiral of its own making, will naturally resort to further doses of the measures that caused the situation to worsen in the first place—*unless compelled to do otherwise.*

The words I have emphasised are important, and serve to illustrate the costly folly of the party system. During its first year or more in office, the Wilson government of 1974 embarked on the spending spree implicit in the two Labour Programmes of that year. When inflation, which had been running at about 10 per cent a year, rose dramatically to 30 per cent, the government borrowed heavily from foreign or international sources, mainly the International Monetary Fund (IMF). The IMF loans or credits fortunately came with 'strings' in the form of necessary restraints on public expenditure. The ideological dose of socialism (the required price of support from the Marxists in the trade unions and constituencies) was therefore followed by an unsocialist dose of good housekeeping (the price of the rescue operation from the international banking system). It would have been more rational to avoid the socialist follies of the first period and avert or reduce the need for foreign aid. But rational government and the party system do not cohabit amicably.

Apart from the defence cuts (mentioned earlier), social security benefits were increased several times (a necessity, given the inflationary nature of the government's programme: first make living costs rise, then squeeze the taxpayer further to meet the rise). The unnecessary or damaging legislation included:

—New regulations to phase out grant aid to 173 grammar schools—rightly described by the Opposition spokesman on education, Mr Norman St John-Stevas, as 'an unprecedented step of educational vandalism' which would 'deprive parents of modest means of educational opportunity'. The grammar schools, among the finest in the world, had been found guilty of 'selection', that is of giving special opportunities to brighter pupils; this was intolerable in the name of 'equality', so they had to go.

—The Housing, Rents and Subsidies Act.

—A well-meaning Sex Discrimination Act so drafted as not merely to protect women from exploitation or discrimination but also to deprive employers of the common-sense right to distinguish between the sexes in matters not involving discrimination. Henceforth, it became an offence to advertise, for example, for a 'girl Friday' and the all-purpose word 'person' came neutrally into its own.

—The vicious Trade Union and Labour Relations Amendment Act 1976, which effectively confirmed the status of trade unions outside the law by repealing most of the admirable provisions of the ill-fated Trade Union and Labour Relations Act 1974.

—The Industry Act 1976, creating a National Enterprise Board with funds up to £1,000 million (of taxpayers' money) to be invested in projects (not of the taxpayers' choice) approved by the government and the unions.

—The Employment Protection Act 1976—in a sense the most obnoxious of the discriminatory labour laws of the Wilson government. It offered employees protection against any employer who might try to stop them joining a trade union, but none against unions that might try to bully them into joining against their will. 'Religious belief' was the only recognised reason for not joining a union. The Act set up an Advisory, Conciliation and Arbitration Service (ACAS), including representatives of the Trades Union Congress and the Confederation of British Industry. Despite its ostensible motives, however, ACAS was soon to demonstrate over the Grunwick dispute that it was decidedly biased in favour of the trade unions. (The issue at Grunwick, a small photo-processing plant in north-west London, was essentially whether the largely Asian work-force could be compelled to join a trade union. Despite massive and, at times, violent picketing, the unions lost.)

—The Health Services Act 1976, under which private pay beds were to be phased out of National Health Service hospitals. The effect of this doctrinaire measure, enacted in the name of 'equality', was to make it more difficult for leading doctors and surgeons to play their full part in the NHS, since instead of being on the spot they would have to travel between private clinics and NHS hospitals. In consequence, it was feared that an increasing number would either opt out of the Service altogether or emigrate.

It was ironical, in the light of such measures—costly, counter-productive or frankly retrogressive as they were, taken as a whole—to read the Chancellor's chastened words on 22 July 1976 and again on 15 December, when he told the House of Commons of the imperative need to reduce government borrowing from £11,500 million a year to less than £9 million over two years. The Marxists had had their way; now it was the turn of the bankers. Was this what the 'mixed economy' meant? If so, it made little sense. In money matters as in the other minimum requirements of the State, Britain was badly governed.

TWO

THE FRENCH SICKNESS

The title of this chapter is drawn from that of a remarkable book by the French politician Alain Peyrefitte, *Le Mal Français* (1976). It is a work of great richness and percipience, and is surely required reading for all who are interested in France and read the language. Since it has not, to my knowledge, been translated, I shall try to summarise its arguments and occasionally quote from its store of illustrations. In so doing, I shall inevitably over-simplify the author's profound and complex presentation. May he forgive me.

Briefly, then, the 'French Sickness' in Peyrefitte's eyes was simply centralisation, and the great culprits, and authors of France's prolonged relative backwardness, were two men greatly celebrated in the French history-books: Louis XIV and Colbert. This was the author's thesis, which is almost blasphemous to anybody brought up in France (as I was for seven years). As every schoolboy knows, Louis XIV the Sun-King said: '*L'État, c'est moi.*' And he meant it literally. In domestic affairs, the permanent top priority was the power and glory of the King. To this end all the resources and energies of the provinces were drained away toward Paris and Versailles. While the world admired the wit and glitter of the royal palace, the provinces starved or suffered in other ways. If the King's indefatigable Finance Minister, Colbert, had been alive today, he would be called a workaholic. Every day and all day he toiled for the greater power and glory of his master. Colbert wanted to centralise everything, and this meant not only the administration of the country but its entire commerce and industry. Everything was to be ordained from on high, by royal edict. Colbert, with the King behind him, would decide in the minutest detail how to build ships, how to manufacture steel, how to weave textiles. Those doing the work should be told how to export it, and how much, and at what price.

For a while his tremendous energy seemed to bring results, but in the long run this total control by the State had a paralysing effect on French development, in competition with neighbouring countries. In 1800, French industry was still producing 70 per cent more than Britain, but France's population was three times as large. By 1810, there were still only 200 steam engines in France, compared to 5,000 in Britain. By the beginning of the twentieth century, British industry produced 60 per cent more than the French. When the victorious French troops in the Great War entered Alsace in 1918, they were astonished to discover that after fifty years of German rule, the entire province had an advanced sewage system, running water, electricity, a telephone service and a social insurance scheme. French Alsace had remained a backward agricultural community, like most of France. Moreover, it is now known that between 1648 and 1662, between 1693 and 1695, and again between 1709 and 1720, France's population had declined drastically. France was a stagnant nation. What there was of private enterprise was successful, but suffered from the excessive preponderance of the State in areas that did not concern it. All through French society, the prevalence of the hierarchical principle had a paralysing effect. Nobody wanted to take a decision, which was always referred up and then further up, until it reached the top, when it had to come down again stage by stage and from official to official. The great French stagnation was hidden from public view by the spectacular deeds of men like Napoleon, and by the brilliance of France's performance in the arts. It was difficult for the French to admit the truth to themselves, and the history-books, with their emphasis on national glories, did not help.

Alain Peyrefitte recounts a rather pathetic story, which illustrates the inertia of the French State. After being elected as a deputy to the French National Assembly in 1958, he was taken, suitably clad, to visit the clay pits in his department. He was shocked by the working conditions of these men who spent their days kneeling in mud. The health record was equally shocking, with a high prevalence of lung trouble and advanced rheumatism. He promised to help them, and in particular to introduce a retiring age of sixty instead of sixty-five. In the end he kept his promise and did even better, introducing a bill which brought the retiring age down to fifty. But incredibly, it took him *eighteen years*, and from the time the bill was adopted to its actual application, six years elapsed. At every stage he encountered either indifference or hostility, or the entrenched blocking mechanism of the civil service. After the elections of March 1973, a local employer had said to him with a cynical grin: 'I warned you. The clay-pit workers didn't vote for you. In other words, you gave yourself all this trouble for nothing.'

Peyrefitte's comment is worth quoting for its relevance to this book: '*We must really be spiritually a long way from democracy to suppose that every public action is motivated by its electoral usefulness.*'

It is one of the merits of Peyrefitte's book that he sees the incompatibility between democracy and a liberal economy on the one hand, and an authoritarian and centralised State apparatus on the other. He dwells less than one would like on the feebleness of the party system, especially under the Fourth Republic, in which governments lasted on an average only six months. General de Gaulle's great achievement on returning to power in 1958 was to give his country a constitution which largely circumvented the party system by concentrating greater power into the hands of the President of the Republic, and thus conferring upon a volatile nation the inestimable benefit of governmental stability. The same volatile nation, unfortunately, turned out General de Gaulle without allowing him to introduce his major proposed reforms, loosely called 'participation' but intended in fact to decentralise power.

Peyrefitte does not really dwell on the mysterious transformation in the relative fortunes of France and Britain during the last twenty years. In 1954 and 1955 France was still the stagnant, centralised and backward country that Peyrefitte was writing about. But twenty years later the French gross national product had doubled, and was 45 per cent higher than Britain's, and with a smaller population. It is not difficult to see the causes of Britain's decline in the universal provisions of the Welfare State (rewarding the idle relatively more than the resourceful) and of a tax system which deprived the country of the necessary incentives to individual effort and merit. In other words, and in its fashion, Britain had caught the French sickness. The State was meddling everywhere and economic decisions had been taken out of the hands of those best able to exercise judgement. The result was stagnation.

The causes of France's sudden spurt forward were of course complex. Some credit must be given to those, including Jean Monnet (the 'father of Europe'), who rebuilt France's economic infrastructure —not least the railways—after the devastation of the Second World War. But it is not, I think, by accident that the real expansion did not take place during the feeble and party-ridden Fourth Republic, but under de Gaulle's more stable regime.

The French Fourth Republic is perhaps the archetypal example of the party system rampant, of what that percipient Spanish writer, diplomat and politician, Gonzalo Fernández de la Mora, called *La Partitocracia.** With a purely ornamental President as Head of State, the party leaders were free to play the game of politics in all its self-indulgent irresponsibility. The story was well told by the then Political Editor (and later Editor-in-Chief) of *Le Monde*, Jacques Fauvet, in his book *La IVe République* (Fayard, 1959). The fall of

* See Short Reading List.

the Fourth Republic is of course well-known, the Algerian agony having demonstrated for the last time its utter incapability of coping with a major challenge. General de Gaulle was called out of the tent in which he had sulked for years, to master the crisis and bury the Republic whose birth he had vainly opposed after the liberation of France. But its impotence had often been demonstrated, notably in the two great crises of 1953.

If a biographical note may be allowed, I have good reason to remember the second of these crises, which was over the election of a new President of the Republic (the first having been over the election of a new Premier). Returning to Europe in the late autumn, after five years in Australia and South-East Asia, I spent weeks in the tiniest hotel-room in Paris waiting to see the bureau chief of a news agency, who was covering the presidential election, having previously been absent on other reporting duties.

It was December, and a cold one. In the huge and underheated Hall of Mirrors of the Palace of Versailles, a few hundred shivering deputies amused themselves and the world for a week, casting vote after vote for candidates emerging from the hazards of the fluctuating parliamentary arithmetic. In the end, on the thirteenth ballot, the mild and well-meaning René Coty was chosen by his peers as President of the Republic. It was 23 December, and the deputies could go home for Christmas. Wryly, Coty commented: 'I have no illusions. If I am President of the Republic it is because I had my prostate operation. This prevented me from taking sides for or against the EDC.'

The EDC? Would any young participant in a quiz show identify these initials? In retrospect, for one of maturer years, the European Defence Community stands as a monument to the lost opportunities and the follies of party politics. The EDC would have created European armed forces out of contributions in manpower and arms from the original signatories of the Treaty of Rome, including Germany. If the French Assembly had voted for it, it is fair to assume that by the 1970s 'Europe' would have ceased to be dependent upon the armed support of the United States (which was no longer credible) against the overpowering threat from the Soviet Union. But this is a digression: Coty was right. Able-bodied politicians were divided irrevocably into supporters and opponents of the EDC and neither side could produce a presidential candidate with enough support to get elected. Coty, out of action because of the state of his prostate gland, could. Of such irrelevancies is democracy compounded.

The EDC issue (which was not finally resolved, negatively, until

August 1954, when Pierre Mendès-France allowed the project to be defeated in the Assembly as part of a deal with the Soviet Foreign Minister, Molotov, to bring peace to Indochina) dominated the earlier ministerial crisis of 1953. For thirty-six days France was without a government. The weary outgoing President, Vincent Auriol (whose decision not to stand for re-election was a form of protest against the impotence of his high office) invited one party or faction leader after another to have a go at forming a cabinet and surviving the ensuing vote of confidence in the Assembly. The eighth candidate, Joseph Laniel, got his majority on 26 June and went on against all expectations to last for eleven months, falling at last with the fall of the isolated fortress of Dien Bien Phu in distant Vietnam. Had it not been for this uncontrollable military circumstance, Laniel might indeed have gone on and on, for he had discovered the recipe for survival in a 'partitocracy'—to do nothing. Hence, Laniel became known as an *immobiliste* and his tenure of office as *immobilisme* entrenched—in itself a perfect commentary on the party system.

The arithmetic of the Fourth Republic is, in this context, instructive. Between its birth with the Constituent Assembly of 21 October 1945 and its death by auto-destruction on 9 December 1958, France had twenty-five governments. Of these, two (Schuman and Queuille) were overthrown the day they were formed. The last of its governments, under the returning de Gaulle, in fact lasted until 8 January 1959, when the Fourth Republic yielded formally to the Fifth.

By the criteria of this book, France was unquestionably far better governed under the Fifth Republic than under the Fourth. It is worth asking why.

De Gaulle's contempt for political parties was well-known and he made no attempt to disguise it. When he launched his Rally of the French People in 1947, he made it quite clear that this was to be no political party in the ordinary sense, but a mass organisation which people of many persuasions were welcome to join. He saw it as the vehicle whereby the French nation could be united under his leadership. This pretension inevitably provoked comparisons with the earlier ideas of Mussolini and Hitler and attracted the all-purpose epithet of 'Fascist'. But de Gaulle, as he later demonstrated, was no Fascist. In the terms of French history, he was a very unusual kind of Bonapartist, with a deep sense of the majesty of the State and an awareness of the need for authority.

The Rally grew rapidly, crested on a wave of popularity, then faded fast. De Gaulle retired to Colombey, nursing wounded pride and awaiting the call he felt sure would come from a distressed nation in need of a saviour. The Rally, meanwhile, and much to his disgust, turned into just another political party like the rest, so that today (1979), nine years after the General's death, Jacques Chirac's Gaullists (known after several changes of name as the UDR or Union des Démocrates pour la République) compete for power with other political groups; which is just what de Gaulle hoped the Gaullists would never do.

Having been unable to defeat or destroy the party system, de Gaulle was nevertheless able so to emasculate it as to prevent a return or continuation of the worst excesses and absurdities of the Fourth Republic. The new constitution, drafted under his general directives by Michel Debré, concentrated the ultimate power of the State in the hands of the President (himself, for a decade). Not only would the President himself appoint and dismiss the Prime Minister, but the ministerial team would be outside parliament and therefore no longer subject to the whims and plots of the politicians.

The outcome was a governmental stability unknown to the notoriously volatile French people since the *ancien régime*—until, perhaps to compensate for years of suppressed desires, pent-up feelings exploded in the 'events' of May 1968. The governments of the Fourth Republic had lasted weeks or months; those of the Fifth had several years of life. Debré, Couve de Murville, Pompidou: these men knew that the President would remove them if he felt their usefulness was temporarily at an end. But they also knew that they would be given enough time to do the job and that their survival did not depend on the factitious willingness of politicians to combine for or against the man in power.

Moreover, de Gaulle's Constitution (strikingly in contrast to Franco's in neighbouring Spain) survived the death of its creator. President Pompidou and President Giscard d'Estaing, each in his own style, were the beneficiaries of the far-sightedness of General de Gaulle (although it is clear enough that de Gaulle was thinking of himself and not his successors when he caused the Constitution of the Fifth Republic to be drafted).

Let us now look at the Gaullist experiment from another angle. I have said that France was better governed under the Fifth Republic than under the Fourth; and so it was. But it continued to be badly governed and over-governed in absolute terms. It was a question of degree. De Gaulle signally strengthened the autonomous defences of France against external enemies; although paradoxically he may have weakened France's security to the degree that he weakened its contribution to NATO by withdrawing from the integrated command structure of the Alliance. Under his successors, France has shared in the general decline of Western countries in regard to the physical safety of its citizens. Moreover, de Gaulle himself diminished the security of the realm by dismantling the entire machinery of the existing anti-Leninist psychological war centres throughout France (the co-called *Cinquième Bureaux*) and severing links with the corresponding organisations abroad.

True, the unwonted political stability his authority provided made possible the great economic expansion of France during the years 1962 and 1968, when France's gross national product grew spectacularly. Early in his reign he had called in the respected Antoine Pinay to deal with the perennial troubles of the franc, and Pinay had done what was expected of him, restoring confidence by the simple expedient of lopping two noughts off the face value of banknotes and calling the result a 'heavy franc'. Thus cured of their monetary ailment, the French obstinately went on reckoning in old francs, a conservative habit they persisted in well into the seventies. Inflation was never entirely cured, however, and was the main reason why Giscard d'Estaing, himself an economist with years of experience as Finance Minister, appointed the man he considered as his country's outstanding economist, Professor Raymond Barre, as Prime Minister some years after de Gaulle's death.

De Gaulle was not particularly interested in either economics or domestic affairs. His authoritative and reassuring presence was nevertheless a factor in France's astonishing great leap forward, as was no doubt the intangible factor of national pride, which he had largely restored single-handed. These were great achievements, but some would attribute France's economic growth at least equally to membership of the European Economic Community, which was not de Gaulle's favourite organisation; although, inheriting it from the Fourth Republic, he soon learned to use it (through the French veto) for the relentless pursuit of French interests, sometimes at the expense of France's partners.

A mixed bag, then. The General had grasped the main causes of French weakness and taken advantage of fateful circumstances and the luck of his own outsize personality to bring remedies of a kind. By divesting parliament of power to the advantage of the Elysée Palace, he had drastically reduced the irresponsible role of the political parties. But he had not succeeded in abolishing them, nor of curing the system of its potential for self-destruction. Subversion went on unchecked, and in the elections of May 1974 and March 1978 it brought France to the verge of destruction of free institutions. (It was never really clear, incidentally, what de Gaulle would have done if he *had* destroyed the political parties; and indeed he never seriously tried to destroy them after the failure of his Rally of the

French People. It must be assumed that he would have replaced them by a single ruling organisation, perhaps on the style of the *Movimiento* in Franco Spain, his admiration for General Franco being on the record. But since this did not happen, further speculation is useless.)

General de Gaulle's attitude towards communism is relevant to our concerns. It went through several phases. In his first provisional government after the Liberation, it was politically impossible for him to exclude the Communist Party which had played an outstanding part in the Resistance to German occupation (though only after the German invasion of Russia in 1941). It was clear that they were after a monopoly of power, and he narrowly averted a take-over bid between the Normandy landings and the end of hostilities. During the Rally-of-the-French-People period, he denounced them with contemptuous venom as 'the separatists'—in his mouth the ultimate insult. He could not accept them as, in the full sense, Frenchmen because of their primary allegiance to a foreign power.

During his second and major period of power, his attitude was more confused. I have mentioned his dismantling of the psychological war centres. His primary concern was with the role these centres were playing in Algeria, where their commitment to continuing French hegemony ran counter to the General's plans for a negotiated peace. The destruction of the counter-subversive apparatus in metropolitan France was an accidental casualty of the Algerian war. The fact remains that it was destroyed, and on his orders.

By then, de Gaulle was embarking on an essentially anti-American foreign policy, in pursuance of which he deluded himself into believing that he could negotiate on equal terms with the Soviet leaders. He could see some political advantage for himself in domestic terms in that his policy did, to some extent, take the wind out of the sails of the French Communists. Moreover, he envisaged his own rather hazy notion of 'participation' in industry as a move towards some kind of Gaullist 'communism' which would make the appeal of the Communist Party itself seem irrelevant.

There is no evidence, however, that de Gaulle—for all his erudition —had ever taken the trouble to understand Marxism, and still less Leninism. I write these words with some confidence as in the course of writing my biography of Charles de Gaulle, I read or reread all the General's published works and speeches. His references to communism display only a rudimentary knowledge of the subject. There are grounds for believing that the theme of the best-selling novel by Leon Uris, *Topaz* (about the planting of a Soviet agent of influence in the Elysée) was based on fact. And de Gaulle's decision to take France out of the NATO machinery in 1966 is cited as a Soviet success in the KGB training-schools, in the revelations of a Soviet defector, Aleksei Myagkov, *Inside the KGB* (Foreign Affairs Publishing, 1976).

In 1964, on learning of the death of the former leader of the French Communist Party, Maurice Thorez, de Gaulle went so far as to write to the latter's son: 'I do not forget that during a decisive period for France, Chairman Maurice Thorez as a member of my government contributed to the maintenance of national unity.' More perhaps than anything else he did or said, this statement conditioned French public opinion to acceptance of the CP as just another party competing for power. For Thorez had spent the war years in Moscow, having deserted from the French Army, and de Gaulle had allowed him to return in safety as part of his deal with the party.

There were of course other reasons for the CP's gradual acceptance. One was its masterly inaction during the riots of 1968, when its refusal to make common cause with the Leftist students contributed to the restoration of law and order. And more recently, there came the party's belated conversion to 'Eurocommunism', which meant the formal repudiation of one or two awkward doctrinal tenets, such as the 'dictatorship of the proletariat', and occasional criticisms of Mother Russia, without any essential change of objectives; but that is another story.

At all events, a revived French Socialist Party, under the leadership of François Mitterrand, was ready, in June 1972, to sign a Common Programme with the CP. This was a sinister and significant event. The Communists had been kept out of all French governments since the birth of the Fourth Republic at the end of 1946, because the Socialists, in common with all other parties, rejected the CP's claim to be a democratic party. Now the CP made a bow in the direction of democracy by accepting the principle of 'alternation'—that is, they declared themselves ready to step down from power if rejected at the polls. But Mitterrand committed himself, in return, to a programme of sweeping nationalisations which would, if carried out, have produced a fundamental change in the nature of French society in the direction of collectivism. There would have been seven or eight Communist ministers in a Mitterrand cabinet. France's defence secrets would no doubt have been made available to the Soviet Union, and the party would have gained access to the secret files of the French security service, the Direction de la Surveillance du Territoire (DST).

In May 1974, Mitterrand stood as candidate for the Presidency of the Republic and polled nearly 13 million votes, or 49·3 per cent of the total, to Giscard d'Estaing's 50·7 per cent. This was a narrow squeak indeed. 'Respectable' at last in the eyes of many French voters other than its traditional supporters, the Communist Party was ready for the great leap forward of the municipal elections of March 1977. Before polling, there were 14,000 Communist council-lors; the voting doubled that figure to 28,000. The public opinion polls inevitably translated these gains into dire prophecies for the general elections in March 1978. In the event, however, after electorally damaging polemics between the Communist and Socialist leaders, and an unprecedented anti-Communist campaign by banks and industries threatened with nationalisation, the Common Pro-gramme coalition (which included the small Left Radical Movement as well as the main Left-wing parties) was decisively defeated, and France (and the world) breathed again.

The threat of collectivism had been laid low, at least for the time being.

To understand how the threat had been allowed to grow one must remember de Gaulle's destruction of the official counter-subversive apparatus, and examine the partial take-over of the Socialist Party by Marxist-Leninists. What happened, in fact, was strikingly similar to what had gone on inside the British Labour Party.

There had always been a small Marxist-Leninist group within the French Socialist Party: nothing new in that. But in the early 1970s, a new and highly organised group, styling itself the CERES (*Centre d'études, de recherches et d'éducation socialistes*) made rapid inroads into the party. By 1975, the CERES controlled a quarter of the Socialist membership. Alarmed, Mitterrand kicked the CERES out of the key posts it held within the party's secretariat (but not out of the party itself).

The CERES, in fact, was typical of the New Left groups that proliferated in European countries after the occupation of Czecho-slovakia in 1968: highly critical of the bureaucratic terror in the USSR, but committed to collectivist policies, and in this particular instance deeply committed to making the Common Programme work—in other words, to collaborating with the Communists. Undoubtedly the Communist Party itself had penetrated the CERES; and possibly controlled it in the Communist interest.

The extent of the Marxist-Leninist take-over of Mitterrand's party has been authoritatively described in the French publication *Est & Ouest*, in a special issue dated 16–30 January 1978. The old Socialist Party of reassuring figures such as Léon Blum and Guy Mollet had gone. In its place was a party that was Socialist but had ceased to be social democratic. Mitterrand continued to advertise his belief in freedom, but seemed (perhaps sincerely) to be unaware of the logical contradiction between 'alternation' and a programme of 'irreversible' change. How like the Labour Party! It had become rather like the Socialist Party of the late Chilean President Salvador Allende—whom Mitterrand had publicly praised to the skies: a party which, if in power, would have rapidly brought social chaos and economic decline, paving the way either for a military take-over or (more likely, in France and with the Communists in power) a take-over by the real totalists, and the death of democracy.

THREE

TARNISHED MIRACLES

It was fitting that the term 'economic miracle' was first applied to the extraordinary success story of West Germany, emerging shattered from the Second World War and given its rebirth when Dr Erhard cut the shackles of the Occupation and gave the Germans their freedom of choice. I have described this *Wirtschaftswunder* elsewhere.

Interestingly, the German experience was repeated in each of the two other defeated Axis Powers—Japan and Italy—and in each case because free enterprise was allowed (in Italy's case for too brief a period) to flourish. Broadly speaking, the 'miracles' have gone on and on in Germany and Japan. Both are living examples of the unparalleled capacity of the market economy (misnamed 'capitalism') to create wealth. In Italy, the 'miracle' was less successful than elsewhere because too great a share of industry is in State hands; because a large and powerful Communist party was able to apply the brake at will; because the State bureaucracy was too large and inefficient; and above all because the party political system has proved a dismal failure.

My main concern in this chapter is the security problem which all three of these dynamic and industrious countries share in varying degrees.

The German Case

Democracy has shallow roots in Germany. The Kaiser was an autocrat, and the Weimar Republic, handicapped as it was by the burden of reparations imposed by the Allies at Versailles and without a real tradition to draw upon, committed suicide when the German voters handed themselves over to a madman named Hitler. The West Germans have nevertheless made a striking success (on the whole) of their post-war democratic experiment. For one thing, they passed the real test of a dual-party system when they voted themselves a change of government in 1969: the Christian Democrats, who had seemed set for ever, were out, and the Social Democrats were in.

This undoubted triumph for electoral democracy was not, however, a corresponding triumph for good government as defined in this book. On the contrary, the advent of the Social Democrats, who were heavily penetrated by Marxist ideas and personalities, almost immediately raised question-marks over the readiness of the new Germany to stand up to the threat to its existence posed by the presence of a hostile German State to the East, with the backing of the arch-enemy in the Soviet Union. This readiness had never been in doubt so long as the CDU–CSU was in power.

Chancellor Willy Brandt's notorious *Ostpolitik* seriously weakened the security both of the German Federal Republic and of the Atlantic Alliance as a whole, in ways I have analysed in detail in *Strategy of Survival*. The internal security of the country has been still more seriously undermined.

It would be unfair to blame the German Social Democrats for the wave of student unrest and political extremism that swept through Germany in the late 1960s and which was still a major problem when I wrote these lines late in 1978. For many other advanced countries experienced similar challenges during the same period. The feebleness of the Sate's response, especially in the initial stages, showed that in Germany as elsewhere the party political system is peculiarly vulnerable to violent internal challenges. In recent times it cannot be said on behalf of the West German Government that it has protected its people adequately. When it is possible for groups of terrorists to murder a leading banker, the head of the industrial employers' federations and a leading State prosecutor, the government in power must plead 'guilty' to a charge of failing to meet the first requirement of the Minimum State.

It must be admitted that the security problem in the Federal Republic is by its nature hideously difficult. At the end of the war large portions of eastern Germany were awarded to Poland in compensation for Polish provinces forcibly incorporated into the USSR. Millions of refugees poured into West Germany. In one sense they were welcome as they provided ready manpower at a time of urgent reconstruction. But it must be assumed that the Soviet secret police (at that time known as the NKVD) planted a fair sprinkling of spies among the truly dispossessed.

Later, with the gradual consolidation of the Communist regime in East Germany (which the Germans, incidentally, regard as 'central Germany'), and with the consequent deepening repression, refugees by the tens of thousands began to pour into West Berlin, whence, after a period of screening, they were transported to West Germany. This too gave the Soviet KGB (as the NKVD is now called, after

several name-changes) an excellent opportunity to plant spies, which
they are now known to have put to the best use. The drain on
manpower was running at nearly 30,000 a month when the Russians
abruptly ended it in 1961 by putting up the infamous Wall dividing
West Berlin from East Berlin.

It must be remembered that East Germany (the 'German Democratic Republic') is in the fullest sense a Soviet satellite, under
occupation by some twenty Soviet Army divisions and utterly
subservient to its Russian masters. The East German secret police
and espionage organisation, known as the Ministry for State Security,
has no independent existence, and is at the disposal of the KGB.
Since Germans speak the same language and are the same people
on either side of the ideological boundary, it is easier for the Russians
to plant agents in West Germany than anywhere else on earth. Still
further opportunities came with the opening of a Soviet consulate-
general in West Berlin in the wake of the signing of various East–
West treaties initiated by Chancellor Brandt.

About a thousand people a year are recruited for spying in West
Germany by the intelligence services of the Soviet bloc. Estimates
of the number of East German spies living in West Germany have
varied considerably, but an authoritative figure of 2,000 to 3,000
was available in 1975.

To deal with this threat, the Federal Government has two main
agencies: the BfV (Office for the Protection of the Constitution) set
up by the British occupying authorities as a security service operating
within strict constitutional limitations; and the BND (Federal
Intelligence Service), set up with American support after one of the
heads of Hitler's intelligence service, Reinhard Gehlen—one of the
most remarkable men of our time—came over with the accumulated
archives he had saved from destruction. By definition, the BND is
more concerned with spying on East Germany and other countries
of the Soviet empire than with the spies on West German soil. The
burden, then, falls mainly on the BfV. From all accounts, it appears
to be a very efficient and professional organisation. It undoubtedly
did an excellent job under the original Federal Chancellor, Dr
Konrad Adenauer, and his Christian Democrat successors; under
the Social Democrats, it has been hampered, at times, by the
objections of principle raised by Left-wing members of the ruling
party, or by a disinclination on the part of the government to act on
information received. Thus, it is known that the BfV tipped off
Chancellor Brandt that he had a spy right in his own office, but the
Chancellor refused to do anything about it for months. In the end,
his personal assistant, Günter Guillaume, was unmasked and gaoled

as an East German spy (but working for the Russians) and Brandt lost his job.

In another sense too, West Germany's security declined sharply during the disastrous Brandt Chancellorship. For shortly after coming to power, he issued a directive to the BND, requiring it to disclose the *sources* of secret intelligence to him and to his ministers. Since reliable intelligence requires the absolute protection of sources (whose lives or at the very least whose usefulness would be imperilled by disclosure of their identity), this was a body blow to the organisation that had been patiently built up by Gehlen, and a number of senior officers of the BND resigned in protest. The organisation was thus seriously weakened at a time when the espionage threat from the East was on the increase. It is worth noting, in the context of this book, that this weakening of the internal and external defences of the Federal Republic was the direct consequence of the party political system, since it resulted from the replacement of a government that cared about these matters by one that did not, or cared a good deal less.

Espionage is, of course, only one of the security problems that face the BfV. Another one, of growing gravity, is terrorism, and with it subversion of milder kinds. Subversion is a systematic attempt to undermine a society and its government. By definition it is an active process, carried out by organised groups. In Germany, ultimately the most important of these groups is the Communist Party, now known as the DKP (*Deutsche Kommunistiche Partei*). The party, formerly known as the KPD (*Kommunistische Partei Deutschlands*) was banned under the Adenauer government in 1956, and the ban stuck for twelve years. Although it changed its name (because the KPD had been declared unconstitutional by the Federal Court), it was essentially the same party with the same leaders. As in Britain, the party is small (with some 34,000 members in 1972, when the problem of subversion was becoming really acute). But its importance lies in the fact that it is basically an extension, a branch office, of the ruling Socialist Unity Party of East Germany, from which it gets abundant funds. It is an orthodox Marxist–Leninist party, dedicated to ridding West Germany of the free enterprise system that has made the country one of the richest in the world, and to turning it into a collectivist society on the Soviet model.

Around the DKP, and not necessarily on harmonious terms with it, is a profusion of Marxist–Leninist or anarchistic groups dedicated to violent revolution. There are also a number of neo-Nazi organisations; but despite a powerful and sustained Communist campaign to denounce them as a threat of Hitlerian dimensions, they are far less of a menace than the Marxist–Leninist groups, their memberships and appeal being minimal. There is indeed considerable evidence that many of the so-called neo-Nazis are Communists in disguise, and that some of the 'right-wing' incidents that rightly attracted much condemnation (such as the daubing of walls with anti-Jewish slogans) were in fact the work of Communist provocateurs.

Broadly speaking, the Marxist–Leninist groups outside the DKP constitute the so-called New Left, in Germany as elsewhere. One of its leaders, a young revolutionary named Rudi Dutschke, coined the significant slogan: 'The long march through the institutions'. The onslaught of the German New Left, which involved a good deal of intimidation and some actual violence, was concentrated on the political parties, the trade unions, education and the armed forces. They were less successful in the trade unions than elsewhere, partly because most of the young Marxist–Leninists were the affluent sons and daughters of middle-class parents; and partly because the German trade unionists, more sensible in this regard than, say, their British counterparts, were well aware that West Germany owed its prosperity to the market economy, which they had no interest in destroying or undermining.

Elsewhere the New Leftists had striking successes. They captured the youth movement of the Social Democratic party (*Jungsozialisten* or Jusos), seriously penetrated schools and universities, and brought two universities (Bremen, and the Free University in West Berlin) entirely under Marxist–Leninist control. As for the armed forces, the Marxist–Leninists sponsored a vigorous and successful campaign against military service—that is, in defence of conscientious objectors. As a result the number of young recruits declaring themselves to have a conscientious objection soared rapidly, reaching nearly 28,000 in a single year. A particularly disruptive feature of this campaign was a new technique whereby the young 'objectors' revealed themselves as such only after recruitment and on receiving their uniforms.

A determined attempt to counter this menacing progress was made early in 1972, when the Federal Chancellor (Brandt) and the Minister-Presidents of the Länder (provinces) issued a directive banning the employment of members of extremist organisations in the Civil Service. The test was to be loyalty to the Constitution, and applied to teachers as well as to other civil servants. This measure undoubtedly reduced penetration of West Germany's institutions, although nothing could be done about those already employed by the State.

The difference between those who used intimidation and minor violence (for example in demonstrations) to gain their ends and those who resorted to real acts of terrorism was one of degree not of kind. Since 1968 West Germany has been plagued by a wave of terrorism which has revived more than once after apparently being suppressed.

At the centre of this plague of violence is the so-called Red Army Group, better known as the Baader–Meinhof gang from the names of two of its leaders, Andreas Baader and Ulrike Meinhof. Although the German authorities term this sordid gang 'anarchist', it is undoubtedly of Marxist–Leninist origin. Indeed it was learnt long after the gang had started its terrorist campaign that the publication which expressed the 'ideology' of the gang, *Konkret*, was financed by East German Communist secret services on behalf of the KGB.

They made their debut in April 1968 by setting fire to a department store in Frankfurt. Over the next few years the gang were responsible for many hundreds of outrages, including bomb attacks on US military installations, on the publishing premises of the Right-wing Axel Springer group in Hamburg, and attacks on judges and public prosecutors. One of the activists was a young lawyer called Horst Mahler, who wrote a paper entitled *An Armed Struggle in Western Europe*, in which he quoted Lenin as the sanctioning authority of the group.

Nearly all the leaders of the gang were arrested in the summer of 1972. The arrests halted the violence, but only for a while. New groups sprang up, inspired by the example of Baader and Meinhof. The trial of the accused leaders was protracted and served as a rallying point for hostile demonstrations by sympathisers, and as a continuing occasion for legalistic obstacles raised by the defence lawyers, who were found to be acting as couriers for the terrorists. In May 1976 Ulrike Meinhof committed suicide by hanging herself in her cell, and Baader and other leaders followed her example in October 1977 (though in their case with firearms which, incredibly, had been smuggled into their cells, presumably by the defence lawyers: Meinhof had used lengths of towel as a rope).

On 7 April 1977, three weeks before the close of the trial, a motor-cyclist with a pillion passenger drew alongside the car of the German Chief Federal Prosecutor, Dr Siegfried Buback. The passenger was armed with a sub-machine gun, which went into action. It was an easy target, as the car was stationary at traffic lights. Dr Buback and his chauffeur were killed. Responsibility was claimed by a body styling itself the 'Ulrike Meinhof Commando'.

On 30 July 1977 a young woman called Susanne Albrecht called at the home of Dr Jürgen Ponto, chief executive of the Dresdner Bank, in Oberursell near Frankfurt. She was a friend of the family and was admitted with a smile of welcome. With her were two companions. When Dr Ponto entered, they shot him dead. This time, a group calling itself 'Red Morning' claimed it had done the deed.

The third in a trio of ghastly acts began on 5 September 1977 when a gang ambushed the car of Dr Hanns-Martin Schleyer, president of one of the employers' federations. The ambush took place near Cologne. The chauffeur and three policemen were killed. Schleyer himself was kidnapped. Six weeks later, telephone calls in Paris led to the discovery of his body in the boot of a car at Mulhouse near the German border.

Had the West German authorities been too soft? Probably they had. It must be said that there were strong extenuating circumstances. The Germans were bowed down by the memories of official horrors under Hitler's rule, when many of those of middle age and over had served: not everybody is, or is capable of being, a resistance hero, and under the Nazis membership of the party or at least acquiescence in its misdeeds (not all of which were publicly known at the time) was the road to promotion. It was hard for Germany's youth to give their elders the respect to which the latter felt entitled. In the light of recent inheritance the German government, in all its manifestations, was determined to lean over backwards to show that it was not infected by authoritarian tendencies, and was truly democratic and tolerant.

But the shock of the appalling events I have recalled was salutary. On 3 August 1977 the Federal Cabinet decided to expand and strengthen the three organisations primarily responsible for internal security and law enforcement in the Republic: the BfV, mentioned earlier; the Federal Criminal Office (BKA); and the Federal Border Police (BGS). Terrorist suspects were denied access to their lawyers. One of these, Klaus Croissant, had taken refuge in France, but was extradited amid stormy demonstrations, bomb attacks and the protests of 'civil rights' groups in France (demonstrating yet again that the main concern of civil rights groups is invariably with the rights of terrorists and their accomplices and not with the right to life of their victims).

The reaction had come late, but was a welcome sign that in West Germany at least, the State was ready to defend itself. In 1976, shortly before the worst outrages resulted in the new security measures being taken, a man who for years had run the Office for the Protection of the Constitution, Günther Nollau, published a book under the significant title: *Wie Sicher ist die Bundesrepublik?* ('How Secure is the Federal Republic?'). He examined the problems discussed above in greater detail and concluded that for a country that had become one of the freest in the world, the Federal Republic was indeed remarkably secure. This amounted perhaps to saying, although he did not say it, that West Germany was as secure as its citizens wanted it to be—in other words, that they preferred individual freedom to remain uncurtailed rather than opt for greater security. Or in still other words, that West Germans were prepared to live with terrorism.

The fact remains that within months of the appearance of Nollau's admirably objective book, a judge was murdered because he was a judge, a banker because he was a banker, and an employer because he was an employer. Can a civilised society tolerate such outrages? This is a question which ultimately only the Germans themselves can answer.

Japan's Red Terrorists

The Japanese economic miracle is if anything still more astonishing than the German (although physical destruction was less complete), if only because the archipelago is mountainous, overcrowded and lacks all major raw materials. It is enlightening to compare Japan's party democracy with West Germany's. Unlike West Germany, Japan has never yet established its democratic credentials by peacefully changing its government at the polls. This is undoubtedly a blessing, for it has enabled the Japanese to avoid some of the problems inherent in party politics. Ever since democratic life began under the American occupation, the Japanese have been ruled by the same set of people: the Liberal–Democratic Party, which, despite its fancy double-barrelled name, is simply a conservative party. Almost any conceivable change would be for the worse in that it would hand the country over to socialists, communists or religious fanatics. Fortunately for the ruling group, the opposition parties have always been weak. In effect, Japan has very nearly had a no-party State, or to be more accurate, a one-party system without the disadvantages of one in that the political liberties have been freely, but unsuccessfully, exercised by opposition groups.

There was no democratic tradition at all to build on, not even a Weimar Republic—only centuries of imperial despotism with, in the recent past, a militarist regime of unparalleled ferocity. The Japanese emerged from the war humiliated and psychologically shattered. They took to democracy because it was the creed of those who had defeated them; and because in General Douglas MacArthur they had a despot of another kind, determined and able to impose democracy upon them. It was MacArthur, the uncrowned foreign emperor of the moment, who gave the Japanese a land reform which brought satisfaction to landless farmers, and a constitution which not only enshrined party democracy but also contained a clause (Article 9) under which the Japanese renounced war as 'a sovereign right of the nation', and undertook never to maintain 'land, sea and air forces, as well as other war potential'.

After recovering from the stunned apathy of defeat, the Japanese people got down to work. They worked for democracy and they worked to better themselves. They canalised all their ingenuities and energies into the peaceful pursuit of economic expansion. In the process they transformed their island country from an unevenly developed and in some respects backward one into an economic giant, the third in the world, and potentially the second after the United States.

My concerns are not with this well-known and important background, but with the requirements of good government. How does Japan score? The short answer is, 'rather well'. But some nuances are needed:

1. On the safety and security of the citizens: fairly well, for a bustling industrial nation.

2. On defence against external enemies: also fairly well, but in special circumstances that call for comment.

3. On the value of money: abroad, excellent. The yen is at or near the top of the world league in the exchange charts. At home, not so well. Japan's heavy dependence on imported oil from the Middle East (90 per cent of domestic needs) caused an inflation rate of 22·7 per cent in 1974, the year of maximum impact of the Arab oil embargo. Even in 1977, the rate was about 9 per cent.

Working backwards, I don't propose to elaborate on my summary remarks on Japan's handling of money: despite inflation at home, the Japanese must be reckoned among the most successful governments in the world on the third requirement of the Minimum State.

In defence, Japan has been both helped and hindered by special circumstances, both connected with defeat at the hands of the Americans. Having renounced war to please the Americans, Japan signed a security pact with the United States, in effect entrusting its defence to that country. The emergence of a Communist regime in China, the Korean war, and the French military involvement in Indochina, caused the Americans to change their minds about keeping Japan disarmed, and in the early 1950s they began to press the Japanese government of Shigeru Yoshida to rearm.

This presented Yoshida and his cabinet with a dilemma that was both moral and constitutional. The exact wording of the Article headed 'Renunciation of War' in the Constitution of 1947 is worth quoting so that its sweeping nature can be appreciated:

> Aspiring sincerely to an international peace based upon justice and order, the Japanese people for ever renounce war as a sovereign right of the nation and the threat or use of force as means of settling international disputes.
>
> In order to accomplish the aim of the preceding paragraph, land, sea and air forces, as well as other war potential, will never be maintained. The right of belligerency of the State will not be recognised.

Note the key words: 'for ever' in the first paragraph, and 'never' in the second. Certainly the successive Japanese governments have never given the slightest sign of bellicosity since the Second World War ended 'not necessarily in Japan's favour' (to quote the euphemistic Imperial Rescript with which Emperor Hirohito obliquely recognised defeat). For many years any foreign suggestion that Japan should, for instance, manufacture nuclear weapons aroused howls of the most sincere popular and political indignation. Japan remains the only country in the world in which atomic bombs have exploded with hostile intent. The suggestion that Japan should acquire the enormously more destructive weapons available today is viscerally resisted. By and large, MacArthur's aim of a demilitarised and unbelligerent Japan was accomplished.

And yet, the Yoshida government yielded fairly swiftly to America's pressure in favour of rearmament, or at least of *some* rearmament: enough to keep the Americans quiet, but not enough to cause a storm at home. This readiness to rearm was clearly in breach of the Constitution, so a formula of suitable verbal hypocrisy had to be found. Yoshida took the view that the acquisition of armaments for 'defensive' purposes was consistent with the letter and the spirit of the Constitution. Today Japan's 'Self-Defence Forces', although minute in comparison with the nation's awesome potential, constitute a formidable enough military machine: 238,000 men under arms, with a mechanised division and twelve infantry divisions, fifteen submarines and thirty destroyers, and 364 combat aircraft. The fiction that this capacity does not constitute 'land, sea and air forces, as well as other war potential' is tacitly accepted.

The Japanese State can legitimately claim that it does provide for defence against external enemies, both by its security pact with the United States and by its Self-Defence Forces. There is, however, an air of impermanence about these dispositions. For one thing,

America's defeat in Vietnam and its subsequent failure to aid its South Vietnamese allies, exposed the United States as an unreliable ally. What, in these new circumstances, is the real value to Japan of the security pact with America in any potential crisis in which it might need to be invoked? This question is being asked with increasing frequency in Tokyo.

Another comment must be made. General MacArthur imposed his 'no-war' Constitution on Japan by right of conquest. In 1947, the United States was the sovereign power in Japan, and MacArthur was its executant. But sovereignty effectively reverted to Japan in 1951 with the signing of the Peace Treaty of San Francisco. Although it has suited Japan to look to America (and to that broken reed, the United Nations) for protection, it can be predicted with absolute certitude that the day will come when Japan will reassert its sovereign right to be a power in its own right; which, given the country's enormous economic capacity, can only mean a super-power.

When it comes to internal security, Japan has a heavy inheritance of political violence. The ritual suicide of the right-wing author Yukio Mishima in 1970 was part of that tradition; and so are the endless student riots and the violent ecological demonstrations that delayed the opening of Tokyo's new Narita airport for several years. The Japanese contribution to transnational terrorism is a gang of singular savagery, the Rengo Segikun, or United Red Army. It was this group which shocked the world in May 1972 when three of its members bombed and machined-gunned passengers at Lydda airport, Israel, killing twenty-five and wounding seventy-eight. It was later established that they had been trained in North Korea, had gone to Germany for passports and to Italy for arms, and had done their deed on behalf of the Popular Front for the Liberation of Palestine. It was this and similar incidents that caused me, at that time, to coin the term 'transnational terrorism'.

The Japanese security forces must be given high marks for the determination with which they pursued and eventually broke up the United Red Army. In 1970, this gang of fanatics numbered about 300. By late 1977, its number was down to between twenty and thirty, and nearly all its activities took place abroad.

On the first requirement of good government, then, Japan must be given a higher rating than its wartime ally, Germany.

Collapse in Italy

Comparisons between nations as disparate as Japan and Italy should not be pushed too far. But it is interesting to note that in

Italy, as in Japan, one political party has exercised power ever since the restoration of national sovereignty after defeat in the Second World War: the Christian Democrats. In Japan, this *de facto* one-party State (with freedom for other parties) has worked rather well; in Italy, after a brilliant start, it has proved a total failure and has led to the breakdown of the State. Italy's only rival as the 'sick man of Europe' is Britain; and Italy is a good deal sicker. The phenomenon is worth analysing.

First, the days of success. Both Germany and Italy, the defeated Axis Powers, were fortunate in having an outstanding statesman to guide their post-war recoveries: Alcide de Gasperi was to Italy what Konrad Adenauer was to West Germany. As Prime Minister in four successive administrations between 1948 and 1953, de Gasperi appeared to have laid solid foundations for both prosperity and unity, in a country of great historical achievements in which unity had come late and was notoriously fragile. But the lesser men who followed de Gasperi proved incapable of building durably on the foundations he had laid. By the mid-1970s the Christian Democratic party had degenerated into self-seeking cliques flawed by corruption and incompetence.

The Italian economic miracle was scarcely less notable than Germany's or Japan's. By 1970, though devoid of coal and iron ore, Italy ranked among the ten major industrial countries of the Western world. During the 1960s, industrial production had increased by 7 to 8 per cent a year, and the growth in the gross national product exceeded 12 per cent a year between 1969 and 1970.

Then things started going wrong: 1971 was the year of disappointment when growth went into reverse, with a decline of 3·5 per cent in industrial output. Strikes and labour unrest became the norm. There was less money in people's pockets and demand fell. Profits were therefore down, and so was investment. Wage costs, moreover, rose by 18 per cent in 1970 and by a further 14 per cent in 1971. Prices rose accordingly.

Political violence began to settle in with the student riots of 1968, which lasted longer, were more violent and had deeper consequences than the far more publicised troubles in neighbouring France. In France, the rioting dominated May 1968 and started petering out in June. In Italy, it began in June 1968 and went on for a full two years.

Governments succeeded each other in monotonous impotence. By the mid-1970s violence was endemic in Italy. Some of it was new-Fascist (New Order), but most of the terrorist gangs were of the extreme Left, and of those the most active were the Red Brigades and the Armed Proletarian Nuclei. A symptom of the general decline in public order was the growth of kidnapping as the lucrative crime of the moment. The terrorists had popularised this device, which had proved its value in South America where enormous sums were extorted from the families or business associates of those inhumanly deprived of their liberty and often of their lives. A crime is a crime, whatever the claimed motivation. Suffice it to say that in Italy many of the gangs who kidnapped for gain did not even claim political motives.

The grisly climax came in the spring of 1978. On 16 March the most important Italian politician, Aldo Moro, aged sixty-one, was kidnapped in a street ambush in Rome, in which his five bodyguards were shot dead. Signor Moro, one of the leaders of the Christian Democrats and several times Premier, was the author of the so-called 'opening to the Left' policy of the 1960s, which he felt was the only way to provide Italy with a stable coalition that could introduce reforms while keeping the powerful Communist Party (PCI) at arm's length. Essentially this *apertura a sinistra* involved a coalition between the Christian Democrats, the Socialists, Social Democrats and Republicans. It was not, incidentally, a success; but Moro was unrepentant and shortly before being kidnapped he had just persuaded the PCI, for the first time, to support the parliamentary majority. He had been generally expected to become the next President of the Italian Republic.

The terrorists demanded the release of fifteen Red Brigades leaders then on trial in Turin, within forty-eight hours, as the price for Moro's life. There was no response, and they announced that Moro was to be 'tried' by a 'people's court'. From time to time, Moro himself was allowed, and doubtless encouraged, to issue pathetic appeals to his political colleagues to do something to save his life. A massive man-hunt, involving tens of thousands of police and army units, was abortive. Eight weeks after the abduction, the terrorists deposited Moro's bullet-ridden body in a car which they left, with obviously intentional symbolism between the headquarters of the Christian Democrats and of the Communists.

This was the pass to which Italy had been reduced.

How did it happen? There can be no doubt that the great, the overwhelming responsibility for Italy's deepening plight rests on the Italian Communist party. It is the existence of this huge and well-organised party, the largest in the world not actually in power, that most clearly differentiates Italy from Japan in political terms. The PCI emerged from the Second World War with the prestige of the leading role it had undoubtedly played in inspiring and leading the Partisans in national liberation and the struggle against Fascism.

The same was broadly true of France, but there was an important difference: France had General de Gaulle, and de Gasperi, although a statesman of high quality, was not a corresponding counterweight.

From the start of the post-war period the PCI enjoyed full legal rights. It took part in the first Republican government, when its leader, Palmiro Togliatti, was Minister of Justice. Later, de Gasperi decided to exclude them. Togliatti toyed with the idea of an insurrection but soon gave it up as impractical at a time when Italy was being rapidly incorporated into the Western community under American protection. Instead, he decided that power would be achieved by legal means.

The long-term strategy of Italian Communism had been laid down many years earlier by one of the founders of the party, Antonio Gramsci. An original thinker for a Marxist, Gramsci had perceived that in an agricultural and Catholic country such as Italy, power could not be seized by anything so crude as a workers' revolt. The peasants had to be won over to form an alliance with the urban workers; and even the middle classes had to be wooed. In the end, the existing system would be destroyed from within, both by the harassment of class warfare and by the ideological penetration of people's minds.

Gramsci had done his thinking under the Fascist regime and largely in their prisons. But Togliatti adopted his strategy as his own in the vulnerable post-war Republic. In a brilliant study (*The Long-term Strategy of Italy's Communists*, Conflict Studies No. 87, London, September 1977), Vittorio Pons demonstrated with what precision the PCI executed this long-term programme. The party played in the truest sense a double game. On the one hand it posed as a serious and responsible party of government, running the municipalities it controlled, such as Bologna, as model and uncorrupt administrations. In this moderate role, and with its pretensions of social justice, it won over many Catholics and made deep inroads into the Church of Rome. On the other hand, meanwhile, it was creating mass discontent by its pervasive penetration of the educational system at all levels and by the dominant voice it achieved in radio and television.

The negative side of this parallel policy was extraordinarily successful. In practice, the party had a veto on industrial activity. It controlled the largest trade-union group, the CGIL, and could call strikes at will; moreover, it tolerated and covertly facilitated the wrecking activities of the extreme Leftist *gruppuscoli*. It was a 'heads we win, tails you lose' situation. Hundreds of thousands of small and medium enterprises were harassed by wildcat strikes, clashes, or actual sabotage. Officially, the PCI deprecated such activities; covertly, it encouraged them. But in Emilia-Bologna, which the party controlled politically, private industrialists, businessmen and professional people were protected against disruption, given public contracts and taxed in moderation, in return for support, including monetary gifts to party funds.

The game was so subtle, and the public-relations techniques of the party so sophisticated, that many people, abroad as well as in Italy, fell for the line that the PCI had ceased to be a Communist party in the true sense, although there was no sign that it was about to abandon 'democratic centralism' (the core of Leninist party organisation) or its long-term aim of a collectivised Italy.

Perhaps the worst aspect of the Gramsci–Togliatti programme (which the party's latest leader, Enrico Berlinguer, pursued with intelligent doggedness) was its debilitating effects on the machinery of the State. For three decades, the PCI constantly attacked its country's institutions: the State itself, the regime, the government, the political parties, free enterprise, the army, the police, the security and intelligence services. There was a tragic irony in the hypocrisy with which one of the party's leaders, Pietro Ingrao, the first to preside over the Chamber of Deputies, appealed on 29 May 1977 for mass intervention in defence of law and order. True, the party had not, at least publicly, incited anybody to break the peace or in any way to indulge in violence. Yet for years it had systematically undermined every institution charged with maintaining law, administering justice, bringing criminals to account or keeping watch on the activities of extremists. Nor should it be forgotten that the Red Army Brigades were themselves an outcrop of the PCI. Both called themselves Marxist–Leninist.

The ideological permeation of the armed forces and the police had grave implications. Soldiers were enjoined to remember their social origins and to disobey the 'bosses' army'. Anti-militarist slogans were spread around and soldiers were encouraged to discover as many military secrets as possible. The long-term effects of this kind of propaganda are hard to calculate. But in the 1970s, the best-informed opinion tended to the view that in the kind of crisis which NATO was designed to counter, a fully mobilised Italian Army would be, at best, of uncertain reliability; at worst, an asset to a potential enemy.

One of the shocking aspects of the Moro case was the passivity of the Italian body politic. True, police and troops had been mobilised in their thousands to find the criminals, though without success. But in Turin the trial of the Red Brigades leaders went on its tranquil course, yielding in the end a moderate sentence of seven years on the terrorist chief Renato Curcio. The politicians themselves gathered in conclave to elect a new President, choosing in the end, and after repeated ballots, a Marxist of a rather mild kind, Sandro Pertini. The spectacle of their manoeuvres and of their shifting voting patterns irresistibly recalled the protracted search for a president of the French Fourth Republic at Versailles at the end of 1953, which I have described elsewhere in this book.

Commenting on these events in the Paris review *Est & Ouest* of 15 July 1978, the distinguished French observer Georges Albertini found himself reminded of a striking passage in that masterpiece of Italian and world literature, Tasso's *Jerusalem Delivered.* In it, Tasso, whose great poem was published in 1581, described an officer whose head had just been chopped off in battle, and who continued to walk because he hadn't noticed that he was dead.

It is hardly worth asking my usual questions. In all three of the requirements of good government, Italy provided a dismal picture of failure: insecurity at home, weakness abroad, an inflated currency.

The Italian case, above most others, demonstrates the ultimate absurdity of tolerating the activities of political ideologies dedicated to the destruction of the pluralist and representative system. The Italian Communists claim to be defenders of law, order and moderation; yet their responsibility in the destruction of the Italian State had been overwhelming. They do not say: 'Give us power and we shall abolish free speech, competing parties, independent justice, free travel and the other normal rights.' On the contrary, they demand to be tolerated on the ground that they themselves are prepared to tolerate others. Yet the political ground is littered with the short-lived promises of Communist leaders such as Ulbricht of East Germany, Dimitrov of Bulgaria, Gerö of Hungary, Gomulka of Poland, and Gottwald of Czechoslovakia, which they forgot as soon as power was in their hands.

It cannot be said too often that no Marxist–Leninist party is, or can be, a political party like other parties; nor indeed can any totalist party be so considered. By accepting them as such, party political systems condemn themselves to death; even if they were not, in other respects, doomed.

FOUR

COLLAPSE IN LATIN AMERICA

At the beginning of 1964, democracies appeared to flourish in Brazil, Argentina, Chile and Uruguay. Twelve years later, with the seizure of power by the armed forces in Argentina, all four of these countries had passed under military rule. All four were, of course, *party* democracies, and in three of them at least the party system fell victim to its own built-in absurdities and contradictions, yielding in the end situations of chaos, discomfort and even danger for the population, so that the military felt bound to intervene. So deeply ingrained is the intellectual fallacy that democracy is 'good' and military rule 'bad' that the generalised press reaction in the West was to blame the soldiers, sailors and airmen for killing 'freedom' and democracy, whereas the blame in all cases rested squarely on the shoulders of the politicians for making an unbelievable mess of the situation when power was in their hands.

The men who deprived the politicians of the power they had abused or squandered were in no sense akin to the traditional *caudillos* of Latin American and Spanish history. They were not 'strongmen' seizing power because they liked the pomp and spoils of office. They were, on the contrary, products of the excellent military colleges of their respective countries, well-educated men of goodwill, who intervened out of a sense of duty and as ultimate repositories of the well-being of their nations. In general, this new breed of military statesmen, though convinced of the moral rightness of their actions, lacked a clear concept of long-term political strategy. They were very clear about the short term: it was their job to clear up the mess created by the party politicians. They were considerably more vague about the further future, about how long they would need to stay in power, about the kind of regime they would like to create, about how, when (and possibly whether) power should be returned to the civilians. General Augusto Pinochet Ugarte alone appeared to have a political vision for the future. At all events, he alone had understood that the political parties were ultimately responsible for the Chilean mess, and he was determined to deprive them of their political monopoly.

Brazil

Chronologically, the first of these party systems to collapse was Brazil's. I first visited that vast and exhilarating country in the late winter of 1964 (that is, in the late summer on the European side of the earth), in the course of a long journey in Latin America which I recorded at the time in a journal published by *Encounter* magazine (December 1964 and January 1965). I have been rereading what I wrote fourteen years before these lines, less from narcissism than from a desire to recapture the impressions of the moment. At the beginning of April—some months before my arrival—the civilian regime of President João Goulart had been overthrown by the armed forces in an almost completely bloodless coup: the fact that no blood was shed was significant, since it showed that there was not much spontaneous popular support for the politicians. The reverse was true, indeed, and great street demonstrations sparked off by the women of São Paulo had made Goulart—a vain and wily man—realise that the game was up.

Why, then, did the military step in? There was a specifically anti-Communist tone to the initial announcements of the new regime, but that was not all there was to it: there were deeper reasons and immediate causes.

The deeper reasons first. In 1930, first year of the Great Depression, Brazil hit the world headlines and provided ready fuel for the international Communist propaganda machine, by burning the coffee crop or dumping it in the sea. Getulio Vargas, the gaucho governor of Rio Grande do Sul in Brazil's deep south, marched on Rio de Janeiro, carried to power on the backs of military and political malcontents. These were his friends and he never forgot them. Vargas was the populist leader incarnate. He did a lot for Brazil, and a lot *to* it as well. He can be praised for sparking off the great Brazilian expansion, and blamed for the great Brazilian corruption.

He opened schools and factories; and he made sure his friends grew rich. A later President, Kubitschek, who created that Dali-esque dream of a metropolis in the Amazonian outback, Brasilia, was the political descendant of Vargas in both the favourable and the pejorative senses. As for Goulart, he had been Vargas's Minister of Labour, and he took populism to the point where it was bound to collapse; for by then it was drained of substance and over-ripe with corruption.

When the army intervened in 1964, they set out to liquidate the social and political heirs to Vargas and make a fresh start. Goulart had come to power fortuitously when his predecessor, the mercurial

President Jânio Quadros, unexpectedly resigned after nine months, complaining that 'occult forces' made it impossible for him to rule. The occult forces he had in mind ('hidden' would be a better translation of the Portuguese *ocultas*) consisted of a kind of Mafia of corrupt politicians and speculators who were doing nicely on the grand scale from property development. Goulart had been Vice-President and he stepped into Quadros's shoes. Naturally enough, he had himself confirmed in office and with full presidential powers in the national referendum of January 1963.

Goulart's power-base was narrow and insecure, however: he led the Left-wing minority party, Partido Trabalhista Brasileiro (Brazilian Workers' Party). He thought he would be safer if he appointed his own men to senior command posts in the army, and in so doing created resentment. In Brazil perhaps even more than elsewhere in Latin America, the army had a deep, almost religious conviction of its predestined role, and liked to think of itself as a 'priesthood at arms'.

Rashly, Goulart attempted to unionise the non-commissioned officers of the three services as a preliminary to forming a popular front government. In September 1963 he sponsored a 'sergeants' mutiny' in the air-base of Brasilia. A mutiny of 1,400 sailors and marines, in support of political demands, followed towards the end of March 1964. This was one of the immediate causes of the take-over. Goulart granted a presidential amnesty to the mutineers. This was more than the army could stomach, and it took only forty-eight hours for the Goulart regime to crumple.

Among the secondary causes was the great Brazilian inflation, which by the end of 1963 was running at 90 per cent and still gathering momentum: by April, it had reached 140 per cent. But this was only the economic reflection of a policy of demagogic irresponsibility. Goulart was hell-bent on his Popular Front, and in a speech to a mass meeting in Rio on 13 March 1964 he demanded the closure of Congress, called for the immediate expropriation of agricultural land for redistribution, and a new constituent assembly of 'the people'. Appropriately, he was flanked by his brother-in-law Leonel Brizola, who had been organising strong-arm squads known as 'groups of eleven', by militant trade-union leaders and by top Communists. For the past three months, with presidential encouragement, groups of militants had been seizing land illegally. The veteran Brazilian Communist leader, Luiz Carlos Prestes, who presided over one of the world's oldest CPs (founded in 1919 by the Comintern), had come back from a visit to Moscow with a precise plan for a Popular Front coalition.

Although it would be wrong to suggest that there was a Communist plot to seize power when the army moved in, it was clear enough that Goulart, himself no Communist, was moving into an alliance with Prestes and seeking power outside the constitutional processes. In addition, Brazil was being ruined. It was the army's duty to step in to rescue the country from the folly of its top politician and his henchmen.

Turbulent Argentina

The history of Argentina is a good deal more turbulent than Brazil's; yet the Argentinos may be said to be democratic by disposition and are not handicapped, as the Brazilians are, by the existence of a vast number of illiterates living outside the monetary economy. With all its troubles, Argentina is the most literate, the best educated country in Latin America. Nearly all its people are of European origin—most of them either from Spain or from Italy—and they dispose of a bountiful land with plenty of space for all. In the 1920s it was one of the richest and most advanced countries in the world, and a prodigious destiny was held to lie ahead. Instead, it has either stagnated or gone backward, with long periods of violence and runaway inflation to sour the people's hopes.

When I say that the Argentinos are democratic by disposition, I refer to their natural tendency to speak their minds and allow others to speak theirs. They are convivial people who consume great quantities of meat and wine and are naturally friendly. Their politicians, however, have served them ill, reducing this great country more than once to anarchy and ruin.

It would be straining my thesis to ascribe Argentina's political troubles to party democracy when it has been under military or authoritarian rule of one kind or another for twenty-two of the past thirty-one years. Yet it is worth noting these facts:

—Argentinian voters freely elected Colonel Juan Domingo Perón as their President in February 1946 and gave his supporters a majority in both houses.
—The elected Chamber of Deputies voted unlimited powers for Perón two years later, enabling him to establish a thinly disguised dictatorship.
—It was as a result of free elections in the spring of 1973 that Perón was allowed to return to Argentina after his years of exile in Madrid.
—When Perón died in July 1974, his third wife, Isabel, a

former nightclub entertainer, succeeded him. The succession was perfectly legal and democratic, since she had been freely elected Vice-President in the joint presidential campaign of 1973. On paper, at least, Argentina had a normal party democracy between 11 March 1973 and 24 March 1976, when a military junta deposed the inadequate creature who had presided over her country's rapid decline into revolutionary anarchy.

One man bears an overwhelming responsibility for the troubles of Argentina: Perón, one of the evil geniuses of this century. He has been called a Fascist and certainly his regime had much in common with Mussolini's Italy. But I believe the term 'populist' fits him better. A populist makes extravagant promises to one section of the population, whatever the consequences to other sections or to the nation as a whole. This is exactly what Perón did. He sought to woo the working class as the mass power-base he initially lacked; and succeeded brilliantly from the standpoint of his ambitions, and disastrously from that of his country. He made extravagant promises to the workers, and delivered the goods, regardless of the consequences. And he left the country bankrupt.

Through the years of his maximum power he was aided and abetted by his second wife, the glamorous and charismatic ex-actress Eva Duarte (Evita to her beloved *descamisados*—the mythical 'shirtless ones' who rallied to the demagogic charm of the Peróns) until she died of cancer in 1952.

He had carefully paved the way for his future regime. As a young army officer he had served as military attaché in Italy, where he became an admiring observer of Mussolini's state. In 1943, he was one of a group of military men who seized power from a rather colourless civilian administration. He was already clear about his political strategy and all he asked for was the apparently modest portfolio of Labour and Social Welfare. Soon he had the working class backing him for the top job.

His hour came on 17 October 1945. By then his fellow-officers were worried about Perón's ambitions, and had locked him up. That day Eva Duarte rallied 300,000 Peronist trade unionists in Buenos Aires and marched them on the presidential palace, the famous Casa Rosada. They chanted '*queremos a Perón*' (which offers the advantage, in Spanish, of meaning either 'we want Perón' or 'we love Perón') over and over until the military lost their nerve and allowed the ambitious colonel to appear on the balcony where, to the massed cheers of the workers, he announced that he was going to stand for the presidency. He was duly elected in February 1946.

Perón censored the press, bullied the employers, showered the workers with wage increases and fringe benefits, nationalised the railways, and launched a massive programme of public works. He paid for all this, while the money lasted, from accumulated foreign exchange reserves and agricultural funds (the workers were his power-base, not the peasants). His regime rapidly became corrupt as well as repressive. After his wife's death he developed a taste for the sexual favours of Lolita-age girls, evading legal retribution by the fact of his power. In 1955 the Pope excommunicated him, though probably less for his personal immoralities than for his anti-Catholic policies: he had deprived the Church of Rome of its tax exemption and banned religious instruction in the schools.

In September, after various clashes and disorders, the army decided it had had enough and Perón was ousted. He settled in luxury in Madrid with a new wife for company; tended his roses; and kept up a steady programme of speeches and articles which placed him constantly in the public eye in Argentina. Absence did what the proverb says it does, and the mystique of Perón grew in the collective minds of the trade unionists. It was impossible to ignore the absent demagogue, whether from the veneration or from the execration in which his name was held. The last thing the military or civilian rulers, who alternated in power after his departure, wanted was his return. Yet they could not rule satisfactorily without him.

In 1971 the government of General Lanusse decided to make its peace with Perón. Lanusse himself had no reason to love the formidable exile, who had interned him for five years. But there seemed no other way out. He ordered the exhumation of the remains of Evita Perón, which had been kept concealed in an effort to damp down the almost religious cult they had inspired, and had them sent to Madrid. Emissaries went back and forth, and in November 1972, the old dictator, now in his late seventies, came back for a brief visit. Thoughtfully, the Lanusse government had waived all criminal charges against him, and returned his passport and citizenship.

Elections, both for the presidency and for the two Chambers, had been announced for March 1973. The wily strongman decided not to stand in person, but allowed a surrogate, Héctor J. Cámpora (by trade a dentist), to stand in his stead. He duly won, as did the Peronist candidates for the legislature. Then on 20 June, Perón himself made his long-awaited return. It was a bloody occasion. His followers of the Marxist Left and the Fascist Right had massed on the grandstand in opposing groups at Ezeiza, the airport for Buenos Aires. The rival groups opened fire on each other and hundreds died. Perón's plane was diverted to another airport. He cannot be held responsible for the violence that had been spreading like a bush fire since 1970; but his violent homecoming showed that his mere presence was not going to be enough to unite his followers, let alone the country as a whole.

Many countries have suffered outbreaks of terrorism in the 1960s and 1970s, but Argentina's outbreak is by any standards the world's worst. Two political gangs were mainly to blame: the People's Revolutionary Army (ERP), a Marxist-Leninist outfit; and the so-called Montoneros, who rather cleverly styled themselves 'Peronist' and may even at the beginning have meant it, but who turned out to be no less Marxist–Leninist than their ERP rivals. The Montoneros had burst into the news in 1970 when they kid-napped a former President, General Pedro Aramburu, and murdered him after a travesty of a trial by a 'people's court' of self-appointed terrorists.

Thereafter the ERP and Montoneros competed with each other in the size of the ransoms they could extort for the return of kid-napped businessmen. The Montoneros set (and still hold) the world record in this sinister game when they received $60 million for the brothers Jorge and Juan Born in 1975.

The aged Perón proved no more capable of restoring order than lesser men, and when he died in July 1978 his widow, the new President, was completely out of her depth. For advice she turned to a curious figure, López Rega, who in turn consulted the stars. López Rega was Minister for Social Welfare and held Isabel Perón under some kind of a spell. His name was linked with a counter-terrorist group known as the Argentine Anti-Communist Alliance (AAA), which drew up death lists and worked through them methodically. When he tried to pack the cabinet with his nominees, the labour unions forced a crisis and he was driven into 'voluntary' exile—to Madrid, where Perón's luxurious home was available to him.

Faced with a breakdown, Isabel Perón was ordered to leave the capital for a complete rest, and handed over power temporarily to the moderate President of the Senate, Italo Argentino Luder, who had replaced López Rega's son-in-law during the late crisis. Under the Constitution, the President of the Senate was next in line for the presidency, since there was no Vice-President. The country began to breathe in hope.

Too soon. 'Isabelita' was back six weeks later, incapable of ruling but unwilling to step down. Inflation was spiralling and violence was becoming a way of life. On 24 March 1976, in what must have been the best advertised *coup d'état* in history, the army arrested the

President (who was later to face charges of corruption) and took over.

It is not part of my purpose in this book to examine in any detail what the armed forces did, in Argentina and other countries, once they had taken over. My aim is simply to show that they had no alternative to taking over. There are grounds for pointing to Argentina as, among civilised countries, the one in which party democracy reached its lowest point. Universal suffrage gave Argentina its Perón, as it had given Germany its Hitler. And party democracy in the end yielded President Isabel Perón, than whom it is difficult to imagine anybody less qualified, whether by intelligence or by character or by ability, to preside over a large nation.

The Long Decline of Chile

If Argentina is the ultimate example of the failure of the democratic process (which is of course debatable) then Chile runs a close second. Much has been written about the late President Allende's Marxist experiment, and the circumstances that moved the armed forces to take over in 1973; and I have contributed my bit to the debate, which became one of the fiercest in recent times, rivalling even the Spanish Civil War in the intensity of the emotions aroused on either side of the barricades.* I propose in this chapter to look at the Chilean problem in historical perspective over the period from 1891, a period long enough to trace the decline and final collapse of party democracy in this interesting country, which long enjoyed a reputation as perhaps the most politically sophisticated in Latin America.

The most sensible starting-year is 1891, when the parliamentary principle was established after a short civil war. The President, José Manuel Balmaceda, felt so strongly about being deprived of his prerogatives that he committed suicide. Party democracy had come to Chile.

The Chileans were poor but proud. They had utterly defeated the Peruvians and Bolivians in the War of the Pacific a few years earlier, and the future seemed bright. What went wrong? The short answers are these:

1. The party system, although it had some successes, gradually disintegrated through factionalism, demagogy and the opportunities it gave to anti-democratic parties, principally Marxist-Leninist.

* The best account, which is partisan but objective, is Robert Moss, *Chile's Marxist Experiment* (David and Charles, 1973). See also my book, *A Theory of Conflict*.

2. Throughout the period, there was a considerable expansion of education, but a qualitative deterioration. In latter years its curriculum was excessively divorced from national feeling. Its contribution to national unity was thus negative.

3. The Church, initially a conservative force through its teaching of traditional moral values, veered increasingly to the Left, reflecting changing attitudes in the Vatican.

4. The independence of the judiciary, which was sustained throughout the period, was largely nullified during the Allende period, when unfavourable decisions were ignored or only partially implemented.

5. The professional and other occupational associations (*gremios*) were inadequately represented by the parties which, of course, had the monopoly of political power, except when deprived of it by the intervention of the military as in 1924 and 1973.

6. The armed forces which, as in most Hispanic countries, regarded themselves as responsible for maintaining national unity, lacked institutional political links with the central authority.

7. The increasing influence of Marxist-Leninist ideology fanned the flames of the class struggle.

Points 5 and 6 above may suggest a plea for a corporative State as in Mussolini's Italy or Franco's Spain. But that is not what I have in mind. I am simply drawing attention to sources of frustration in Chile. The frustration of the *gremios* is very important, for it was they (especially the association of lorry owners) who in the end brought the Allende government to a standstill on the eve of the military intervention in 1973. The armed forces, too, were frustrated, for although some army officers had themselves been infected by Marxist ideas, they were in a tiny minority. Most of the officers watched in increasing anger as the politicians drove the country into chaos and revolutionary anarchy. It all comes back, then, to the politicians—that is, to the political parties.

Let us now look at the developing situation in greater detail.

From 1891 to 1924, Chile was a typical example of total *laissez-faire* in the economy, with all the usual results: rapid prosperity (in Chile's case, through the exploitation of rich nitrate deposits), concentration of wealth in very few hands and a good deal of sheer waste. There were virtually no taxes, and no savings or investment policy, nor was much attention paid to infrastructure, such as roads and railways. From 1924 on, the State gradually took charge of the economy, again with the usual consequences: communications developed rapidly, and various State public utility enterprises—

railways, gas and electricity—were set up. The bases for industrialisation were laid, but the new industries were heavily protected and highly inefficient in real terms. Economic growth slowed down.

As peasants flocked to the towns, the normal social problems and tensions appeared. And so did Marxism, from about 1897. The first socialist group, however, advocated anarchism and worker-control. It was short-lived and the Marxists grew influential, first among the workers and later among the students, with their insistence on the international class struggle. As in other Latin American countries, the landed oligarchy thought first and last of their own interests and showed little interest in reform.

The middle class grew rapidly towards the end of the century, and the army officers, who were middle class, began to reflect the political and economic preoccupations of the civilians. The oligarchy was little affected by the inflation and general dissatisfaction that set in about 1920, but the army wanted to do something for those who were suffering most—the workers and the middle class. Various social measures were drafted, but parliament thought it had more important priorities, and in 1924 voted a pay rise for the Senators before considering the draft social laws. Thereupon the Army 'requested' President Alessandri to intervene, and a cowed parliament voted sixteen new social laws in three days. The President then resigned, saying he was a prisoner of the military, who took over for a few months.

There were further military interventions: in 1927 (which yielded the military dictatorship of General Carlos Ibáñez del Campo); in 1932 (twice); and of course in 1973. It is fair to say that all Chile's military interventions were motivated by social or political concerns rather than by the mere thirst for power. The 1924 one, as we have seen, was to force the politicians to introduce social reforms. Once in power in 1927, General Ibáñez promulgated the social reforms which Alessandri had advocated but not actually seen through. The junta headed by Carlos Dávila in June 1932 wanted to do something about the social unrest that had plagued the conservative President Juan Montero during the depression, when the fall in nitrate and copper prices hit Chile badly. He tried to embark on a socialist policy, but was soon overthrown by another junta who thought he was being high-handed.

Between 1924 and 1932, Chile had no fewer than twenty-one cabinets, counting the military as well as the civilian ones. Over the years every possible political tinge or combination of colours wielded power in Santiago. There were popular front governments, Right-wing ones and populist ones. Remedies were tried by one government and discarded by the next. When demand for Chilean copper was high (as during the Second World War and the Korean war), prosperity returned and discontent diminished—until runaway inflation brought back the discontent.

The progressive decline of party democracy deserves attention. In general, Chile's parties are more or less ideologically motivated. That is, they are reluctant to apply pragmatic measures to deal with the country's very real problems, and would prefer to resort to the dogmatic approach. Moreover, during the entire period there was an excessive proliferation of parties, partly encouraged by proportional representation, partly caused by ideological confrontations within the parties leading to splits and factions, and partly by the clash of personalities.

Unlike, say, Britain where a non-partisan civil service is ready to serve whatever party is in power, Chile suffered from the propensity of the political parties, once in power, to promote men of their choice, on the criterion of party allegiance not competence—hence a good deal of corruption as well as inefficiency in the public service.

Another disadvantage of the party system lay in the temptation, which the political leaders did not resist, to politicise the professional and occupational associations. The *gremios* and *sindicatos* (trade unions), educational organisations and others, were an easy prey for the political parties, who used them for their own ends. The consequence was that such bodies served the interests not of their members, but of the political parties.

But perhaps the major cause of the decline of the party system was the demagoguery of the politicians. The leaders, avid for votes, bid and outbid each other in promises to the voters, going in the end well beyond the capacity of the country to meet the promises made. The familiar phenomenon I have often mentioned in these pages, the politics of the market place, reached extraordinary heights in Chile. The politicians became the prisoners of dilemmas of their own making. Once in power, they had the choice between not carrying out their promises, thus losing popular support; or fulfilling them and ruining the economy, thus increasing Chile's dependence on external aid—with much the same result in the end. Hence a general disillusionment with the traditional parties leading to the growth of new parties or groups, with ever more demagogic promises in reserve.

I have argued elsewhere that demagogy is inherent in party systems, although the degree to which it manifests itself varies enormously. In Chile, an underdeveloped country, a special form of demagoguery consisted of agitation for the continual expansion of the suffrage, with the appropriate talk of the rights of women, young people, peasants, the illiterates, none of which at the time could be said to possess the political sophistication to exercise their rights responsibly, even in their own interests. From 1934 to 1938, for instance, the number of voters increased by 66 per cent, although the total population went up by only 16 per cent in a longer period (1930–40).

The search for magical formulae, which is characteristic of party systems as a whole, culminated in what might be called the 'demagogic spiral' of the Allende regime, leading in the end to the collapse of democracy. The radicalisation of the educational system, with the involvement of teachers as well as students in revolutionary activities, was an extreme manifestation of the demagogic spiral. Democracy may be said to have gone mad when the book-lined studies of university lecturers and professors become store-rooms for firearms and ammunition, and when a president recruits violent revolutionaries on their release from gaol (by his orders) for his presidential guard. These things happened under Allende.

The 1925 Constitution had much to answer for in the disintegration of the Chilean system. Under it the parliament had the right to choose a president between any two candidates who had obtained the first and second largest number of votes in a presidential election. It was this feature that enabled Salvador Allende Goossens, who had obtained only 36 per cent of the votes in the triangular contest of 1970, to attempt to impose a Marxist regime on his country. The French voting system, with its provision for second thoughts in the shape of a second ballot in national elections, might have enabled Chileans to avoid the folly their system inflicted upon them.

The Chilean people was sovereign, but its parliament had un-limited legislative powers. As in other party systems, the result was a kind of legislative diarrhoea: 17,000 new laws on the statute book between 1925 and 1973, many of them contradicting previous ones, or in turn to be contradicted by future ones, according to the advent or disappearance of transient political groupings.

In theory, the Supreme Court and the Controlaría (the highest court of appeal) could pronounce on the constitutional propriety of contested laws, but Allende ignored or vetoed judicial judgements that conflicted with his programme. Nor was there any outside authority to impose standards of behaviour on the parliamentarians. The 1925 Constitution, which sanctioned political parties, made no rules for them: they could run themselves as they pleased, and find money wherever it might be on offer, including foreign sources with their own axes to grind. In the fairly frequent political cases tried during the Allende 'experiment', the parliamentarians were told how to vote by their parties before they had had time to hear the evidence.

The 'reform' of 1971, moreover, gave the widest latitude to extremist parties or groups (of the Left, of course), even those advocating the violent overthrow of the existing system. Nor was it practicable for independents to challenge the parties through the electoral process: the parties controlled the machines which controlled the votes. Add to all this the many irregularities that came to light at election times, such as double or false registration of voters, and the breakdown of the system becomes still easier to understand.

The paradox to which I have drawn attention in this book—that is, the constitutional toleration of anti-democratic political parties—flourished in Chile. Under the 1925 Constitution, parties that wished to destroy the system enjoyed exactly the same rights as those who were prepared to abide by the rules of the democratic process. Unfortunately, the Chilean Communist Party was the largest and best disciplined in Latin America, and eternally loyal to Moscow. Under the Right-wing presidency of González Videla, the Party was outlawed in 1948 and its leaders gaoled. The ban lasted ten years. In Chile, as in Spain, the common assertion that Communist parties flourish in clandestinity was disproved. Its influence in the trade unions, for instance, greatly diminished during the ten-year ban.

It is truer to say that Communist parties, unlike ordinary parties, do survive in clandestinity because they have well tested techniques for survival. It is worth remembering that the party at no time in its history has polled more than 16 per cent of the popular vote. Yet its participation in the Popular Unity coalition directed by Allende gave it a chance to destroy private enterprise as the preliminary to introducing a full Communist programme in Chile. Unfortunately for Moscow, the violent extravagances of the extreme Left parties, which Allende tolerated if he did not sponsor them, provoked the military intervention that blocked the road to a 'people's democracy'.

The absurdity of tolerating totalist parties and partisans of violence was as great in Chile as elsewhere. On the one hand, the Chilean Communist Party professed to abide by the democratic rules. On the other hand, the party's press and its declarations showed that it considered the judicial system as 'class justice' and not as an independent power in accordance with the law; that it regarded the executive power and parliament as the 'general headquarters of the bourgeoisie' and not as the legitimate delegates of popular representation; and elections not as a legitimate mechanism of selection but as a kind of class fraud. To give a party with such views a share in political power is to invite the destruction of the system from within. Moreover, if society is considered as consisting exclusively of antagonistic and irreconcilable social classes, not only is democracy impossible, but any kind of national unity is illusory.

Chile in 1973 was a country at war with itself, or more precisely it was a country in which a powerful section of the body politic was waging a unilateral war of aggression against the rest of society. On seizing power the military embarked on a period of determined, and even ruthless, repression, in which many people, both guilty and innocent, were tortured, lost their lives or disappeared. The same is true of conventional wars. On 12 March 1977 the head of the ruling junta, President Pinochet, abolished all political parties by decree. His constitutional speeches have indicated, though without absolute precision, that he has no intention of returning the monopoly of political power to the parties. Should he embark on a no-party experiment, I for one shall follow it with the greatest interest. Meanwhile, the gaols have been emptied (as they have not, for instance, in Cuba), the abuses of the period that followed the overthrow of the Allende regime have ended, and an amnesty has allowed many political exiles to come home.

A particularly important decision was an economic one: the Chilean economy has been freed, and much attention has been paid in Chile to the teachings of that arch-priest of the market economy, the Nobel Prize-winner Milton Friedman. The economic consequences were felt immediately, with a boom and rapidly returning prosperity. Inflation was reduced in a couple of years from 1,000 per cent a year to about 40 per cent (still, of course, an intolerably high rate by European standards). The political consequences are bound to come also: free enterprise and the market economy are the natural habitat of political freedom. It will be interesting to see how the junta conciliates economic freedom with the need for authority during what is bound to be a fairly prolonged transitional regime.

Perhaps the most striking recent event as these lines were written was the decision, in August 1978, to arrest the former head of the secret police, General Contreras, on alleged complicity in the murder, in Washington, two years earlier, of a Chilean diplomat named Orlando Letelier. No decision could better illustrate the determination of the junta to move away from the excesses of the immediate post-*coup* period and return to normality.

Welfare and Collapse in Uruguay

Uruguay, in common with its larger neighbours, has suffered from political violence in an extreme form, yielding in the end to military take-over. Here, as in Brazil, Chile and Argentina, the subversive challenge to the State came from the Marxist-Leninist Left, and in all cases Moscow's hand was clearly visible. I have argued in *Strategy of Survival* that these outbreaks are local or regional manifestations of a 'Third World War' which began in about 1944 or 1945.

The Uruguayan case is, however, less relevant to the present book than the other three. Democracy was better established in Uruguay than anywhere else in Latin America, and this small country—sometimes known as the Switzerland of Latin America—could claim the oldest Welfare State in the world, dating back to the enlightened presidential rule of José Battle y Ordóñez in the early twentieth century. Uruguay's democracy was destroyed by a desperate economic crisis which left a heavily bureaucratised Welfare State without the necessary means of support; followed by a ruthless outbreak of terrorism; followed in turn by a no less ruthless police and military repression.

But it would be misleading to blame this tragic sequence of events on the Blanco and Colorado political parties which alternated in power in Montevideo, except to the extent that the parties proved incapable of dealing with the terrorists within the Constitution. Nor is it fair to blame the politicians for the economic crisis, which was beyond their control in that it was due to a fall in the world demand for wool and for Uruguayan meat exports. Left to itself, the system would have muddled through to better times; it would be seen that Welfare for all is a luxury if you can't afford it. But it was not left to itself: a murderous gang of young middle-class fanatics calling themselves Tupamaros instituted a reign of violence and called the tune for about five years until the army stepped in in 1972. The Uruguayan case illustrates the vulnerability of democracy; but tells us relatively little about the shortcomings of the party system.

Perhaps for this reason the military junta, when I talked to some of its members late in 1977, were planning to move back to the party system, albeit with some kind of watchdog device to save the politicians from themselves. It seemed doubtful whether the politicians could cope with a post-revolutionary crisis in a small country in which about two out of three citizens were State employees, many of them unproductive. Perhaps, however, a boom in the market would save the situation.

EPSIA REMINDER...

OUR RECORDS INDICATE YOU NEED TO FULFILL YOUR TWO YEAR RENEWAL MEMBERSHIP CREDIT. THERE ARE MANY VARIED PROGRAMS BEING OFFERED THIS SEASON INCLUDING A RACE PROGRAM, INSTRUCTOR **TRAINING** COURSE, MASTER LEVEL PROGRAM, NOT TO MENTION OUR EXAMS AND SPECIALIZED WORKSHOP CLINICS. YOUR **PROFESSIONAL SKI TEACHER NEWSLETTER** HAS THE FULL SCHEDULE OF EVENTS WHICH LIST EACH EVENT, ITS LOCATION, AND DATE FOR YOUR REVIEW. PLAN TO ATTEND AN EPSIA EVENT TO OBTAIN THE LATEST PROFESSIONAL SKI TEACHING INFORMATION AND TO COMPLETE THIS MEMBERSHIP REQUIREMENT.

EPSIA
1202 TROY-SCHENECTADY RD.
LATHAM, NY 12110

FIVE

AMERICA'S DEATH-WISH

Any society that ceases to defend itself is courting destruction, for it must be presumed to have lost the will to live. In the wake of defeat in Vietnam and the Watergate affair, the Americans, through their elected representatives, decided that they no longer wished to defend themselves. As a result, their society was in grave danger when these lines were written, and its survival was in serious doubt.

Of course the decision not to defend itself was not couched in those terms: if it had been, it is conceivable that the elected representatives of the American people would have recoiled from their self-destructive course. Legislative language is often designed to obfuscate real motives and intentions, and this was a case in point. The motives, as expressed in the interminable sittings of the various House and Senate committees involved, were of the highest: the legislators professed themselves appalled by the revelations of reprehensible behaviour on the part of the two organisations mainly concerned with the defence of American society—the Central Intelligence Agency and the Federal Bureau of Investigation—and approved steps and measures designed to curb the activities of these organisations by bringing them under Congressional scrutiny and throwing them wide open to public scrutiny as well.

While they were about it, they made it virtually impossible for the main law-enforcement agencies, principally the police and customs department, to do their jobs as well.

If America comes to its senses and reverses the unbelievable decisions of the past few years, historians of the period will undoubtedly describe it as an interlude of collective folly unparalleled in the story of the American people. And if the decisions are not reversed, and American society succeeds in destroying itself, there will be few people to read this book anyway.

Let us begin at the beginning. No police force or security service, and no intelligence agency, can do what it is supposed to do unless it has an effective machinery for gathering information that is not readily available. It is unfortunate, perhaps, but true, that this kind of information can be obtained only by secret agents or informers,

by tapping telephones, by electronic eavesdropping or the inter-
ception of secret or coded signals. Some people think such activities
are immoral, or at any rate distasteful. So is the bayoneting of a
live enemy soldier, the dropping of a nuclear bomb or the hissing
of a nerve gas in anger. If the world lived at peace and harmony;
if human beings were less aggressive and mutually antagonistic; if
peaceful societies were allowed to pursue their peaceful purposes
unthreatened by external or internal enemies; if the ordinary law-
abiding citizens had nothing to fear from violent criminals because
there were none; if only these conditions were fulfilled in whole or
in part, then the unpleasant activities briefly described would be
unnecessary, and a great country like the United States could inflict
the kind of damage it has been inflicting on itself and get away
with it.

But the world is not like that, nor is life. There *are* violent criminals
and terrorists. There *are* enemies of our kind of society, both within
it and outside. There *are* powerful enemy agencies with all the
apparatus of espionage, bribery, extortion and repression at their
disposal. There are hostile powers that wish to destroy us.

What the Congressmen and Senators, incessantly egged on by
the unelected and self-appointed journalists of press and television,
have done is to destroy the intelligence-gathering capacity of the
FBI, the CIA, the police and the customs department. For they
passed the Freedom of Information Act, subjected the CIA to
Congressional approval for projected actions, and made it illegal
for any government agency to keep files on any individuals or
organisations, regardless of their colouring and intent. The predictable result was that informants dropped out by the hundreds or
the thousands, afraid that their identities could no longer be protected; while subversive organisations were officially protected
against official investigators. This is the lunacy that has been done
in the name of public morality.

I should not expect any readers to take my word for these asser-
tions, so I shall produce some witnesses.

Witness No. 1 is Glen D. King, executive director of the International Association of Chiefs of Police, who appeared before a
sub-committee of the Senate Judiciary Committee on 27 July 1977.
Mr King said:

> . . . the Washington State Patrol reports that, because the FBI
> can no longer conduct surveillance operations except in open
> investigative cases, the Patrol no longer has access to information
> it was once provided by the Bureau. Specifically, on two occasions,

organised crime figures travelled into the State of Washington and the police agencies knew nothing of their presence until after their departure from their State. Prior to the enactment of the Freedom of Information Act and Privacy Act, the FBI would have monitored the movements of these figures and notified the State of Washington of their activities. As a result of this cutback the State of Washington is forced to monitor the movements of organised crime figures as well as the normal activities Washington monitors. Washington currently has an intelligence field force consisting of six persons. In essence, the free flow exchange of intelligence information is no longer done on a nationwide scale.

Mr King concluded his testimony with these words: 'Rather than risk the effects of intimidating lawsuits, media scrutiny, and legislative regulation, law-enforcement officials are limiting the scope of intelligence operations to a point where they have become less than adequate to protect the citizens of our country.' In other words, gangsters can now move around with impunity in the United States, safe in the knowledge that the law makes it impossible for the authorities to keep an eye on them.

Witness No. 2 is a collective one: the eleven experts consulted by another sub-committee of the same Senate Committee in 1977 in connection with possible terrorist and other threats to the security of the Trans-Alaska Pipeline. On becoming operational, the pipeline was initially to transport 600,000 barrels of oil a day, building up to a capacity of 2 million barrels a day by the mid-1980s, or about 10 per cent of the United States's domestic needs. Indeed by the 1990s, Alaska gas and oil will account for more than half of the domestically produced energy consumed by the Americans. The protection of the pipeline from sabotage and of the personnel against terrorism was obviously of high importance.

In its published findings, the sub-committee referred to 'the catastrophic erosion of law-enforcement intelligence gathering capabilities nationwide, and the near stoppage of the exchange of intelligence information between the Federal, State and local law-enforcement agencies'. Although some abuses in the field of intelligence were conceded, and there was recognition of the need to protect the constitutional rights of American citizens, there had been a 'general anti-intelligence hysteria' in recent years. But

. . . the excessive and unreasonable restrictions that have been placed on . . . intelligence gathering activities made it much more difficult . . . to do an effective job of protecting society against violence-prone and other criminal elements.

In the sphere of intelligence on subversive and violence-prone organisations, State and metropolitan police files built up laboriously over a period of decades, have in some cases been destroyed outright; in other cases, locked up so that they are unavailable for use; and in still other cases, reduced to the point where, as Chief Davis of the Los Angeles police department stated, they 'cannot be classified as intelligence'.

Law-enforcement and intelligence capabilities have also been badly hurt by the drastic reduction in the exchange of intelligence resulting from the Freedom of Information Act and the Privacy Act.

Witness No. 3 represents a department with which constant travellers, including the author of this book, have no natural sympathy: he is Robert E. Chasen, head of the US Customs Service. There is more, of course, to Customs than the petty and sometimes deliberately obstructive readiness of officials to prevent travellers from indulging their human right to consume Scotch whisky or offer perfume to their wives or girl-friends. A more important activity concerns the prevention of the smuggling of narcotics and other dangerous drugs—an activity of overwhelming social importance. Testifying before the Senate sub-committee on Criminal Laws and Procedures on 5 October 1977, Mr Chasen pointed out that his service monitored some 96,000 miles of land and sea borders. 'To a great extent,' he went on, 'our effectiveness is . . . dependent upon the timely gathering of intelligence and other information regarding all aspects of international travel and trade, but particularly potential or ongoing unlawful activities, and the effective maintenance of such data.'

As with my previous witnesses, Mr Chasen found that the Freedom of Information Act and the Privacy Act were making it increasingly difficult for the Customs Service to gather and maintain the information they needed, and keep it confidential. There was a 'new reluctance to voluntarily pass on or release information to a Federal law enforcement agency' and 'confidential informants are particularly concerned that their identity may be revealed' through public disclosures under the Freedom of Information Act.

Similarly, international law-enforcement agencies were less willing to provide information in the knowledge that the American Customs Service could no longer guarantee to keep it confidential. Finally: '. . . our law enforcement mission would be handicapped if information on intelligence gathering methods and surveillance techniques were made available to the public. Nevertheless, on occasion, we have been required to release manuals or materials which would reveal investigative and surveillance techniques.'

In other words, the great army of Mafia and other gangland providers of death for the young at the highest prices could breathe more easily as a result of the zeal of the legislators in Congress. And the press and television could congratulate themselves on protecting the human rights of the drug-pushers.

The last of my witnesses, Mr Alan K. Campbell, Chairman of the US Civil Service Commission, deals with a question of perhaps still more fundamental importance: the loyalty of the civil service of the United States of America. I say 'perhaps still more fundamental' because, in modern times, a country's civil service has become the visible symbol of the permanence and continuity of the State. I do not wish to press the point too far, since in many States the appointment of civil servants is still at the whim or discretion of incoming politicians. But in the United States (as in Britain) the civil service does represent a permanency, a body of men and women whose services (and presumed integrity and incorruptibility) are at the disposal of an incoming administration irrespective of party allegiance. Nor is this normal assumption invalidated by the enormous powers of patronage that go with the attainment of high office.

But efficiency and integrity are not the only qualities required of a civil service: an equally important one is loyalty. Recognising this, at least tacitly, the British, while in occupation of their zone of Germany after the defeat of Hitler, created a security service with the significant name of Federal Office for the Protection of the Constitution (*Bundesamt für Verfassungsschutz*). This explicit function has enabled the BfV (as it is known) to protect the German Federal Republic from the worst consequences of the ideological penetration of the Social Democratic Party (a point explored more fully elsewhere in this book).

How, then, is the loyalty of entrants into the civil service to be established? Clearly, vetting procedures are inescapable. (If better vetting procedures had been devised in Britain before the Second World War, traitors like Philby, Burgess, Maclean and Blake would never have been appointed to the Foreign Office or intelligence service.) But vetting involves files. And the files will have to record the activities of organisations dedicated to the subversion and overthrow of the State (whether by violence or not is in this context immaterial) or the undermining of the Constitution. Mr Campbell's testimony, given before the sub-committee on Criminal Laws and

Procedures of the Senate Committee on the Judiciary of 9 February 1978, brought out the following startling facts:

—Since 1975, no applicants for civil service posts, even in sensitive departments, had been asked whether they were or had been members of the Communist Party, the racist Ku Klux Klan (KKK), the American Nazi Party, the Maoists and Trotskyists, and even of avowedly terrorist organisations such as the Weather Underground, the Jewish Defence League and the Palestine Liberation Organisation.

—In the absence of any overt act of a criminal character, mere membership of such organisations was not a bar to Federal employment.

—The Civil Service Commission had decided to destroy its security files on alleged subversive and disloyal activities.

In other words, the tiny minority of subversives and terrorists were being protected, at the expense of the huge majority of law-abiding and loyal citizens.

Summarising the findings of the hearing in a letter to Mr Campbell on 1 March 1978, Senator Strom Thurmond, who had taken the chair, went on: '. . . I find it difficult to avoid the conclusion that over the past five years or so, without the knowledge of Congress and contrary to statutory requirement and the Commission's own regulations, there has been a progressive dismantling of the Federal Loyalty-Security Program—until today, for all practical purposes, we do not have a Federal Employee Security Program worthy of the name.' Senator Thurmond called on the Commissioner to desist from destroying the security files: a request which appears to have been granted, at least temporarily.

The hearing had revealed that since 1967 no Federal employee had lost his or her job for security reasons, and no applicant for the civil service had been turned down on grounds of doubtful loyalty. And this was during a period of striking expansion of extremist activities, marked by the bombings of the Weather Underground, the revival of the KKK with its burning crosses, and the murderous exploits of the Symbionese Liberation Army, in which Patty Hearst, the heiress to the newspaper fortune, had found herself involved after being abducted.

Only one more thing need be said: the witnesses quoted above made it clear that in the 1970s the gigantic State apparatus of the USA ceased to provide the minimum requirement of protecting its own citizens against crime and subversion.

Freedom for Enemies

The abdication of the State in its responsibility for the defence of the nation against external enemies—the second requirement of the Minimum State—has been less complete than in the field of internal security, but extensive enough to arouse grave disquiet. One point should be made clear at the outset. Defence is too often measured simply in terms of weaponry and gadgetry. Does Super-Power A have more Inter-continental Ballistic Missiles, or more powerful ones, than Super-Power B? Is the accuracy of Super-Power B's death-dealing devices sufficient to compensate for an inferiority in numbers and 'throw-weight'? And so forth. I do not wish to minimise the importance of such questions, but they are emphatically not the only ones that matter. The security of a country against external enemies is also, and perhaps primarily, measured by its capacity to discover an enemy's intentions and capabilities, and above all else by its will to do something about it once it knows. It is in the vital field of intelligence and the will and capacity to conduct clandestine operations that the United States has been most severely crippled by the follies of its legislators and the irresponsibility of its media.

While internal security and the war against crime are the province of the Federal Bureau of Investigation (FBI) and the overt law-enforcement agencies, the defence of the United States against external enemies—through the collection, evaluation, and eventually the use, of intelligence—is divided between several organisations, of which the principal ones are the FBI and its 'foreign' counterpart, the Central Intelligence Agency (CIA). This shared responsibility, while it is perhaps unavoidable, has inevitably led to disputes over the exact demarcation lines between the two, especially during the lengthy reign as head of the FBI of the late J. Edgar Hoover, who was fiercely, almost pathologically, jealous of his prerogatives and the integrity of his empire. For example, counter-espionage (the watch on potential foreign spies on American soil) is the domain of the FBI. But the CIA has (or had) a counter-intelligence department which was naturally interested in the validity of whatever revelations were made by captured spies, and had a prescriptive right to debrief defectors and evaluate the results. Obviously, these circumstances made some overlapping inevitable.

The Watergate affair was followed by an inordinately prolonged campaign in the media to 'expose' the wrongdoings of both the FBI and the CIA, both real and imaginary. This campaign uncovered the utterly unimportant fact that during the Vietnam War, the CIA

had unconstitutionally opened the mail of American citizens suspected of aiding the enemy. That this was done is not in dispute,
but it was unimportant because academic: the FBI had the right to
open mail, but for complicated reasons was not doing what was
required of it. From the standpoint of the outraged citizens and
their supporters, it made no difference at all whether their letters
were opened or their telephones tapped by one agency or the other.
What is clear, and much more important, is that nowadays home-
grown subversives are absolutely protected from such 'outrages' by
the Freedom of Information and Privacy Acts. As for foreign spies
and agents, they now enjoy an unprecedented immunity.

Let two key examples tell the story: Congress and the United
Nations. It is common knowledge that KGB agents pullulate on
Capitol Hill. Indeed there is nothing to stop them, since this holy
citadel of American democracy has been ruled out of bounds to
the FBI. On 17 June 1975, Senator Henry 'Scoop' Jackson, a
Democrat whose awareness of the Soviet threat is well known, said:
'There is no doubt in my mind that the KGB is showing closer
interest in Congress than ever before and has established a spy
network on Capitol Hill.' He might have added that spying wasn't
the only thing the KGB was up to on Capitol Hill. For the Russians
are equally interested in making ideological converts and feeding
false information to those who will listen to them. A Congressman
or a Senator is a major catch in these terms, but to catch such major
fry it is not absolutely necessary to work at the top level: a well-
placed staffer is easier prey and can yield much the same result in
the slanting of speeches or the drafting of resolutions, or in vetoing
unwelcome measures. A young member of one of the Congressional
staffs is sometimes flattered by the congenial attentions of apparently
well-heeled Soviet 'diplomats', and not necessarily aware that about
three-quarters of those so accredited are in fact members of the
KGB.

The advantage of Capitol Hill, from the Soviet standpoint, is that
it is amenable to penetration by accredited Soviet members of the
diplomatic corps, since it is in Washington, where they have freedom
of movement.

For the United States at large, however, the Soviet embassy is
hampered by restrictions on the movements of its diplomats imposed
by the State Department to reciprocate similar restrictions on the
movements of American diplomatic people in Moscow. That is
where the UN comes into its own. For Soviet personnel seconded to
UN headquarters in New York are, *ipso facto*, international civil
servants for the duration of their tour of duty, and enjoy the

unrestricted right of travel in America. As a result of this privilege, the UN has become the biggest Soviet spy centre in the world. Further details of the use the Russians make of this abnormal privilege will be found in my book *Strategy of Survival* (London and New York, 1978) and in John Barron's authoritative work, *KGB* (1974).

To sum up: in the post-Watergate area, the United States and its capital have been made safe for enemies and difficult for defenders.

The great wave of hostility against the CIA began in December 1974, when the *New York Times*, the most famous newspaper in the United States, published a series of articles by Seymour Hersh claiming to expose the misdeeds of the CIA against American citizens. It gathered strength and continued in full flood for several years. Indeed, it had not fully abated when these lines were written late in 1978. However, there were occasional signs of awareness that whatever good may have been done by some of the disclosures was vastly outweighed by the harm done to the security of the US as a whole. In its issue of 6 January 1978, *Time* magazine, a publication not normally noted for its boldness in departing from a current consensus, carried a cover story on the CIA from which I cull the following significant quotation:

A Soviet KGB agent told a *Time* correspondent in Cairo last week: 'Of all the operations that the Soviet Union and the US have conducted against each other, none have benefited the KGB as much as the campaign in the US to discredit the CIA. In our wildest scenarios, we could never have anticipated such a plus for our side. It's the kind of gift all espionage men dream about. Today our boys have it a lot easier, and we didn't have to lift a finger. You did all our work for us.'

The only comment needed, I think, is that the last two sentences are undoubtedly an instance of Soviet 'disinformation'. It would be true to say that most of the work of destroying the CIA was done by Americans in the media and Congress. But not all. Once the wave had started, the KGB was both diligent and highly successful (on an easy wicket, to vary the metaphor) in swelling the flood by indirectly feeding the journalists and politicians, mostly without their knowledge, with quantities of 'facts' about the CIA. But this does not alter the essentially suicidal character of the whole exercise. Never had the collective American loss of will to survive been more patent.

Another American publication, *US News & World Report*, whose concern with American security is more consistent than that of

Time, complained in its issue of 24 April 1978 that: 'the Soviet Union and its Communist allies are flooding the US with more spies now than ever before—more, even, than in the cold-war days when Communist spying was taken far more seriously than it is today.' (Note the unconscious assumption that the cold war is over, whereas the very facts reported by the magazine in the same sentence make it clear that it is far from over on the Soviet side.) The magazine went on to appeal to colleagues and politicians 'to quit punishing our counterintelligence agencies for past misdeeds by crippling their ability to cope with spies'.

The Hardware Gap

One power and one power only threatens the survival of the United States: the Soviet Union. The defence of the United States, and through the US as leader of the Western Alliance the allies of the United States, is therefore essentially a defence system strong enough either to deter the USSR from using its offensive capacity, or if deterrence proves ineffective, to ensure survival after a clash of arms, including nuclear ones.

It is necessary to restate these self-evident facts because in recent times successive American administrations have given the impression that they have forgotten the facts or prefer not to remember them. Defence is a highly technical subject which one cannot expect the general reader to have mastered. But the essential facts can be expressed very simply. They are these:

—For years, the United States enjoyed absolute and relative strategic superiority over the Soviet Union because of its monopoly of first the atomic and later the thermonuclear bombs.

—In October 1962, the reliable knowledge that the US was still superior to the USSR in nuclear weaponry enabled President Kennedy to outface Khrushchev in the so-called Cuban missiles crisis.

—Two years later, with the removal of Khrushchev, the Soviet leaders launched the biggest armament programme in history with the aim of catching up and surpassing the Americans in total military power.

—Shortly after, the US embarked on a process of unilateral disarmament, which started slowly, but gathered momentum under Presidents Nixon, Ford and Carter. Specifically, in the twelve years from 1966 to 1978, the US reduced its air force from 935 strategic bombers to 415; cut down its navy from 300 major warships to 169; and scrapped all missile defences against both bombers and Intercontinental Missiles (ICBMs). Moreover, it froze the strategic missile strength at the 1967 level.

—In the 1975–76 period, Soviet strategic strength began to outstrip America's. Nevertheless, President Carter unilaterally scrapped production of the B-1 strategic bomber, at a time when the Russians increased their own production of the Backfire strategic bomber and started testing an even more formidable one. He also unilaterally deferred production of the enhanced radiation warhead (popularly and misleadingly known as the 'neutron bomb').

—At the time of writing, the USSR was outspending the US by 3 to 1 on strategic weapons.

More than any other previous President, Jimmy Carter professes the intention of basing his foreign policy upon moral foundations. During his electoral campaign, he repeatedly spelled out his aim of eliminating nuclear weapons from this earth—an aim which, incidentally, it was not within his power to achieve, since he had no power to compel the Soviet Union to follow whatever example he cared to give in reducing and ultimately dispensing with such weapons. Nevertheless, he reiterated this intention in various speeches after his assumption of high office.

I am not here concerned with the philosophical absurdities of President Carter's public professions (which were admirably exploded by Dr William Kintner of the Foreign Policy Research Institute in Philadelphia in a splendid article in the 1 September 1978 issue of the New York Magazine, *National Review*). I am concerned simply with establishing the fact that the great American party democracy of the United States no longer provides for the proper defence of its citizens against the one external enemy that represents a real threat to their survival. The fact of America's decline, in absolute as well as relative terms, is indisputable.

Whether this decline has, in fact, deprived America of the capacity to survive a confrontation with the Soviet Union is one which, mercifully, will remain untested until such time as a confrontation takes place, when it will be too late to do anything about it. All that can be done is to quote the grim calculations of the strategic mathematicians. At one time, the American nuclear deterrent was totally 'credible'—that is, it absolutely deterred the Soviet Union from even planning to launch a nuclear attack against the United States in what the strategic jargon terms a 'first strike'. The deterrent worked because the Russians knew that if they attempted a first strike their main centres of population and most of their economic and military capacity would be wiped out in an American 'second strike'.

Today this American credibility has gone. It has gone because the Russians have more missiles than the Americans and more powerful ones; and because the Americans decided they needed neither an Anti-Ballistic Missile (ABM) system nor deep-shelter protection for the civil population, whereas the Russians decided they needed both. As a result, it has been calculated that if the Russians decided to launch a first strike against the US strategic forces, and the Americans decided to retaliate against Soviet cities, the USSR would lose no more than 4 per cent of its population. But a further Soviet retaliation against American cities would slaughter 60 per cent of America's people.

I am of course over-simplifying an exceedingly complex set of problems, but the foregoing paragraph is basically what it comes down to. The American political system must therefore be awarded dismally low marks for its failure to meet the second requirement of the Minimum State: America's people are now unprotected against aggression by the only Power with the capacity to inflict mortal damage on the United States. It does not follow that the Russians will in fact attack the US, for there are many other ways, not involving massive destruction, in which the Soviet leaders might achieve their political and strategic aims. But the possibility can no longer be ruled out.

The Dwindling Dollar

The value of a nation's money may be measured in two principal ways: its purchasing power at home, and its exchange rate abroad. By either standard, the value of the American dollar has dwindled drastically during the past seven or eight years.

The effects of inflation are cumulative. When politicians talk of 'cutting the rate of inflation' and feel virtuous, they conceal from the ordinary citizen the fact that their money is going to buy still less in the next period. Thus between 1972 and 1977, the purchasing power of the US dollar at home declined by nearly 50 per cent. The actual figure was 49·64, which is what happens when inflation (as measured by increases in consumer prices) rises by: 3·3 per cent (1972), 6·2 per cent (1973), 11 per cent (1974), 9·1 per cent (1975), 5·8 per cent (1976) and 6·5 per cent (1977).

This was bad enough, but 1978 brought worse news still. In April that year consumer prices in the US rose by 0·9 per cent, which brought the annual inflation rate up to 11·4 per cent. But (as *Time* magazine pointed out on 12 June 1978), food prices were rising more than twice as fast at 23·8 per cent.

The citizens of the richest country in the world were thus being cheated of much of the value of the money they were earning, after the tax man had finished taking his cut of their incomes. Moreover, if they travelled abroad or traded with foreign countries they found the experience increasingly painful (depending on the country that welcomed them or traded with them). Between 4 November 1977 and 10 March 1978, all the major world currencies (including the battered British pound) rose against the dollar, by the following percentages:

French franc:	0·3
Italian lira:	2·9
Japanese yen:	5·5
British pound:	5·5
German mark:	10·9
Swiss franc:	16·4

(Source: *Time* magazine, 20 March 1978)

The rot began with President Nixon's decision in August 1971 to allow the dollar to float in relation to the price of gold. Thus, at a stroke, he dismantled the whole basis of the Bretton Woods arrangements which had regulated international trade and finance since the Second World War, for that basis was the gold-exchange standard, tying the price of gold to the dollar, and allowing dollars to be freely convertible into gold.

I am not here concerned with the rights and wrongs of Nixon's decision in itself. It led, by 1978, to chaos in the world's currency system. It helped US exports by making them cheaper, but transferred enormous dollar holdings into foreign hands and created a disastrous loss of confidence in the financial leadership of the United States. But these are symptoms and consequences, and I am more concerned with causes.

Under the party system, an incoming administration is saddled with the errors and follies of its predecessor. Nixon inherited the mistakes of the Johnson Administration. A paragraph in *The Memoirs of Richard Nixon* (1978) explains the situation with admirable succinctness:

The economy that Eisenhower had bequeathed to Kennedy in January 1961 was remarkably stable, with a rate of inflation of about 1·5 per cent. By 1969, largely because of the effects of the

Vietnam war, inflation soared to 4·7 per cent. But the war was not the only cause of inflation. Johnson had tried to satisfy everyone; he had encouraged the American people to believe that even in time of war they could have butter as well as guns. The fact was that the expansion of the Great Society was financed by deficit spending [pp. 515–16].

Even allowing for the natural tendency of a politician to blame his predecessor for present troubles, this was, I believe, a precise description of the consequences of President Lyndon Johnson's optimism and budgetary indiscipline. Nixon inherited an economic and financial mess. Welfare programmes attract voters in the lower-income groups, but if they are financed out of budgetary deficits, there is a delayed price to pay in inflation from which the entire population will suffer. As my late boss Geoffrey Crowther once wrote in the *Economist*, the British could hardly expect to remain bankers to the world if bankrupt at home. A similar vanity was implicit in the assumption that the dollar would continue to be the linch-pin of the world's currencies if it lost its value at home.

Two generations of Keynesian and pseudo-Keynesian economics accustomed politicians to think that the State was immune from the consequences of failing to balance a budget. A State, it was thought, could never go bankrupt. And this was true in a way, but only in the sense that in a world of sovereign States nobody could force a debtor State to pay its debts short of military occupation. It was cheaper and less damaging to bail the bankrupt out; which was what happened time and again with Britain when the International Monetary Fund came to the rescue.

It was to the political (that is, electoral) advantage of the parties to foster the illusion that there would always be money for the State to pick up the bills. And indeed there was: if tax income was insufficient, one could always print the money or borrow it. Those who pointed out that if there was too much money around in comparison with the goods and services being produced, the result would be inflation, were denounced as 'monetarists', which became a dirty word almost overnight—until in time the hard realities made monetarists of many politicians who had been using the word as a term of abuse in the speeches of the day before yesterday.

Let us heed the words of the great American exponent of realistic economics, Professor Milton Friedman: 'There is one and only one basic cause of inflation: too high a rate of growth in the quantity of money—too much money chasing the available supply of goods and services.' (*Newsweek*, 3 October 1977.)

The cause, then, is purely technical. But the reasons why governments print too much money are usually political, when they are
not rooted in ignorance. Governments spend more than they earn
to provide Welfare (a bottomless pit), or to preserve or create jobs.
(Thus, in Britain a Tory government stepped in with subsidies to
prevent Rolls-Royce from collapsing, and a Labour government did
the same for British Leyland. There is little to choose between the
parties in this respect. It is the party system itself that is to blame.)

This is what happened in America, as it happened elsewhere. In
America as in Britain, governments resorted to wage controls and
in both countries were unwilling to learn the lesson that the relief
which wage-controls bring is temporary. They palliate but do not
cure inflation.

There is no need to explore the subject further. The point at issue
was whether the American party system was delivering the third
requirement of the Minimum State by preserving the value of money.
The answer was painfully negative. Thus the system was in default
in all three of the requirements of good government. What it did
provide, at an exorbitant cost to the citizen, was gross over-
government.

So gross indeed was the over-supply of government that one day
it happened, as perhaps it was bound to: the great tax-revolt came.
It happened, perhaps appropriately, in the richest State of the
Union: in California, where everything can happen, smog, quick
fortunes, race-riots, earthquakes, high technology, mass murders,
Richard Nixon, and even common sense. A local business man in
West Los Angeles, Howard Jarvis, collected more than 4 million
signatures for a petition to slash the property tax by 57 per cent.
The petition, known as Proposition 13, made fiscal history. Mr
Jarvis had picked the right issue for his campaign. As property
values inexorably rose, house-owners found themselves paying more
and more in property tax. For the State, Proposition 13 meant a
loss of revenue of $7 billion.

Not only had Howard Jarvis made history, he had also started a
kind of rolling earthquake that rumbled through the United States
as similar petitions were drafted within weeks in half a dozen other
States.

As James Burnham pointed out (*National Review*, 21 July 1978)
there were going to be losers as well as winners in the great tax
revolt. The winners would include all property owners, among them
hotel and summer camp proprietors, and the owners of industrial
and commercial property. But the losers would probably include
government workers, many of whom faced unemployment, those

renting their accommodation who were probably not going to have their rents reduced, and those on Welfare.

It was too early to say, when these lines were written, what the long-term consequences of Proposition 13 were going to be. The important thing was that the taxpayers of California had found a way of showing they had had enough of big government and the confiscatory taxes that sustained it. Whatever happened later, it was a move away from over-government, and quite possibly a move in the direction of good government; although the second proposition did not follow from the first, since party politics went on unhindered.

SIX

THE SWISS EXCEPTION

In July 1937, the engineering and metalworking trade unions of the Swiss Confederation announced a Peace Agreement: from that time forward, they declared, they would renounce the strike as their normal way of getting what they wanted. This alone would account for the arresting fact that the standard of living in Switzerland, which was about half that of the United Kingdom in 1930, is now about double—a relative rise of four to one. But there are other reasons, all of relevance to any search for the Minimum State.

In retrospect, the Peace Agreement of 1937 (as important in its way as the famous Saltsjöbaden peace treaty of 1938 between labour and capital in Sweden) stands out as one of the three key events in Swiss history, along with the League of the Three Forest Cantons of 1291 (which brought the cantons together for common defence) and the Congress of Vienna in 1815 (which recognised the permanent neutrality of Switzerland). As Britain's outstanding specialist on Switzerland, Professor Christopher Hughes, put it in his book of that name in 1975: 'The spirit of this agreement has become part of the national ethos, and the British way of managing these things is regarded with the sort of disgust and fear which a primitive people feels for leprosy [p. 173].' The metaphor is so robust and expressive that I cannot resist quoting it.

I have no wish to over-simplify the infinitely complex subject of the behaviour of peoples. Although the Swiss are usually thought to be a placid and unemotional lot (not, perhaps, unfairly if the reference is to the Swiss as the average traveller finds them today), there are much violence, passion and in particular labour troubles in their history. Events appear to have changed the national character, or at any rate the national behaviour. Why, for instance, should the Swiss trade unions decide that their interests and those of their employers were not necessarily antagonistic; while British ones still favour a continuance of the hostilities that so visibly impoverish the country as a whole, while providing members of the stronger unions with an illusory and temporary relative well-being—which, in the end, leaves them half as well off as the workers of neighbouring countries?

There is an explanation for the industrial peace of Switzerland. The Swiss felt mortally threatened by Nazi Germany. There was a great upsurge of national solidarity, and in 1936 the country launched a vast rearmament programme which cost the Swiss more *per capita* than Britain's corresponding effort. The Social Democrats supported the rearmament programme, and the unity forged in the face of the Nazi danger enabled the Peace Agreement of 1937 to be concluded.

In Britain, in contrast (and wherever the workers are led by Marxists, as so many British workers are), trade unionists continue to blame all their troubles on the fiction they call 'capitalism' and consider it their duty to undermine the liberal market economy that produces the wealth and tolerates their disruptive tactics. If successful in the long run, the Marxist leaders will produce a political revolution that will turn Britain into a 'people's democracy' with a permanently reduced living standard. Alternatively, of course, the silent majority of the workers could shake off their apathy, rid themselves of their leaders (as the engineering workers did in 1978) and aspire, while still alive, to a Swiss standard of living. In labour relations, as in politics and economics, the Swiss exception stands as the shining model.

One explanation of the Swiss success in this field is of special interest to a country such as Britain, in which labour relations are so bad. A number of the original and beneficent functions of the trade unions—relating to the health, education and welfare of members and their families—have been taken over by the Welfare State; in Switzerland the trade unions retain these functions and are not, therefore, concerned solely with the 'class struggle' against the employers. In Britain, the rank-and-file trade unionists have become, in a sense, 'disconnected' from the unions and from society. In Switzerland, they remain 'connected'. In the larger country, there is alienation; in the smaller, social harmony.

Let us, however, dig a little deeper.

First, some examples of the violent past.

War: the Swiss infantry crushingly defeated Leopold of Austria in 1315 in the Battle of Morgarten. Leopold's mistake was to suppose he could crush the Swiss and punish them for supporting Louis IV against Frederick the Handsome (of the Hapsburgs). The international reputation for skill and courage of the Swiss foot-soldiers started that day.

Civil war: for fourteen years, between 1436 and 1450, Zürich clashed with neighbouring cantons over the domains of the Count of Toggenburg. French and German armies joined in the fun, but in the end the Emperor Sigismund made the peace of Constance (Switzerland being but a part of the sprawling 'empire' that was neither holy nor Roman, although so-called) and the Confederacy was strengthened not weakened. Thenceforth, the long Swiss internal peace (the rule) was punctuated by occasional civil wars between Protestant and Catholic cantons (the exceptions).

War again: in 1460, the Confederation conquered the Thurgau from Austria, thereby gaining a frontier on Lake Constance. Between 1474 and 1477, the Swiss defeated the predatory forces of the French Charles the Bold (of Burgundy) at Grandson, Morat and Nancy: it became ever clearer that it was a mistake to tangle with the Swiss, who had become the leading military power in Europe. In 1478 they defeated the Duke of Milan's army at Giornico. The Pope, at this point, decided it was a good idea to employ Swiss soldiers: hence the picturesque Swiss Guard admired by tourists visiting the Vatican. In 1499 the Swiss took on the Emperor, no less, inflicting upon him a series of defeats. In the end, the victorious Swiss brought Basle, Schaffhausen and Appenzell into their Confederation, nicely rounding off its northern border. War brought great military prestige to the Swiss, but at the usual cost in peasant unrest and urban hardship. It also brought its share of despotism, and it is salutary to reflect that in the 1480s the ruthless and cynical Hans Waldmann ruled as Burgomaster over what is now the solid citadel of Swiss material success: the canton of Zürich.

Fervour and Persecution

A sense of innate sin is deeply engraved in the conscience of the Genevan citizens—a circumstance for which the French religious fanatic and reformer Jean Calvin was directly responsible. His spirit broods still today over the old quarters of Geneva; although the modern city, perhaps through the natural cosmopolitanism of the headquarters of the old League of Nations and large portions of the United Nations, has developed a rather sinful atmosphere. There is of course no contradiction there: for Calvinism without sin would be like fish without sauce.

Twice Calvin lived in Geneva, and on his return in 1541 found a reign of disorder and irreligion. He soon set about remedying conditions which he held to be displeasing to God, and indeed the theocratic State he created was styled the City of God. Not only, he preached, are we all born with the sin of ancient Adam within us, but we are all guilty and deserve to be punished, including babes and infants.

Since almost anything we might think of doing was sinful, especially if it brought pleasure, Calvin sought to suppress everything that offended against doctrine. His euphemism for such offences was Godlessness. When Jérome Bolsec, a rival theologian, attacked Calvin's form of predestination on the logical ground that it seemed to identify God as the author of all evil, Calvin had him expelled from the City of God.

He was the lucky one. When a still more formidable exegetist, the Spaniard Miguel Servetus, challenged him on points of doctrine, Calvin had him arrested and burnt at the stake—a course of action which the Genevan city fathers thoroughly endorsed. An anti-Calvinist uprising in 1555 was suppressed with appropriate ruthlessness; religion being the ideology of the day.

Intolerant Calvinism, then, is part of the heritage of the Swiss (or at any rate of Canton Geneva, which may help to explain why two foreigners—let alone two Swiss or one of each—not joined together in holy matrimony, if misguided enough to share a hotel room in Geneva, will both be liable to arrest). But the legacy also includes the softer reformist doctrines of Hyldrich Zwingli, and the medieval character of the Church of Rome.

Wars, Strife, Riots and Uprisings

The seeds of strife were inherent in the conflicting religious inheritance of the cantons, and Protestants and Catholics were frequently at each other's throats. There were the First Villmergen War of 1656, in which the Catholic cantons defeated Berne and Zürich; and the Second Villmergen War of 1712, which gave dominance to the Protestants after a smashing Bernese victory.

Nor was religion the only source of conflict. As long ago as 1314 the herdsmen of Schwyz sacked Einsiedeln Abbey and carried off the monks into servitude. In 1653 Nicholas Leuenberg rallied peasant insurgents and laid siege to Berne. Other cantons came to the rescue and the peasants were suppressed. Then there was Peter Fatio's popular insurrection in Geneva in 1707; but once again, other cantons joined in and the revolutionaries were defeated. Berne was held to be a particularly oppressive canton, and Abraham Davel of the Vaud decided in 1723 that he had had enough of the Bernese. He captured Lausanne, before being outmanoeuvred, captured himself and executed.

More uprisings followed in Geneva in 1734 and 1737. Then came the great French Revolution and its inevitable contagion of ideas. The Bernese government crushed an incipient insurrection in the

Vaud, but in Geneva the revolutionaries actually seized power at the end of 1792.

Marxism came to Swiss awareness at the turn of the nineteenth century and ushered in three decades of industrial unrest. It was from Zürich that the famous sealed train set off in 1917 bearing Lenin and the incalculable consequences of the Bolshevik Revolution. The new regime promptly opened an embassy in Berne, which became a centre for Communist subversion, and as such the forerunner of a long line of embassies, trade missions and the like, unto this day. With the collapse of the Kaiser's empire and the proclamation of a Republic Germany was in full revolutionary ferment at the end of 1918. The workers of Zürich called a one-day strike on 9 November, which turned into a nationwide general strike. Four days later, the army had restored order and the workers were back in their factories. On 8 December the Confederation broke off diplomatic relations with Moscow and did not resume them until 1945, an interesting illustration of the ideological boundaries of Swiss neutrality. But strikes broke out time and again, in accordance with a militant tradition that long ante-dated Marxism, as witness (for instance) the riot of 1832 in the township of Uster (Canton Zürich) when the factory of Corrodi and Pfister, which had pioneered mechanical weaving, was burnt to the ground (Hughes, p. 183).

The Time of Peace

These highlights of a turbulent past are in no sense, of course, a history of the Swiss. But they do show, I hope, that the Swiss did not begin placid, peaceful, reasonable and infallibly industrious. It is all the more remarkable that they exchanged strife for peace, persecution for tolerance, division for unity, and war for neutrality.

How did they do it? It is easier to chronicle than to explain. It is as though the Swiss people as a whole decided that they had had enough of the convulsions that had racked their mountain country's history, and wished to bury the past. It did not happen from one day to the next: it was an organic process spread over more than a century, from the proclamation of Switzerland's permanent neutrality by the Congress of Vienna in 1815 to the Labour Peace of 1937 (two key events already mentioned in this chapter). The period was, however, punctuated by fresh convulsions from time to time. The Protestant cantons liberalised their constitutions in the late 1820s, then banded together to defend themselves under the Siebener Concordat of 1832. Some years later the Catholic cantons, in which Jesuit influence was very strong, banded together in a league called the Sonderbund to protect their interests. The Catholics were defeated after a short civil war (yet another) and in 1848 the Swiss at last gave themselves a federal constitution, not unlike that of the United States, which recognised the cantons' local rights but introduced a strong federal government. There was a further strengthening of the federal government under the constitutional revision of 1874.

Switzerland's unique military system, with its standing militia, was conceived in 1847 and revised in more or less its present form in 1907. All males aged twenty to sixty are under conscription. There is a basic military training-period of seventeen weeks, followed by eight years of additional training-periods of three weeks each. In the event of war, the country could mobilise an army of half a million men, plus 200,000 men as home guards and in auxiliary services. For a country with a population of around $6\frac{1}{2}$ million, this is a formidable force. The system itself served as a model for Israel's, with its capacity to mobilise the entire population within a day or so. Unlike Israel, Switzerland has not needed to put its system to the test of a response to actual war.

There can be no doubt that if attacked the Swiss would prove a formidable foe, not only because this is what history teaches about the Swiss and the facts on paper suggest, but because of the mountainous configuration of their country, which favours a durable last stand. Surrounded by Axis-controlled territory during the Second World War, the Swiss warned Hitler that if he was thinking of invasion, they would destroy roads and railways across the Alps, including long stretches of tunnel that would take years to repair, and fight to the last Swiss in an inner redoubt in the high Alps. Hitler did not attack.

It is sad to have to add that in June 1977 a former commander of the Swiss Civil Air Defences, Brigadier Jean-Louis Jeanmaire, was gaoled for eighteen years for passing on defence secrets to the Soviet Union over a period of thirteen years. It was Jeanmaire himself who had supervised the construction of Switzerland's elaborate system of underground defences, full details of which he had passed to the Soviet KGB. No system, however good, is better than the men who administer it, and none is proof against treason. But this nasty blemish does not alter the fact that Switzerland amply meets the second of the three criteria of the Minimum State: defence against external enemies.

It is fair to add that the Swiss security service (Police Fédérale or Bundespolizei) is highly efficient, and would doubtless have exposed Jeanmaire long before it did instead of allowing him to

retire at sixty-five in the belief that he had got away with his prolonged bout of treachery, if he had behaved as spies normally do
and parted with his country's secrets for cash. Instead, he did what he
did for confused motives that included spite after being passed over
for promotion in mid-career; friendship for the very able Soviet
KGB official who flattered him over the years, to the extent he
allowed the Russian to become his wife's lover; and a perverted
sense of his own importance. A sorry tale.

As for the Swiss citizen army, it should be remembered that the
Swiss soldier, virtually alone in the world, has to keep his arms and
ammunition at home, and performs his annual gunnery duty in
civilian clothes. Where else does such trust exist between a government and its citizens? It is often argued that the prevalence of guns
in a community (as in the United States) must of necessity be a
major factor in the incidence of violent crime, but the Swiss case
disproves the assertion. There is virtually no violent crime in
Switzerland, although highly efficient means of murder are in every
Swiss household. It takes murderers to kill people.

Here again, the concept of 'connection' and 'disconnection' is
useful. A professional army of the usual kind, even if it includes
conscripts, lives apart from the population and tends to be 'disconnected' from it—a thing apart. A citizen army, such as the Swiss,
permeates and is part of society.

Government by Reference

I have often said in these pages that democracy is impossible; and
indeed it is. But the Swiss come closer than any other nation to
making a reality of it, partly because the Swiss canton is the nearest
contemporary equivalent to the ancient Greek city-State (that is,
small enough for the principle of popular suffrage to have a meaning),
and partly because of that uniquely Swiss contribution to the art of
politics: the referendum.

The Swiss electorate (all Swiss citizens over the age of twenty)
does not delegate its sovereignty to its elected parliament as does,
for instance, the British. Sovereignty continues to reside in the
people, which can both block legislation of which it does not approve
and initiate constitutional change. The sovereign Swiss electorate
exerts its direct powers in three principal ways: the Facultative
Referendum; the Popular Initiative; and the Obligatory Referendum.

If 30,000 voters band together and all sign the requisite document,
they have the right to demand that any legislative measure passed
by parliament or any decisions taken by the Federal Council be

put to popular vote. This is the Facultative Referendum. Moreover, the signatures of 50,000 voters can force the government to draft and submit to parliament either partial or sweeping amendments to the Constitution. This is the Popular Initiative, and it is restricted to constitutional questions. The constitutional sovereignty of the Swiss people is maintained all the way, for any decisions affecting any part of the Constitution, if deemed 'urgent', must be put to a popular vote: this is the Obligatory Referendum. It should be added that on the level of the canton—which to the Swiss is the real State—the devices of the Referendum and Initiative are even more strongly developed in favour of the voter. In most cantons, any kind of legislation can be initiated by popular demand—that is, by a comparatively small number of signatures (the requirement varying from canton to canton). The referendal principle also applies on the level of the commune.

If a canton proposes to spend more than a certain sum, there will be a Finance Referendum to determine the views of the citizens; below the agreed sum, the canton may proceed, but only if not challenged by the voters. And who, it may be asked, are the voters? I have already defined them as Swiss citizens over the age of twenty, but this short definition does not do justice to the complexities of Swiss citizenship. There is, in fact, no Swiss citizenship as such. A Swiss citizen is a citizen of a canton (the *real* State, as I have noted) and cantonal citizenship in turn is based on citizenship of the commune—the commune (town or village) being, historically, the original country in which one lived and worked. Moving from one town to another meant the crossing of borders. A passport, or document of origin and identity, was therefore needed. Hence citizens of Swiss cantons have a 'Document of Origin' (*Heimatschein*, in German).

In certain important ways, apart from historical origins, a Swiss canton is still a sovereign State: for instance, the canton raises its own tax revenues by its own system, and in total independence of the central government. To move from one canton to another still means crossing a border. A Swiss therefore has to inform the communal authorities of any move to a new place of domicile and give the new address. At the new domicile, the internal passport or Document of Origin will have to be deposited with the local authority.

To the stranger, these requirements have an authoritarian ring, if not worse. They may recall, for instance, the internal passport without which Soviet citizens cannot change their place of residence, and in most cases their jobs. But the Swiss do not look at it that way, and there is no comparison between the Swiss and Soviet internal passports. The latter constitute one of the many means of enforcing control by the secret police. The Swiss are proud and happy to have a Document of Origin, because it guarantees the holder's right to live and work in his place of origin. Should a Swiss fall on bad times, he is entitled to 'poverty assistance' and to a place in the local almshouse. In practice, the financial benefits have been superseded by the Federal Old Age Pension, but the Swiss values the *Heimatschein* because it guarantees a domicile and records the responsibility of his or her community of origin (even if the last person who actually lived there was a long-deceased great-grandfather).

Since the *Heimatschein* (in effect, the Swiss equivalent of a birth certificate) has to be deposited with the local authority, each Swiss is issued with an identity card with picture. In this, they are no different from the citizens of most Continental countries (though not of Britain, which issued identity cards in wartime, then dropped them—as indeed the Swiss did for a while). In all this, there is no flavour of Gestapo or KGB. But it is fair to add that the universal registration of domicile undoubtedly facilitates the State's task (No. 1 in my criteria for the Minimum State) of providing for the safety and security of its citizens, and the prevention of crime.

In this, as in other spheres, the decentralising federal principle helps the average citizen, for police authority is exercised mainly by the cantons and by some of the larger communes. The federal police corps, which is small, enforces federal laws on certain offences, including forgery (a tempting offence in a banker's paradise) and treason.

An inconvenience of another kind lies in the multiplicity of occasions for voting. A Swiss citizen is always voting on *something*, at the communal, cantonal or federal level, whether in elections or to stop a law or initiate an amendment. At times this must be a nuisance. A British citizen probably does not vote more often in a lifetime than a Swiss in one year. But at least the Swiss voter knows that his vote counts for something. He may delegate legislative responsibility to the two national assemblies, but the final say lies with him. He is consulted more often than any other voter. And consultation is infinitely preferable to 'participation': the one is consistent with individual freedom, the other is not.

The Great Swiss Prosperity

In a way, the wealth of the Swiss Confederation is as mysterious as the current placidity of the Swiss. Certainly it is not inherent in either the geography or the history of the country. It has a little iron but not much; and hydro-electric power; and that is about all. About 70 per cent of the surface is mountainous, and nothing can be grown on rock, water and ice, although the Alpine economy has traditionally supported pasture and agriculture. (Not that a shortage of raw materials has prevented Japan from becoming an economic super-power, nor an abundance of them brought an economic miracle to, say, Indonesia.)

As for history, for centuries the Swiss were poor and exported labour either in civilian form or as mercenaries for other countries' armed forces. But the tradition of disputatious poverty that is part of the Swiss legacy has not prevented the country from soaring to the top of the economic league in recent decades. There can be no better demonstration that the richest natural resource is simply people.

How have they done it? The answers, I suggest, lie in the following factors, separately and together: the Labour Agreement of 1937 (already mentioned) which brought industrial peace; peace in the wider sense of the absence of foreign wars, after Napoleon had done his bit; the national habit of hard work, forced upon the Swiss to some extent by a long and cruel winter which obliged many rural families to cultivate a handicraft as a secondary occupation; the Puritan ethic; the rule of law; and not least, a faith in and reliance upon the market economy, served by an efficient and accommodating banking system and by a sensible taxation system which leaves profits and earnings largely in the hands of those who make them. Incentive is rewarded in Switzerland, as it is not in Britain and some other countries where socialist ideas have ruined the economic system without satisfying the dogmatists. Private enterprise works where it is allowed to work, and Switzerland, so far, has allowed it to work.

Another factor to be mentioned is the availability of relatively cheap migrant labour—an economic asset and a political liability. By the 1970s, about one worker in three was a foreigner—Turks and Greeks, Spaniards and Italians and Portuguese poured in from the relatively penurious south of Europe, as they had into so many other prosperous countries. They brought with them willing arms, and sometimes skills, but they also created social tensions, and in the end political problems, which are not strictly relevant to our concerns here.

It should be added, however, that such tensions are in no way comparable to those created by the irresponsible immigration policies of successive British governments. In Switzerland, there has been no blanket permission to settle, with citizenship thrown in.

Unlike the British, the Swiss were consulted, by referendum. And foreign workers were normally admitted on nine-months renewable contracts, which if not renewed left no legacy of bitterness.

In inventiveness, the Swiss would not claim to be primary innovators, as the British are. Like the Japanese, they tend to exploit other people's inventions. But again like the Japanese, they are important secondary innovators. Very often a British or French or American idea is developed to its utmost in Switzerland because the idea has been improved, or because some technological adaptation has made it marketable by the ingenious Swiss.

The outcome has been a remarkably steady growth rate, not at spectacular levels but singularly free of the distortions and maladministration that cloud so many other countries' economic prospects. The Swiss suffered, as everybody else did, from the oil crisis of 1974 and 1975, which brought a price-inflation of about 9·8 per cent for each of these years. On the other hand, Britain's inflationary rates were 16·1 and 24·2 per cent for the respective years, and Japan's 22·7 and 12·2 per cent. Likewise, real growth declined by 0·2 per cent in 1974 and by as much as 7·3 per cent the following year (compared with Britain's 0·2 and 2·1 per cent, and Japan's 1·3 per cent for 1974 with a positive growth of 2·4 per cent the following year). But the overall record of Switzerland is extraordinary. In 1977, inflation was down to 1·5 per cent, with 1 per cent of unemployed and a real growth of 2 per cent. At the time of writing, the estimates suggested that inflation was running at no more than 0·5 per cent—that is, that it was negligible.

The ready availability of capital has played a leading part in the Swiss economic miracle and so, obviously, has the Swiss banking system. Much has been written about its secrecy—as if British banks, for instance, published details of their clients' accounts. The fact remains that a law of 1934, revised in 1971, does make a breach of banking secrecy a criminal, as distinct from a civil, offence. This undoubtedly provides exceptional protection not only for the superrich tax-evader (who has my sympathy for philosophical reasons expressed in this book), but also for Communist secret services and, no doubt, the Mafia, as well as Arab terrorists and potentates.

In finance as well as in politics (though not, as noted, in ideology) the Swiss are neutral, and the money, clean, tainted, or freshly laundered, flows in, to the general benefit of the Swiss economy.

The range of services provided by the Swiss banks is, in other respects also, considerably wider than, say, the British or American banking system can offer. A Swiss bank will not only manage a client's portfolio but even exercise his voting rights in companies.

The Swiss National Bank, with its monopoly of the printing press, presides in a sense over several quite distinct types of bank: the Great Banks (such as Swiss Credit and Union Bank); the cantonal banks; the rather aristocratic private banks (corresponding to the merchant banks); the savings and mortgage banks; and a rather shadier category known euphemistically as the 'other banks'.

Until quite recently, the Swiss banks, whatever their secrecy concealed, enjoyed a high reputation for honest dealing and traditional practice. Then the 1970s brought a series of unexpected scandals. To the extent that the 'other banks' were involved, nobody was particularly shaken, except those whose malpractices were unexpectedly revealed. But the summer of 1977 brought a scandal of another dimension: one of the greatest and most honourable of the Great Banks, the famous Crédit Suisse (Swiss Credit Bank, Kreditanstalt) admitted to its horrified shareholders that one of its directors had been siphoning off funds for years, in unauthorised, and in the end disastrous, operations through a company with a Liechtenstein registration. The serenity of Zürich's Bahnhofstrasse was shattered, and the Swiss National Bank, together with the Swiss Bankers' Association, drew up a new and stringent code of banking conduct. Henceforth, anybody opening a Swiss bank account would be required to reveal his true identity (although it was not easy to see how a Mafioso chief could be prevented from using a front man); and bankers were to be forbidden to help customers to evade taxes or export capital illegally. This again sounded more stringent than it was likely to be in practice. The President of the National Bank, Fritz Leutwiler, revealed in an interview (*Time* magazine, 11 July 1977) that Swiss bankers could not be expected to police other countries' foreign-exchange regulations: all that was meant was that Swiss bank managers were henceforth forbidden to travel abroad and actually organise illegal capital outflows.

There are, of course, scandals in all countries, and until human nature changes (perhaps by some biochemical process yet undiscovered), scandals will recur. The Swiss banking scandals of the 1970s are therefore a digression: the system itself has proved itself amply as a machine for bringing prosperity to a country that used to be poor.

The Swiss Polity as a Model

In nearly all respects Switzerland's 'direct democracy' is a model for a practical Minimum State. But in one respect, it is worrying:

along with the many unsatisfactory systems, it is a party democracy. There is a small but active Communist Party and various extremist groups of Right and Left. The federal elections tend to yield a rough equality between the three major parties which may be termed Social Democrat, Radical and Christian Democrat (but the names are changed from time to time and are not necessarily the same at the cantonal and federal levels). The real danger lies in the existence of the Social Democratic Party, which includes mild people who think the Swiss should introduce more sharply progressive taxation to make the rich poorer and would like more Welfare; and wilder people who are ready to include inflammatory aspirations in the party manifesto to appease the Marxists and other revolutionaries. If the party were ever taken over by the extreme Left (as has practically happened in Britain) and came to full power, there would, at least in theory, be an acute danger of a general wrecking operation which would yield much blood and no treasure. Even if the milder socialists had their way, they would, less rapidly but no less surely, mess up a system that has worked admirably to the general benefit.

A more general danger is implicit in Switzerland's century of change from the 1830s, in that the change was so gradual and evolutive that the current outcome does not rest upon any written philosophical basis, so that the Swiss system could be vulnerable to the invasion of false ideologies.

These are the dangers, real or hypothetical. In reality, they have been nullified until now by direct democracy, that is by the referendum and in particular by the Legislative Challenge described earlier. It may be assumed that a socialist majority in the assemblies would be frustrated in no uncertain terms in this manner. But this would cease to be true, and the referendum cease to be a safeguard, should some demagogue of the Left convert majorities to his views in the major cantons. Fortunately, this is at present a remote possibility. But in the long run the prospect cannot be excluded. To quote Professor Hughes: '. . . it is only since 1959 that the party has had a programme which justified socialism's opponents in taking social-ists into their confidence in any way. There is still a certain ambiguity about what happens in practice to anti-socialists, if socialism attains power. Democracy as a means to power is accepted: does it survive, or wither away on attainment? [pp. 165–66].' That is the eternal question about socialism, which unfortunately can be answered only when it is too late.

The direct democracy of Switzerland, closer to the real-but-impossible thing than anywhere else, has much to its credit. Not least, it makes a doctrine of the mandate impossible. Even if a Swiss party ever achieved an absolute majority in parliament, it could not hope to impose its views on the whole nation (as the British Labour Party can) because the people would reject such pretensions. Essentially, and in the best possible sense, the referendum is a conservative device, militating against change for the sake of change and asserting common sense over hare-brained political proposals.

And yet, in my view, the Swiss system could be still further improved if the Confederation abandoned the obsolete party concept in favour of the No-Party State. Let the political parties survive as pressure groups, along with the banks, and the employers' federation and the trade unions, but without the power to compete for office. In Switzerland more than in any other country, a No-Party State would perpetuate, through direct democracy, the economic bases of continuing prosperity and freedom. To sum up: because of the referendum, the political parties are less of a danger to the future of the Swiss Confederation than they might otherwise be. But in themselves they contribute nothing to the national well-being and ultimately threaten it. The Minimum State that is the glory of Switzerland deserves better than a party system.

SEVEN

ABSOLUTE PERFECTION:
THE MAXIMUM STATE

The totalist States can legitimately claim to provide the three requirements which the democratic ones as a rule no longer provide. In general, that is, they can guarantee the safety and security of their citizens; defence against external enemies; and a stable currency. The trouble is that they also provide over-government on a horrific scale. The totalist polity is the Maximum State not the Minimum: Hobbes's Leviathan in monstrous and hypertrophic form.

My main concern is to draw attention to the features that distinguish them from authoritarian States and make them infinitely less tolerable.

The Soviet Union need not detain us very long: I have already written a great deal about it in other books, and Soviet specialists of high quality are thick on the ground. Although it is difficult (for me at least) to understand how anybody with the dreadful example of Russia to contemplate could advocate communism or place any faith in Marxism–Leninism, it is encouraging to note that in general Russia gets a bad press in most countries. Even so Marxist-permeated a body as the National Executive Committee of the British Labour Party, or the Trades Union Congress, has felt compelled in recent times to protest against the Soviet treatment of dissidents, or the continued occupation of Czechoslovakia; although this has not stopped these bodies, in particular, from welcoming to Britain such archetypal representatives of the Soviet tyranny as Alexander Shelepin and Boris Ponomarev. Still, it is possible to speak of progress when even the normally Stalinist French Communist Party can protest about the confinement of Soviet dissidents in psychiatric wards.

The real criterion of the totalist State, the one that most clearly distinguishes it from the authoritarian, is that it is virtually impossible, or at any rate very difficult, for the ordinary citizen to escape from the political process. In countries such as Portugal under Salazar, Spain under Franco, or Chile under Pinochet, on the contrary, the ordinary person could be reasonably happy and be left in peace, on condition he or she kept *out* of politics. Mussolini, whose speech-writer coined the word 'totalitarian', meant his Fascist State to embrace the entire people and involve all citizens in politics. This was even truer of Nazi Germany (except that German Jews were not regarded as human), and of Stalin's USSR.

Ghastly though the Soviet regime still is in the late 1970s, nobody could assert with conviction that it is as bad now as it was under Stalin. To a perceptible degree, Russia has become less totalist than it used to be. Certainly it is less totalist than the Chinese People's Republic which therefore, in this context, deserves more space. That it really *is* less totalist can be shown by the simple test of the criterion already mentioned: it is obviously far easier for ordinary Russians to opt out of politics than for ordinary Chinese. (By 'ordinary', I simply mean men and women who are not members of the ruling party.)

A sign of the times is that we know much more about the daily life of ordinary Russians than we were allowed to know in Stalin's day. A couple of years before this chapter was written, an American journalist of 'liberal' inclinations, Hedrick Smith of the *New York Times*, brought out a long but highly readable book entitled *The Russians* (Times Books, 1976). The picture that emerges from these pages is of a squalid and extraordinarily cynical society whose technological achievements are skin-deep, in which the weight of the Russian tradition is still heavy; of a society in which the knowledge of failure and shortcomings is as universal as the pretence that all is well: a gigantic Potemkin village. But it is quite clear from the many examples he gives that it is possible, given ingenuity and courage (and not a little sheer cheek), to beat the system and live reasonably well; in other words to get away with a lot. Hedrick Smith's massive account is confirmed by the tales of defectors such as Aleksei Myagkov (mentioned earlier), and foreign students back after a year in the USSR.

Of course no system is ever 100 per cent totalist, just as the true Minimum State does not, as far as I know, exist anywhere. Russia indeed shares with China the peculiarity that both consider it necessary to allow individual peasants to till private plots of land in such spare time as labour in the collective or commune leaves them. Without this 'capitalist' contribution to the collective food supply, the peoples of both countries would on occasion go hungry. Certainly the private plots make an altogether disproportionate contribution to food produce in countries where collective agriculture has been a disastrous failure.

One other point needs to be made about the Soviet system: despite the ideological addiction to the dogma that crime is the outcome of class conflict and exploitation under capitalism, the crime rate appears to be soaring in the USSR. I say 'appears to be' because there no crime statistics are published: if they were, the proposition that crime is a capitalist symptom would too easily be disproved. Even so, the Soviet press continues to declare that 'there are no socio-economic causes of crime in our country'. This leads to the pretence that crime, which visibly exists and is probably on the increase, must be something left over from 'bourgeois culture', or an infection due to imports of films and books from the capitalist West.

Perhaps the most interesting point about the crime wave in Russia is the observable fact that young people are responsible for most of it. Rapes, muggings, gang attacks on lone pedestrians, enable Moscow, in at least this particular, to compete with New York or Detroit. Hedrick Smith reports the case of a young psychopath who killed several women in Moscow. An arrest was made, but the newspaper *Evening Moscow* quoted one of the city's top policemen as saying: 'No dangerous crimes have been committed in the city in the last ten days [p. 347].' Ordinary Muscovites knew better. A more detailed, and widely accessible, report on crime in the USSR may be found in the *Reader's Digest* (UK edition) of September 1978, supplemented by quotations from the weekly *Literaturnaya Gazeta*.

Soviet and Russian specialists, however, can turn to the Soviet press for the evidence. They will find both the denial of the fact of crime and proof of its prevalence. In one of its frequent outbursts of ideological lyricism, the Party paper *Pravda* repeated the familiar claim on 18 November 1977: 'Under conditions of Socialism, an historically new type of personality has taken shape—Soviet man— who combines ideological conviction with great vital energy, culture, knowledge.' When the Soviet press is recording rather than extolling, it paints a picture of a society much like others, with drunkenness, casual violence and flourishing rackets.

Compared with the 1920s, twice as many offenders are drunk at the time of the offence, according to the *Herald of Moscow University* (*Law Series*) No. 3 for 1977. On 24 July that year, listeners to Moscow radio heard that 'over 50 per cent of crimes involving bodily harm and 80 per cent of murders are committed by persons under the influence of alcohol'. The speaker, A. Yudkin, went on to note that 'crimes committed in a state of drunkenness are generally without motive, cruel and savage'.

Back in the realms of ideological fantasy, the Soviet Interior Minister, Nikolai Shchelokov, said there had been a substantial reduction in crime over the past sixty years. As reported in the journal *Sociological Research* (No. 3, 1977), he claimed this alleged reduction as 'a major social achievement'. Professional and organised crime had long been eliminated, and so had crimes 'for national and racial motives'. Yet the Soviet press and radio continue to give details of the organised and professional crime that is supposed to have been eliminated. The retention of the death penalty for so-called 'economic crimes' is an indication of the seriousness of the problem. On 30 November 1977, for instance, Moscow radio blamed economic crimes on 'shortages and mismanagement'. It quoted the words of a 'big-time thief' awaiting trial who was asked whether he was afraid and replied: 'Well, not very much. Everyone steals, but not many get caught, so why should I be the one who gets into trouble?'

It is clearly going to be difficult for the Russians to eliminate crime if they continue to pretend that it does not exist: they do, however, occasionally execute violent criminals as a deterrent. If the wave of violent crimes continues, the Soviet system will lose any claim it might once have had of meeting the minimum criteria of the State, in that it will not be able to claim that it provides safety for its citizens. *Security* is another matter: the all-pervasive secret police does ensure that enemies of the system are uncovered and put out of harm's way. Thus the survival of the system is ensured; though whether the ordinary people of the USSR are thankful to the KGB for the self-perpetuation of the autocracy under which they live may be doubted. And since there are neither free elections nor public opinion polls, it is not easy to find out for sure.

Absolutism in China

The 'absolute perfection' of totalism, which forms the title of this chapter, does not exist outside the termite heap. But in human societies, Communist China comes closest to it. Naïve and un-sophisticated visitors to China, of whom there have been a remark-able number over the years, invariably report the sea of smiling faces they find wherever they go, and draw the conclusion that communism has brought universal happiness to the 700 million (or 800 million or 900 million, according to demographic fashion) Chinese people. Mass euphoria certainly appears to be a product of this most totalist system on earth.

Not all visitors are thus deceived. One of the more sceptical observers was Professor Edward Luttwak of Johns Hopkins

University who saw through the wall of propaganda erected by the Chinese system to discourage prying eyes. He recorded his observations (in both senses of the word) in a remarkable article in the New York magazine *Commentary*, from which Bernard Levin quoted extensively in his column in *The Times* of London of 17, 18 and 20 May 1977. Luttwak had the good fortune to travel extensively (although under supervision) in Tibet and outlying provinces of China as well as in Peking. He had interesting things to say about the ruthlessly efficient colonialism of the Han Chinese over non-Chinese peoples, and about the inefficiency of the economic system, despite its high growth rate of about 7 per cent (which, however, compares very unfavourably in relative and absolute terms with the growth rates of free enterprise in Japan, Taiwan and South Korea).

Another sceptical observer was Ross Munro, who was the Peking correspondent of the *Toronto Globe and Mail* for two and a half years. He too was quoted at length by Bernard Levin (in *The Times* of 13, 14 and 16 December 1977). In China, as Munro discovered, you cannot change your job, you cannot start even a one-man business, you cannot live where you like, or travel. Most Chinese are assigned a work unit; and this is where they will have to work for the rest of their lives. A transfer, though not impossible, is very difficult to obtain, but may in rare cases be granted if the worker who wants to leave finds a suitable replacement.

In the depressing slums of Calcutta, thousands of people exist and die in the open, surrounded by their own squalor. This you will not find in China, and its absence draws exclamations of approval from those who want to praise. But, as Munro explains, the reason is that no peasant is allowed to move into the cities. If a peasant does move illegally into one of the cities, he will have to do without food coupons and beg what he can from friends or relatives. If caught, he will be punished.

In the madness of Mao Tse-tung's 'Great Proletarian Cultural Revolution', millions of young undergraduates or graduates were sent to distant villages to purge them of the sin of intellectual class-superiority and acquaint them with the spirit of permanent revolution. In the commune they were under the sharp eyes of the party cadres, who would try to persuade them to spend the rest of their lives on the land. The more pragmatic leaders, who have taken over from the dead leader and from the 'gang of four' (Mao's widow, Chiang Ch'ing, and other associates) who were his chosen favourites, are softening some of these fanatical excesses. This will make life marginally easier for many Chinese. But there is no suggestion that

China's special system of all-pervasive party supervision and control is to be dismantled.

A Chinese is expected to live in the compound in which he or she works. This is part of the machinery of thought-control. A man who leaves the compound to go home and commutes to the compound next morning is, to that extent, escaping from the watchful eyes of the party functionaries. He might develop a split personality: faithful to the party by day, living his own life at night; and this would never do.

That aspect of Marxism which is about the class war is interpreted in China as justifying discrimination against young people whose fathers or grandfathers had the misfortune of being classified as 'rich peasants' during the bloody 'land reform' of the early 1950s. Munro estimates the number of Chinese in this situation—bad class background—at about 30 million, or (let us say) the population of Spain or Poland. All their lives they will draw lower wages than the rest, will be denied free medical services and will have to submit to bouts of verbal abuse. This barbarity is characteristic of Chinese absolutism.

Mao's Contribution

There was nothing particularly new in the observations of Edward Luttwak and Ross Munro. Yet Bernard Levin undoubtedly performed one of his public services by quoting both at length. For the suspension of incredulity about China is still the rule, whereas it has become the exception where Russia is concerned. Today's gullible intellectual fellow-travellers find their Utopian fantasies fulfilled in China, not Russia. It is therefore all the more necessary that sober and unemotional observers should repeat the truth from time to time. Nor should the truth be concealed or glossed over merely because China's rulers fear the Soviet Union and denounce its 'social imperialism'. In totalist societies, the current of abuse can very easily be switched off or diverted elsewhere. It may be expedient to be on good terms with the Chinese People's Republic, but there is no reason why expediency should spell blindness.

The truth about China's pervasive tyranny has been known for a long time, not least because occasional periods of relative tolerance have allowed witnesses to emerge. One such witness—a Western-trained engineer—returned to China in 1957 and did not like what he saw. He managed to get out again, and wrote of his experiences under the name of Mu Fu-sheng, in a book which he entitled *The Wilting of the Hundred Flowers* (Heinemann, 1962). All the things discovered fifteen years later by Luttwak and Munro are in this book and the interesting thing is that conditions had evidently not changed during those years.

Mao Tse-tung had virtually ignored Marxist–Leninist prescriptions in his successful struggle for power. The doctrine envisaged a seizure of power in the cities by a disciplined Communist Party as the 'vanguard' of the workers. But China had relatively few urban workers and teeming millions of peasants, so Mao mobilised the peasants. Similarly, he refrained from a slavish imitation of the Soviet model in the apparatus of repression he built for his 'people's republic', and in the techniques for the permanent retention of power he elaborated on achieving it. First, mainly in 1951, there was a coldly calculated terror, when hundreds of thousands of Chinese were publicly executed. There are wide variations in the estimated numbers of those who were deprived of life. The highest estimate—about 25 million—was the one disseminated by Chiang Kai-shek's defeated regime, which must be credited with an incentive to quote a high figure. At the same time (the mid-1950s) the US State Department was giving a low estimate of 15 million and a high of 18 million. British diplomats and journalists who were present in China during that period gave much lower figures, and the one that seemed to me the most likely to be true was 800,000, which happened to be about the same as a figure casually mentioned by Mao himself in a speech.

The people eliminated in 1951 were 'class enemies'—unrepentant landlords, 'reactionaries', bandits and Nationalists. But the physical terror did not go on year after year as in Russia, though force and nastiness were always there in reserve. Instead, Mao developed a technique of mass persuasion which amounted to another kind of terror—a psychological one. With remarkable speed the Chinese Communist Party established committees and branches everywhere— in every street of every town and in every village. Having liquidated the irreconcilable 'class enemies', Mao 'persuaded' the rest to join in and help the revolution. There were, of course, recalcitrants, both among former class enemies and among the rest of the population. In general, they were not liquidated. Instead, a remorseless succession of Party cadres would call and relentlessly—by night, as well as by day, when necessary—talk them out of their recalcitrance. In the end, his spirit broken, the ex-dissident would have to confess his sins publicly and submit to thought-reform in a labour camp.

Nothing like this, and certainly nothing on such a scale, had ever before been attempted in history. This ancient nation, in which the family had always been strong but in which individualism had flourished, this nation of inveterate capitalists—'the Jews of the East'—was reduced to mass conformity.

The term 'Hundred Flowers', the wilting of which Mu Fu-sheng had described in his book, needs perhaps to be explained for the younger readers of today. In 1956, with the cruelties of land reform and punishment behind him, Mao had launched the attractively poetical slogan: 'Let a hundred flowers bloom, let a hundred schools contend.' Nothing much happened, however, until at the end of February 1957 the Chairman decided to explain what he had in mind, in a closed session of the Supreme State Conference. He wanted people to feel free to speak their minds, to voice their criticisms.

Could he possibly mean what he said? The party press throughout China buzzed with exegetical commentaries, as did the street committees everywhere. Then, at first timidly and later more boldly, a trickle of criticism turned into a flood. All aspects of life in Communist China were bitterly attacked, by students and their teachers, by more humble people. It became obvious after the event that Mao was taken aback by the whirlwind he had unleashed. The object of letting the flowers bloom and the different schools contend was to demonstrate the superiority of Maoism over all other forms of thought and over all other schools. The whole thing lasted six weeks. Then Mao brought the curtain down. The dissident voices were stilled more suddenly than they had been allowed to speak. Punishment was meted out to those who had spoken their minds. Total thought-control took over again, and all was quiet.

This thought-control, this total stifling of free inquiry, is part of the exorbitant price the Chinese have had to pay for the 'good government' they have had (but not invariably) under Communism. The exceptions in this respect are no less interesting than the general rule. Mao may have been a great leader, but I have not the slightest doubt that he was insane. He severely damaged China's 'developing' economy in 1958 when he announced a 'great leap forward' and set impossible targets for steel production. All over the country, backyard furnaces sprang up and a great quantity of useless metal was produced, along with an unbelievable dislocation of industry. And he caused even more serious damage to the educational system with his 'cultural' revolution from above in the late 1960s, when he turned gangs of Red Guards loose and allowed them to destroy many art treasures and publicly humiliate teachers and even high party officials. Several years' intake of university students were exiled to distant communes or made to clean latrines or collect night-soil. During the four years of the Cultural Revolution, the Chinese people can scarcely be said to have enjoyed either safety or security. Neither then nor during the 'great leap forward' and its aftermath could they be said to have enjoyed good economic management.

It has often been claimed on behalf of the Chinese system that it has kept China free of inflation. For example, former Peking correspondents have noted on leaving that the prices of foodstuffs in the shops were pretty much the same as when they arrived. I do not doubt this; but over a longer period, the figures suggest that China is not, after all, quite immune to inflation. An Australian specialist, Dr Audrey Donnithorne of the Australian National University in Canberra, produced some interesting comparative figures after an intensive study of Chinese sources. Dr Donnithorne has good reasons for being interested in the subject, for she lived through part of the Chinese hyper-inflation of the 1940s, which did as much as anything else to lose the Chinese mainland for the Nationalists.

Dr Donnithorne originally published her research in *The Three Banks Review* in September 1974, but brought some of her findings up to date for *Current Scene* (an American official publication, issued in Hong Kong) of April–May 1978.

Her study of the index of retail prices in eight major Chinese cities showed a rise of 18 per cent between 1952 and 1963. More recent figures are unfortunately incomplete, and in general any researches of this kind for China (as for some other Communist countries) are hampered by inadequate or non-existent statistics.

In any case, the regimentation of the entire population is so thorough that the concepts of wages and prices are almost without meaning. Most commodities are rationed and price-controlled. If a worker wants better housing or personal transport other than a bicycle, or holiday accommodation, there is no question of a personal choice in the matter: it is the local party committee that decides, on the basis of rewarding merit (especially political conformity). Wage rises are decreed from time to time, but are meaningless beyond a certain point as goods are not freely available for purchase. The fact that there is no income tax in People's China sounds startlingly attractive, but has to be measured against the total absence of personal liberty. (The central revenues are almost entirely raised by taxes on the State's own enterprises.)

What about crime? Probably there is less of it in China than in Russia, partly because the regimentation and universal surveillance of the entire population are so much more thorough. As in Russia, such crime as there is is attributed to 'class enemies' and incorrect political thinking. But crime does exist, and every now and then cases find their way into the party papers. There have even been armed bank-raids, and on 30 August 1976 the *Chekiang Daily* reported the killing of a bank manager in a hold-up.

The criminals must have been on the rampage in Chekiang and Honan provinces at that time, because the standing committee of Chekiang's provincial party, which met from 12 November to 9 December 1976, called for action against 'embezzlers, swindlers, murderers, arsonists, criminal gangs and bad elements who are seriously sabotaging public order'. The committee called for the suppression of those indulging in 'beating, smashing and looting'. One of the 'capitalist' crimes listed would not be regarded as criminal in countries like Britain or the United States: it was called 'working on one's own'. The others, including theft and profiteering, had a more familiar ring.

Paradoxically, most of the wrongdoing in Chekiang was blamed on the 'gang of four' who, whatever they may have done to incur the displeasure of the authorities, were surely *Communists* and not capitalists. But such accusations are a kind of ritual in Marxist–Leninist countries, and not to be taken literally. They are hate-signals to divert the attention of the masses from their current miseries.

Much of the petty crime is done by young people returning to the towns illegally from the distant villages to which the party had assigned them. They have no way of applying for work, since they are registered as living in the villages they have left. They therefore resort to thieving and prostitution. Although crime is not necessarily due to social conditions (as sentimental sociologists aver), here is an apparently clear instance of direct correlation: first create the social problem by tearing young people away from their normal environment against their will, then reap the consequences when some of them return. According to the *Kuangming Daily* (27 September 1976), only a small proportion of the young people sent to the countryside in recent years have come back illegally. But how small is 'small'? No fewer than 14 million youths of both sexes were the victims of this mass enforced internal exile. In Canton early in 1976 a gang of illegal young 'returnees' stole a vehicle, abducted a woman in it and raped her. In Shanghai similar gangs were buying up concert tickets and reselling them to workers.

It is of course impossible to compare the scale of such activities with similar ones in Western countries, for the West reveals all and the Communist East conceals except when the problem is so great that the authorities need publicity to deal with it. Let us just say there is crime in China as everywhere else, and let us add (because that is the logic of relentless regimentation) that there is probably less of it than in Russia or America.

When it comes to defence (the second of my Stately criteria), the Chinese People's Republic must be given high marks. Even more than in the Soviet Union, the entire population is, in effect, militarised. Military service is universal. Those lucky enough to be assigned to the land forces of the People's Liberation Army will serve between two and four years. If they are allotted to the navy or volunteer for life at sea, they will have to serve five years; the air force will claim them for four years. If any outside power were foolish enough to emulate Japan's example of the 1930s and invade China, it would have insuperable problems for it would be up against the whole population, which can be mobilised at next to no notice. It is, after all virtually mobilised at all times, whether for military or for civil tasks. As in other Communist countries, political indoctrination goes hand in hand with the teaching of the military arts. As for the standing army of $3\frac{1}{4}$ million, it was able to demonstrate its prowess by fighting the Americans and their United Nations allies to a standstill in the Korean War of the early 1950s. A fanaticised army is a formidable force.

By now, the Chinese Communists have stockpiled several hundred nuclear weapons, and have successfully tested a multi-stage Inter-continental Ballistic Missile with a range exceeding 3,000 miles. A larger one, with more than double the thrust, is on its way.

At the time of writing, the only serious enemy in sight was the Soviet Union. Any risk of military entanglement with the United States had vanished with the American withdrawal from Vietnam. The Japanese—enemies of yesterday—had become relatively benevolent neighbours and a peace treaty had been signed. There remained the Nationalist regime on Taiwan, with its ritual and reiterated calls for the recovery of the mainland. I have never believed that this 'war aim' should be simply dismissed as merely symbolic. But the Nationalists have always lacked the amphibious means to launch a successful invasion: their chance would come—if it ever did—only if some other power invaded China and if the People's Republic had begun to disintegrate as a result.

Will there be a war between Russia and China? This prediction was fashionable in the late 1960s, on grounds that seemed to me then to be entirely mistaken. There was no point, at that time, in the minds of the Russians in seeking war with China, since there was always a chance that once Mao Tse-tung was dead his successors would seek an accommodation with Moscow. This has signally not happened, however, and a Soviet attack cannot now be ruled out. If it came, it would almost certainly take the form of a surprise attack to destroy all China's strategic capability at one blow: nuclear missiles and launching-pads, military airfields and bombers. Conceivably, this would be preceded by a carefully stage-managed border incident, with the Russians accusing the Chinese of being the aggressors.

This kind of scenario was examined in detail in an interesting but unpublished article by John Carbaugh, a young member of the staff of Senator Jesse Helms. I found it singularly convincing. Should the Soviets decide on a strike of this kind, the likely outcome would be a desperate anarchy in China, possibly leading to civil war. In a situation of this kind, the Nationalists could get their long-deferred chance.

The possibility of strife and division can never be ruled out in China, for all the regimentation of this ultra-totalist regime. Should any future Mao attempt to revive his practice of 'permanent revolution', the great country could again be plunged into chaos. This was what happened during the Cultural Revolution, when a situation curiously reminiscent of the warlord feudalism of the 1920s developed, with the various regional military commanders asserting their local power independently of Peking. The most totalist power on earth could turn out to be less united than the bland appearance suggests.

What conclusions should be drawn from this admittedly rapid look at some characteristic features of the two major totalist regimes of our time? One word of praise is in order. As Professor Hugh Seton-Watson has pointed out from time to time, a ruling Communist Party, no matter how evil the consequences of its rule, is in essence and by its own lights a gigantic 'do-gooding' organisation. It is part of its intentions to provide 'good government' in the sense in which this term is used in this book. The intentions are not necessarily fulfilled, but the failure is kept out of sight by total control over the means of information. Communist governments do not solve problems so much as conceal their continued existence.

Even if they are given every possible benefit of the doubt, however, the 'good government' they provide is overshadowed by the grossly excessive invasion of all areas of life by government. The price is exorbitant beyond toleration. There is nothing in the practice of Marxism–Leninism in power to attract people of goodwill and intelligence. Only the deluded, the ill-informed, or the timid or the ambitious time-servers can hope to find anything of value in it. The Maximum State is an evil monstrosity.

The Cambodian Horror

Although closer to the theoretical perfection of totalism than the rest, the Chinese Maximum State is not the most evil of its kind. If the highly circumstantial accounts of refugees and of some diplomats are to be believed, this appalling distinction belongs to the first Communist regime in Cambodia. The accounts are of such concentrated horror that they are indeed hard to believe in the sense that there is a natural disinclination to accept that such things could be true. Since the accounts tally, however, and have been carefully checked and cross-checked by competent observers, they must be accepted as substantially true.

The tiny group of Marxist–Leninists who seized power in this former French protectorate in the wake of the American collapse in 1975 were animated by a blood-lust unusual even in Communists. In comparison, the Chinese and even the Vietnamese, were mild and gentle. First, the entire population of Phnom Penh, the capital, was driven into the countryside. This alone was an act of supreme atrocity. There were about 3 million people living there at the time. Hospital beds were wheeled into the streets and gravely ill patients emptied on to the pavement. Everybody, regardless of age or sex, was force-marched into the countryside. Those too old and feeble to walk that far were finished off by the Communist military, known as the Red Khmers. The same process took place in other towns.

The aim of the mysterious group at the top, known simply as 'Angkar' was apparently to obliterate all traces not only of the colonial past and of the brief American presence, but even of the country's ancient traditions. Books and archives were burnt. Museums, Buddhist temples and shops were demolished. Even money was abolished.

Anybody connected in any way with the previous government was killed: all members of the government itself; all officials; and all army officers. The entire population was harnessed to the forced cultivation of rice and made to work all day. The slightest recalcitrance was punished by instant death.

How many died in this great slaughter? It is impossible to say with certainty. In a population of about 7 million, probably 1·2 million were simply liquidated. But the estimates naturally vary, from a 'low' figure of 800,000 to a high of about 3 million. On a population basis, it seems likely that the Cambodian massacres exceed those of Hitler or Stalin, and leave Mao Tse-tung's well behind.

When the horrors of totalism reach such ghoulish extremes, the concepts of safety, security and defence cease to have any meaning. And since the Angkar also abolished money, the normal minimum criteria of the State are entirely inapplicable.*

* It is too early to say whether the new communist government imposed on the Cambodian people by neighbouring Vietnam in January 1979 is more than a marginal improvement on the ousted regime.

PART III

THE CURES

ONE

LORD HAILSHAM'S RECIPE, AND OTHERS

Lord Hailsham has several claims to greatness: as an advocate, as an Englishman, as a parliamentarian, and not least as a character. His book, *The Dilemma of Democracy* (Collins, 1978) is both important and profound, and I propose to devote suitable space to it.

It is mildly gratifying to me as an observer of politics that so eminent a practitioner of the art as Lord Hailsham should come up with a diagnosis that is in nearly all respects the same as my own. (There is an important difference, however, which I shall explain later.) When I first noticed that the system was breaking down, and drew attention to the fact as long ago as 1961, nobody wanted to listen, and indeed sage doubts were expressed about my sanity. When Lord Hailsham first startled the world with his diagnosis, in his much-discussed Dimbleby Lecture in 1977, the situation had of course become much graver than it was sixteen or seventeen years earlier. But the seeds of decay were already clearly visible to anybody who took the trouble to look and whose thinking processes were not shackled by inherited inertia and complacency.

Early in his book (p. 15), Lord Hailsham uses a striking image, which perhaps owes less to the Bible than to John Bunyan: the City of Destruction. 'We are living in the City of Destruction,' he writes, 'a dying country in a dying civilisation, and across the plain there is no wicket gate offering a way of escape. We have to stay here and fight it out.' The image recurs throughout the book.

The heart of Lord Hailsham's argument is that the British system, which has worked so well for years, was based on a broad consensus between the two main alternating political parties, but has now broken down and turned into what he calls 'an elective dictatorship'. Conscious of the fact that he will be accused of bias as a Conservative politician, he goes out of his way to be fair to the Labour Party, but feels bound to conclude (as indeed so do I, as a non-party man) that the trouble lies within the Labour Party, which has allowed itself to be infiltrated and largely taken over by the Marxist element.

He points out that the danger was always inherent in the Constitution of the Party, with its notorious Clause 4 calling for the common ownership of the means of production, distribution and exchange. He recalls the late Hugh Gaitskell's abortive attempt to get the offending clause repealed (as a very similar commitment was abandoned by the German Social Democratic Party in the 1960s), and points out that as long as Clause 4 remains, each succeeding Labour government, whether its leading ministers believe in it or not, will feel bound to extend the area of State ownership, while the growing Marxist minority in the trade unions and the constituencies will feel self-righteously intransigent in pushing for socialist legislation.

Given this situation, a 'ratchet' effect ensues: every time it is in power, the Labour Party pushes the country further towards socialism, and the Conservative Party in office is unable to reverse the process, so that there is 'a movement of national policy which is both linear, irreversible, and probably entirely against the determined wishes of the large majority of the electorate [p. 59].'

He is scathing about the 'social contract'—the device which Wilson inflicted on the country as a sop to trade-union power and ostensibly as a device to bring inflation under control. He is certain that one-sided contracts of this kind must not be repeated, lest permanent harm to a democratic constitution result. But he regards it as the ultimate condemnation of the abuse of union power that the actions and attitudes of the unions betray their own membership. 'Wages, which started lower on the Continent are now higher than in Britain whether measured in absolute terms or in relation to prices. In Germany they are something like double [p. 63].' Nor was this due to lack of investment or the quality of management, for the managers were personally penalised by taxation, profits were condemned, prices were controlled and no funds were available for capital expansion, with a resulting absence of confidence.

Lord Hailsham is acutely conscious of the danger of a take-over, through the manipulation of trade-union elections, the fostering of industrial disputes and the initiation of extremist measures decided by an organised minority outside Parliament. The author is at his most eloquent in chapters on 'elitism and democracy', 'in praise of law' and 'in praise of freedom'. He rejects the sophistry which argues that political freedom is useless without economic freedom [p. 93] or that freedom to join the dole queue is no use to the working class. As he says, affluence is no substitute for freedom, and the technological and other changes which have so revolutionised society in the recent past have been due entirely to the freedom of enquiry. In contrast, the collectivist societies of Russia and Eastern Europe have nothing to offer. 'In the West, we have to restrict immigration. But there it requires walls, machine-guns, State trials and a Gulag

Archipelago to keep in place the inmates of the Worker's Paradise, where the proletariat is alleged to exercise a dictatorship, but where in fact government of the people is exercised by the party on behalf of the system [p. 97].'

Lord Hailsham notes, as I do, the sad fact that we are both over-governed and badly governed, and he laments the proliferation of unnecessary laws.

I now come to the main area (for there are minor areas as well) at which I part company with Lord Hailsham. It never seems to cross his distinguished mind that what is wrong with the democratic system is the institution of the political party itself. He seeks the source of the trouble everywhere except where the root really lies. The title of his Chapter VII, 'The Failure of Party Politics', speaks for itself. He sees that the party system has 'temporarily at least' broken down, and he is not wrong in putting the blame squarely on the Labour Party. 'To do it justice, the Labour Party has never been, and has never pretended to be, the same sort of institution as the old Liberal and the present Conservative Parties ... the Labour Party has remained another sort of entity altogether, committed to an ideology, culturally assimilating the Trade Union Movement, and committed to the class struggle.' He simply takes the necessity for political parties for granted in a representative democracy, as in the following sentence: 'To give coherence to the choice of the people and to give consistency to the policy of the government, parties are required and dominate the scene both inside Parliament and at election time [p. 58].'

As all other writers do, he has trouble philosophically over voting systems, pluralism and expediency. He favours two main parties in alternation (because until recently, this has seemed to work out in practice) but is aware of the infinite range of individual opinions. For all his erudition, eloquence and lucidity, his range of examples is relatively narrow and confined almost entirely to the United Kingdom. His natural concern is to find out what has gone wrong with the political system in his own country, and he seems insufficiently aware that the party system is not working well elsewhere, and that it has broken down in a number of countries.

In his search for the deeper causes of breakdown, Lord Hailsham fastens on the peculiarly British phenomenon of the unlimited sovereignty of Parliament. Historically, in the days before universal suffrage, the role of Parliament was as defender of the rights and freedoms of ordinary people against the excessive powers of the Crown and the nobles, and later of the industrialists in the period of the Industrial Revolution. With the advent of universal suffrage and the decline of the independent power of the monarchy, Parliament has become a law unto itself, untrammelled by the restrictions that might have been written into a formal constitution. 'In theory Parliament is supreme. There is nothing legally it cannot do, and practically nothing which, at one time or another, it has not done. It has prolonged its own life. It has taken away the lives or liberties of its fellow citizens without the semblance of a fair trial. It has confiscated property. It has ratified revolutions [p. 125].' It follows that the party which controls Parliament (however the control is achieved) can do anything it likes. If the party itself has been taken over by an anti-parliamentarian and anti-democratic minority (as has happened to the Labour Party), then Parliament could abolish itself and the democratic system along with it. Therein lies the danger.

What of the Crown? In Lord Hailsham's view, the Crown is about the only part of Britain's unwritten constitution that is working as it was intended to work. As the symbol of national unity, the Queen is required of course to be above party politics. Her residual powers are few. The leader of whatever party commands the majority in the House of Commons will be summoned to her presence and invited to form a government. But in a hung House, where no party has a clear majority, it is up to the Queen to decide whom to invite. That is one of her remaining privileges. Another is the power, at least in theory, to refuse a dissolution. If, for example, a Prime Minister seeks a dissolution within a few days of a general election, on the ground that he does not command a sufficient majority to govern, the Queen would be within her rights in refusing one if she judged the request to be frivolous. The monarch's dilemma on such occasions will always be just how far she can assert her remaining prerogatives without jeopardising the throne itself.

Lord Hailsham writes: 'I am, of course, a dedicated party politician. This means it is extremely dangerous to the monarchy to receive too many bouquets at my hands and, for this reason alone, I shall try to avoid bestowing them [p. 142].' His party allegiance inhibits him from raising the only really interesting dilemma. Supposing the leadership of a party fell into the hands of an anti-monarchist and anti-democratic extremist, would the Queen have the nerve (as well as the undoubted right) to refuse to summon the politician concerned?

The question is far from academic. While it is just possible that a secret member of the National Front should worm his way into the Conservative Party and become its leader, the contingency is only very remotely possible. What is far more likely is that a Marxist, or a Marxist supporter, should become leader of the Labour Party. The situation very nearly arose after Harold Wilson's precipitate decision to resign as Prime Minister in March 1976. In the ensuing leadership contest, James Callaghan came out on top, but the runner-up, Michael Foot, attracted a dangerously large minority of votes. The figures in the third and final ballot were: Callaghan, 176; Foot, 137. Although not in the formal sense a Marxist, Mr Foot is on record with his public tolerance of Marxists within the Labour Party. Had he won the leadership, would the Queen have declined to call upon him?* I should like to think that she would, but doubt it: for if she had, she would have precipitated a grave constitutional crisis in which the monarchy itself might have been swept away. But let us carry this speculation still further: supposing in a further period in the wilderness, the Labour Party moved inexorably towards the Marxist Left, and that some Left-wing figure, possibly Tony Benn, became the Leader of Her Majesty's 'Loyal' Opposition. Supposing a further general election brought the new, by now thoroughly Marxist, Labour Party back to power, would the Queen commit constitutional suicide by sending for Mr Benn (bearing in mind that although Tony Benn, like Michael Foot, is not formally a Marxist, he too has defended the presence of Marxists in the Labour Party)? One could also add: by that time would it matter any more?

Lord Hailsham does not put his faith, as do many others, in a Bill of Rights, on the sensible ground that in a Parliament with unlimited sovereignty it would be open to a hostile incoming party to repeal any such Bill passed by its predecessors. He is against tampering with the Crown, on the ground that it is the only element of our unwritten constitution that actually works. His prescription is for a written constitution institutionalising limited government, as distinct from the 'elective dictatorship', and for an elected second chamber. He points out that if the Labour Party is determined, as it apparently is, to abolish the House of Lords, it will do so sooner

* In my hypothetical constitutional crisis over the Queen's refusal to invite Mr Michael Foot to form a Government, the Crown would not necessarily have been the loser. A party leader, thus rebuffed by the sovereign, would of course call a vote of confidence in the House. But even if he had achieved the leadership, Mr Foot would not necessarily have commanded the confidence of his fellow-MPs. For it must be assumed that those who voted against him felt more strongly about keeping him out than those who voted in his favour felt about Mr Callaghan. In a vote of confidence, he might not have attracted substantially more votes than those who declared themselves in his favour during the leadership contest. If the House had demonstrated its lack of confidence in him as Prime Minister, it would have been open to the Queen to recommend a dissolution.

or later. He recognises, as everybody does, that the existing unelected Upper House is an anachronism, despite successive attempts at reform.

What he fears above all is that a still more extreme Labour Party in office might abolish the Lords without putting anything in its place, thus further strengthening the elective dictatorship, since there would now be no restraints whatever on the already unlimited sovereignty of the Lower House. Despite our logically absurd 'first-past-the-post' voting system, which he defends rather unconvincingly, he is against any reform of the voting system, at least for the existing House of Commons. But he sees no reason why his elected second chamber should not be created by proportional representation. At all events, an elected Upper House would be able, as an unelected one is not, to restrain the excesses of the Lower one. He thinks his Conservative Party would be foolish not to give the matter of the second house its immediate attention upon re-election. He would give top priority to constitutional drafting, with a moratorium on unnecessary legislation. A new constitution should be drafted, clause by clause, and each clause embodied in a bill to be submitted to the country by referendum, so that no future Parliament could tamper with the constitution without first going to the people on each and every individual clause.

Such is Lord Hailsham's prescription. Would it work? For the main purpose he has in mind—to prevent the untrammelled growth of elective dictatorship and above all to guard against the constitutional path towards revolutionary change, my short answer is Yes. In the hands of a determined Prime Minister with a united party behind him or her, it would even allow some measure of reversal in the apparently inexorable process that has been taking the country along the road to socialist dictatorship.

It might even reduce over-government. But in my view, it would do nothing to guarantee good or sensible government. The parties would still be competing for the attention and support of the electorate, with promises they would attempt to fulfil upon reaching office, thus inviting retaliatory promises from their party rivals at the next general election. The essential frivolity of the political game would go on as before. If a thoroughly Marxist Labour Party found itself in the wilderness for many years (a possibility not to be excluded), the country would face a prolonged period of single-party rule, with all the temptations this would imply. If, on the contrary, it found itself re-elected, the country might be treated to a prolonged spectacle of governmental frustration, with its bills being systematically rejected by the new Upper House. Worse still, the Upper House could find itself in agreement with the Lower and 'irreversible' change could still ensue.

Having said this, Lord Hailsham's proposals are imaginative and deserve the serious consideration I hope they will have received by the time this book is published. They harmonise with the history of the British Isles and with the English tradition. My criticism of them is that they are insufficiently radical in the light of what is happening to the world, not simply in the United Kingdom.

The Sendall Formula

An interesting set of proposals for the reform of the parliamentary system was made by Wilfrid Sendall in that fascinating, variable format magazine, *Art International/New Lugano Review* in January 1978. Of the author, it could be truly said (as indeed of Lord Hailsham but for different reasons) that he knew what he was talking about: as a veteran lobby and political correspondent for the old *News Chronicle* and the *Daily Telegraph*, he had observed the life of Parliament for three decades, watching politicians, including Prime Ministers, come and go. I find myself in agreement with him on a number of points, especially of diagnosis, but I do not entirely share his view of what needs to be done to put things right.

'Freedom resides,' he writes, 'not in the right of the people to choose their own government, but in the power of the people to get rid of their government without resort to violence. Lose that power and all is lost.' Parliament, in Mr Sendall's view, is in danger of losing the confidence of the people.

Rightly, he devotes much space to an analysis of what he (and I) considers the pernicious doctrine of the mandate, which as he reminds us has two meanings. One is 'the conception that, unless some act of policy has been advertised to the electorate in advance of a general election, the government of the day has no authority to execute it, however urgently the situation might require it.' Then: 'Conversely, the doctrine is interpreted to mean that, if some far-reaching proposal is as much as mentioned in an election manifesto, even though the general election was principally contested on other issues, the government has been, not merely authorised, but instructed to carry it out.' As he points out, either interpretation of the doctrine would, if carried to its logical conclusion, deprive Parliament of its sovereign right to exercise judgement.

Mr Sendall is no less severe than I in castigating the shortcomings of the party system, although he summarily dismisses any notion that we could do without it:

Parliamentary government and the party system go together like a horse and carriage. As Disraeli observed, you can't have one without the other. This self-evident truth has not prevented sentimental sighs for some lost golden age when none was for a party and all were for the State. Do away with the parties and parliamentary democracy would be perfect. When faced with difficulties, have a coalition, a national government of the 'best' men. This sort of twaddle has become a substitute for serious thought about the matter.

Self-evident? In effect, this is what Hailsham is saying, too. But it is self-evident only to the extent that parties grew naturally out of absurd theories about democracy and universal suffrage: democracy being (as I have tried to demonstrate) impossible, and universal suffrage ridiculous perhaps even more than absurd, parties are necessary 'as a response to the problem of gaining and retaining the consent of mass electorates to whom ultimate sovereignty has been devolved' (Sendall's words). But this is a circular argument, amounting to no more than saying that parties are necessary because you can't do without them; or alternatively that you can't do without them because they are necessary.

There is really no question (at least in my mind) of returning to some golden age, because there never was one. The real point is to find a way of preserving what is good in democracy, and discarding what is bad. If, as I think can be shown, all that is bad can be traced back to the political parties, then the case for retaining them seems to me, *a priori*, to be rather weak.

Sendall notes (as I have done) the deplorable consequences of the party system:

—Parties, having chosen successful candidates, expect them, once they are in Parliament, to uphold party interests, thereby depriving MPs of their freedom of judgement.

—In general, MPs are not elected but selected by the party machines.

—The re-election of a party (in Britain) is normally secured by timing an economic boom to coincide with an election. Hence both the major parties have fostered permanent inflation, and non-productive employment. Thus the Conservative Party committed itself in 1950 to building 300,000 houses, which, when they duly won the election, they proceeded to provide—thus inflicting permanent damage on the economy. In 1964, Labour got in 'loaded with inflationary promises of improvements in the social services'.

In his interesting article, Sendall quotes the unexpected contribution of the Moderator of the General Assembly of the Church of Scotland, the Rt Rev Professor Thomas Torrance, who proposed measures of constitutional reform when preaching in Westminster Abbey at a service of thanksgiving on the bicentenary of the American Declaration of Independence. One of the Moderator's proposals was for fixed-term Parliaments, to strengthen the independence of MPs. As Sendall points out, this would deprive Prime Ministers of the power to dissolve Parliament 'which, over the years, they have filched from the Sovereign'. It would also make MPs more independent in that they would be less at the mercy of a Prime Minister's whim than they now are. On the other hand, it would do nothing to undermine the mandate doctrine, nor necessarily do away with attempts to rig the economy.

What, then, is Wilfrid Sendall's prescription? It is simple, yet ingenious, and deserves more publicity than it has had and very serious consideration.

If sovereignty in the British system is held to reside in the Crown in Parliament, it is surely anomalous that Parliament should ever be dissolved. Nobody, after all, 'dissolves' the monarch, and a dead sovereign is deemed at the time of his passing to have been replaced by his or her successor. The permanent Parliament Sendall proposes would, however, remain an elected body. But instead of holding elections every five years or at the Prime Minister's pleasure, one-fifth of the Parliamentary seats would be up for election every year. He believes it to be desirable that a determined effort should be made to draft constituency boundaries that approximate as closely as possible to natural communities. With this reservation, the annual vote would break the vicious circle of electioneering economics, since it would be impossible to contrive an annual election boom. Moreover, the mandate system would immediately become obsolete, since no party could claim a mandate on the basis of one-fifth of the seats contested every year. Each MP would have a five-year security of tenure, but the government would not have a guaranteed majority for five years; and might therefore be forced to govern more sensibly and with less attention to demagogic appeal. Gone would be the electoral heroics of gladiatorial contests between the leaders of the rival parties. Gone too, at least probably, would be the elective dictatorship of which Lord Hailsham complains.

Those are the good points, and I accept Sendall's analysis and the claims he makes on behalf of his very sensible proposals. If reform is required and not the drastic overhaul that would become urgently imperative in the event of total breakdown, then I think the 'Sendall formula' is the best that can be devised. But he probably underrates the price to be paid in time for decades of accumulated follies under the present system. Granted the excessive power of the Prime Minister (an unfortunate reality), would a reigning Premier consent to proposals that would reduce his or her power? Will there be time for reform?

Admitting, however, that circumstances were favourable and that the Sendall system or something like it actually happened, it would reduce some of the evils of the party system as it stands, but it would not go to the heart of the matter, which as I see it is the search for a system that would, of itself, be conducive to good (that is, intelligent and minimal) government. Even the Sendall system would continue to be a 'selectorate' of the unqualified by the unqualified. Nor would he discard the simple majority system ('first-past-the-post') so that more than half the electorate would continue to be, in effect, disfranchised. The quality of our legislators would probably continue to decline, and the guarantee of a five-year security of tenure would act as a disincentive to meritorious performance. Moreover, almost certainly, local as distinct from national issues would tend to loom larger in the central Parliament than they deserve. What, after all, is the purpose of local government?

My verdict, then, is that the Sendall reforms would be a great improvement on the present system and in some respects on Hailsham's more widely publicised suggestions. But neither goes to the heart of the problem.

The House of Lords

The same is true, perhaps self-evidently, of the various proposals for the reform of the House of Lords. The British Upper House is of course an anachronism in democratic terms: it is logically unacceptable that a hereditary chamber should exercise any kind of control over a democratically elected lower one. Logic, however, has never played the dominant role in British institutional concepts (in contrast with, say, those of France). There is a pleasing continuity about the historical origins of the House of Lords, and most unbiased observers would agree that the quality of the debates in the legislative abode of the Peers of the Realm is in general notably superior to that of the more powerful plebs who wield the final power.

The introduction of life peerages after the Second World War was intended in part to 'democratise' the House of Lords, but of course it did nothing of the kind since the life peers were not elected but nominated by the party in power. Some of those selected for elevation merited the honour on grounds of gifts or competence; others were being rewarded for faithful service or for services rendered. The device enabled the Labour Party, in particular, to reduce by patronage the natural preponderance of Conservative Peers.

By the 1970s, the proposition that something had to be done about the Lords was almost universally accepted. The question was: What? The increasingly militant and extremist Labour Party favoured abolition, and its National Executive Committee in October 1977 called for 'the total reform of Parliament into an efficient single-chamber legislating body without delay'. This highly dangerous proposal, if implemented, would leave the British people unprotected against any future government with totalist intentions.

A second chamber with revisionary powers is an essential element in any constitution devoted to the cause of freedom. In Britain's case, the question is whether the existing House of Lords should be replaced by a wholly elected Upper House or Senate, or reformed in a way that would preserve some dosage of historical continuity. I mentioned Lord Hailsham's proposals earlier. In March 1978, the findings of a Conservative Review Committee chaired by Lord Home of the Hirsel proposed a mixed chamber of elected members (by proportional representation, no less) and nominated ones. My own view is that Lord Home's proposals are the best that have been made so far.

Reform of the Upper House alone, however, is not going to be enough to meet the requirements of the Minimum State. More radical measures are needed.

Further Reforms

The guiding principle of reform ought to be:

1. The need to strengthen the authority of government throughout its term of office. (As I argue elsewhere in this book in greater detail, strong government is an absolute necessity for the preservation of freedom; and governmental stability is a prerequisite of economic progress. A government should not be at the mercy of fortuitous majorities on minor issues.)

2. To prevent the imposition of the views of an extremist minority upon Parliament and therefore upon the country as a whole.

3. To encourage a return to the three principles of good government and discourage frivolous or unnecessary legislation.

One measure that would powerfully contribute to these ends would simply be the abolition of the Whip system, allowing voting to be free on all issues. Bills would thus be considered on their merits by elected representatives of the people, by the criteria of intelligence and conscience and not those of party discipline and advantage.

It might be objected that this would put the Government's survival at risk almost daily. But this would be true if the absurd convention that requires a government to achieve a majority for every measure it introduces were left untouched. (In fact, this convention is quite often ignored when a government's majority is very tenuous.) The answer is to introduce categories of legislation in order of importance. All measures concerning the three principles of good government (safety and security; external defence; and money) should automatically get top rating and require a two-thirds majority of all MPs (not just those who happened to be present in the House).

The definition of measures coming within these categories would need to be wide: for instance, sweeping proposals for nationalisation have an obvious bearing on the soundness of money; as indeed do all measures requiring excessive government expenditure, deficit financing and foreign borrowing. (If the constitutional proposals outlined elsewhere in this book were given the force of fundamental law, nationalisation proposals in respect of productive industry would in any case be unconstitutional, either on the ground that they would create monopolies, or because they would necessarily infringe any statutory limitation on the percentage of the economy allotted to the public sector.)

On losing the vote on a major measure, a government would not necessarily have to step down. It would have two options: to withdraw the proposal and substitute another, more acceptable one; or to put the proposal to the country in a referendum.

There is no reason why such measures could not be combined with aspects of the Hailsham or Sendall proposals. In a suitable combination, they could go a long way towards remedying the worst features of the party system. In the next chapter (The No-Party State), I examine the feasibility and desirability of adapting the idea of a profession of politics to the party system.

TWO

THE NO-PARTY STATE

I am deeply conscious that the system I propose could be used either for good or for evil. The fact that this is true of other systems is not necessarily a consolation. Men are more important than institutions, whose original purposes they may pervert. My system is morally neutral: it could provide a permanent framework for a free society; or be used to establish a permanent tyranny, although probably not of the worst kind. That is why it is so important that it should be inseparably linked to a constitution incorporating guarantees of liberty, as suggested in the preceding chapter.

A Profession of Politics

The gravest weakness of party democracy lies in the natural incompetence of the legislators. As we have seen, however much voting-procedures may differ from country to country, this is a feature common to all. Age is normally the only qualification for election. It is not required of a legislator that he or she should show any evidence of intelligence, ability or knowledge. True, the political parties have their own selection boards, but these are composed of people similarly unqualified.

The selection process—inevitably, if it is admitted that political parties should have the right to present candidates—is by its nature fraudulent in that it frustrates the purposes of democratic theory. The voters have no say in the selection of candidates (except, in a minor way, in the American presidential primaries): they vote for pre-selected candidates. If a selection committee has fallen into totalist hands, the pre-selected candidate will be a collectivist, and the voters may have no means of knowing that they are voting for someone who intends to deprive them of their freedom.

That is the system at its most sinister. But even when the candidate is a man or woman of goodwill, there is no guarantee that he or she is in the least qualified to legislate over fellow-citizens. There was a time, perhaps even in living memory, when this anomaly mattered little, when life was simpler than it now is, when communications were more primitive, when populations had not yet exploded, before technology had entered its era of exponential change. England, in particular, fostered the notion of the gentleman-politician who entered politics not as a career but as a disinterested form of public service. That great and imaginative traditionalist, Lord Hailsham, whose views I have extensively discussed, finds it hard to discuss this attractive notion. He is, in fact, mildly schizophrenic on the subject and we find him (*The Dilemma of Democracy*, p. 160) lamenting the fact that we are 'governed by a bureaucracy of mandarins and their subordinates imposing on a people partisan policies devised by a government of amateurs who have achieved their position by a minority of votes under an unfair voting system'. But he also has this to say (p. 138):

> In my view, the professional politician should be the exception rather than the rule among MPs, if only because a professional politician cannot be representative of a constituency, which however constituted, is not composed of professional politicians. There are other reasons equally compelling. A professional politician is thrown on the street if he is turned out. . . . He ceases to be the responsible representative of a free constituency, and, if he is not careful, he soon develops into a disreputable party hack. There are too many such hacks in the present-day House of Commons.

Logically, I have no quarrel with Lord Hailsham's reasoning, but one has to point out that he is talking about professional politicians *in a party system*. I see his objections as yet another condemnation of the party system. For what he is saying is that the professional politician is out of place in such a system. Even then, of course, there are professional politicians, but they tend, as Lord Hailsham says, to become 'disreputable party hacks'. None of these advantages would apply if a profession of politics were created, only members of which would have the legal right to compete for power and office.

The case for a profession of politics is, in my view, overwhelming. If I need a heart-valve operation, I go to a heart specialist, not to the local butcher. If I seek legal advice, I go to someone with the appropriate degree and background. If my teeth are giving trouble I go to a dentist, not to a veterinary surgeon. Is it not astonishing that in a matter of such universal concern as the laws of the land, we entrust our destinies to the unqualified? Not of course that MPs and deputies are necessarily incompetents or unqualified or foolish. Clearly, even a system as haphazard as party democracy will throw up some first-class minds. I would go further and say that the intellectual level of MPs is undoubtedly higher than the average level for the population as a whole. But this is not much to concede: all our legislators without exception ought to be men or women of outstanding intelligence, ability and character.

Although it is rare for a man like John Stonehouse to achieve high office in a Western parliament, the system is in theory remarkably open to men and women of indifferent character. Indeed, since there is no general standard applicable to selection procedures, the danger is obvious. In Argentina, the return of the ex-dictator Perón in 1973 after a long exile, his death and succession by the former nightclub-dancer Isabel, who happened to be his wife, was perhaps an ultimate illustration of the vulnerability of the party system to manipulation by unscrupulous demagogues.

Imagine, then, the *existence* of a profession of politics (I shall deal later with the extremely difficult circumstances which might make one possible, and with the complex problems of creation). How could it be used in the absence of political parties to preserve the two (and only two) essential points in the democratic system—a choice between candidates, and the chance of changing the government peacefully at general elections?

The answers are surprisingly simple. The profession of politics—let us call it, provisionally, the College of Politicians—nominates two candidates for each constituency or electoral division. The voters make their choice—a choice not between equally unsatisfactory party programmes but between men and women on their personal appeal and merit. As in conventional elections, one candidate will receive the majority over the other. However, both candidates enter Parliament or Congress, so that the voters who picked the loser are not disfranchised (as under the British system) but will be represented by a deputy of their own choice. The winners form the governing group for the duration of the Parliament; the losers form the Opposition. At the next elections, there will be a general reshuffle—no candidate may oppose the same candidate as last time, and no candidate may stand for the same constituency as before. Inevitably, then, by the mathematics of chance, there will be a change of government. Some of the winners would doubtless win again but others would lose and losers would become winners. Out of the new pattern, a new administration would arise.

Entry into the profession of politics should be regarded as an honour, an aspiration, a legitimate ambition, the achievement of which would carry lifelong obligations and duties. Entry should be accordingly difficult—the reward of natural ability, or exceptional knowledge, of a well-deserved reputation, of specialised expertise, of the highest ethical standards. Successful entrants would be embarking on (or entering later in life) a career for life, as in the civil service, with absolute security of tenure, subject to the maintenance of the highest standards of behaviour and competence. It would be necessary for the State to provide successful entrants with very high salaries and emoluments, including a house and personal transport for life. Corruption and temptation should be made irrelevant for lack of interest—and to yield on this score would be a cause for instant dismissal.

The selection procedures should be flexible, but one well established principle should always prevail: co-option. Like should pick like—the best guarantee of continuity, assuming the initial kernel to be of the right quality. A School of Political Service should be created, with the object of training potential entrants to the College of Politicians. Entrants into the College should be determined partly by a written examination and partly by an interview. The object of the exam, however, should be less the testing of formal knowledge than the determination of an aptitude for its practical application. The core of it, therefore, would be a creative essay on current problems. Candidates themselves should propose the subject, although the right of acceptance would rest with the original members of the profession. A candidate might, for instance, choose and be invited to write upon the comparative merits of a privately- or publicly-owned telephone service, or on the improvement of a country's defence system, or on possible ways of settling a border dispute, or an ethnic or racial problem.

In isolation, but armed with whatever works of reference or factual matter were appropriate, preferably with an almost unlimited or at least a generous time-scale, the candidate would write his thesis. The interview, held at the outset for eliminatory purposes, would last a whole day and would be designed not only to test general awareness of problems, the ability to switch a mind rapidly from one subject to another, fluency of speech and suitability of personality and temperament; but also to determine the depth of the candidate's attachment to the principles of the Minimum State, opposition to all forms of collectivism, awareness of the Marxist problem and of Leninist techniques, general reliability and probity of character. It would have to be preceded by 'positive vetting' of the kind that determines the suitability of candidates for entry into one of the secret services.

Once accepted, candidates would be given an intensive course in law, history, politics and political philosophy, government, public administration; with optional extras, such as urban planning, rural development and afforestation, transport, trade unionism, industrial management, and so forth. Candidates lasting the course and showing evidence of having benefited from it, would be re-interviewed with a view to admission into the College of Politicians (or Public Servants, or National Service, according to the linguistic norms, or traditional criteria, of individual countries). One important point should be made clear: the College of Politicians must be wide open to the whole population, without distinction of race, religion, class or social origin. Admission would be on merit and character alone; exclusion on the obverse grounds.

The Constitution

The Minimum State will have to have its own *polity*, which must offer the voters a chance to reject their rulers at regular elections, with a free choice between candidates for election. The structure of the State will have to include a *written Constitution*, and a *Constitutional Court* to adjudicate between government and people in the event of a challenge on the constitutionality of a proposed measure. It follows that there must be separation of the *legislative* and *judicial* powers. It is also desirable in the interests of efficiency that the *executive* and *legislative* powers should be separated, so that the *executive* may exercise maximum authority and have the time to govern, undistracted by Parliamentary duties. It is essential that Members of Parliament or Assembly should be qualified for the job—the increasing complexity of technology and society have rendered the age of the amateur obsolete. As freedom cannot be exercised in a strictly controlled economy, it is essential to guarantee freedom of enterprise in a competitive market. It is desirable in principle for the legislation of the assembly to be subjected to revision (and perhaps vetoed) by an *Upper Chamber*, the composition of which should be regionally determined.

The Constitution should be drafted with the requirements of the Minimum State and the free society in mind. It would build in all the rights I have listed, with the possible exception of Nos 15 and 17 over which the legislature must be allowed a measure of discretion.*

---

* For the convenience of the reader, here is a bare summary of my proposed Charter of Rights (see I, 5: 'Democratic Fallacies'):
  1. Protection at home and abroad.
  2. Stable money.
  3. Property rights.
  4. Minimal personal tax.
  5. Legacy and inheritance.
  6. Marriage.
  7. Elementary education. [continued overleaf

An essential clause, however, would guarantee free enterprise by imposing a specific upper limit on State participation in the economy (meaning the wealth-creating process).

Ideally this limit should be zero, but let us recognise that the ideal may be difficult to reach. In the end one might compromise with, say, 25 per cent. This requirement may seem revolutionary, but it has the virtue of elementary logic. The Soviet Constitution and the constitutions of other Communist States specifically limit private property essentially to personal belongings, and allocate all economic resources to the State. This is the Marxist challenge: a State determined to resist it must be prepared to defend free enterprise and the market economy.

It is obviously just as important to guarantee free competition as to limit State participation in the economic processes. There should therefore be a specific interdiction of monopolies, including State monopolies (thus ruling out further nationalisation and rendering existing nationalised industries unconstitutional). Such clauses alone would provide the foundations for a free economy and therefore for a free society.

I have left an important point to the end of this constitutional survey. It is at the regional and local level that democracy is most important. The local democracy of the Swiss Confederation is not the least of the reasons for the success of the Swiss polity. Alain Peyrefitte and Charles de Gaulle were right to see a major cause of France's frustrations in the excessive centralisation of the French system; and the extraordinary growth of the arbitrary power of local councils in Britain, witnessed over the past few years, has been a major cause of alienation. The people of counties, boroughs and urban or rural districts should have the right to be consulted on the amount of money they are required to part with in rates, and the uses to which the money is put. The local referendum is a Swiss device that could profitably be imported into other countries. It should be built into the Constitution of the Minimum State.

------

8. Travel at home and abroad.
9. Choice of employer; right to leave.
10. Right of dismissal.
11. Right to strike for industrial purposes, but not vital occupations.
12. No intimidation.
13. Worship.
14. Inquiry and advocacy.
15. No arbitrary arrest.
16. Equality under the law; no retrospective laws.
17. Assembly; joining or not joining an organisation.
18. Welfare if poor and old or sick.

The System At Work

Under the party system, election time is the babel of the market place, with promises, threats, and pledges rending the air. What does the voter do? In a typical British constituency, he may have a rather personable young Liberal candidate with sensible ideas; but the voter knows that to support him would mean throwing away his vote and as he only has one vote he would rather not waste it. The voter may be a Social Democrat in the Gaitskell mode; unfortunately the Labour candidate chosen by an aggressive Marxist caucus is quite clearly a Trotskyist or Communist under thin disguise. Reluctantly, he thinks he had better vote Tory, not because he likes the Tories, but to keep the Trotskyist out. He goes to a meeting of the local Tory organisation to listen to the Conservative candidate. He is shocked, for this is a town with a few thousand West Indians and the Tory man sounds like a Powellite. The voter is no racialist and doesn't feel he can vote for this particular Tory candidate. What to do? Abstain? Or vote Liberal? Reluctantly, he votes Liberal after all. It is the only protest he has.

Throughout the campaign the leaders and lesser stars of the parties live in a blaze of publicity, whistle-stopping, several speeches a day, television appearances, fallible in the unguarded moment, promising perhaps more than is wise—as with Mr Heath's promise to slash prices 'at a stroke' and in the end to a greater or lesser degree a prisoner of his own party. They are always in the limelight, harassed by the absurd hours and insane discipline of the Whip system. These able men and women, as so often they are despite everything, lack above all *serenity*. They need peace and calm, but this is what they never, or rarely, get.

The members of the College of Politicians would have serenity. With a career before them and an assured living, the demagogue would be at a discount. There would be no party behind them to egg them on to undesirable courses. Each candidate would bring his or her mind to bear on local and national problems *on their merits* and not according to a party ideology. And so it would be once in office.

The legislators would have plenty to do but their work would differ from that of their present-day predecessors in some important respects. For one thing, especially in the early years of the new system, they would not be wasting their time and the taxpayer's money on useless or damaging legislation. Instead, much of their time would be spent in dismantling existing structures and repealing existing laws with the needs of the Minimum State in view. In

Britain, for a start, the Price Commission would have to go; the nationalised industries would be broken up and offered to private tender. Contrary to the popular wisdom, they would be scooped up, for with the constitutional guarantee of the free enterprise State written into the Constitution, the shadow of re-nationalisation would be lifted from the shoulders of *entrepreneurs*. Moreover, as part of the deal, there would have to be massive refunds of company taxes, and of individual super-tax, capital gains tax and other iniquitously acquired public finances. With this giant stimulus, investment would rush in to fill the vacuum and, freed at last, private enterprise would get to work to rebuild the wealth of nations.

The dismantling of the Welfare State (discussed in a separate chapter) would be a delicate and fascinating task. The neediest would have an absolute right to the best treatment. The rest would have a choice between State and private insurance schemes to meet their health requirements. Within a short time, self-exiled doctors would be coming home, eager to develop their skills and to offer their services in the land of their birth.

It would be the same, *mutatis mutandis*, with education. The State would meet its obligation to provide basic education and compete with private education at the secondary and higher level, with a system of vouchers to restore parental choice. Membership of student unions would be voluntary, and grants would not be available for the financing of political activity.

Security in the Minimum State

Since safety and security constitute the first principle of the Minimum State, it is worth looking at the kind of measures that would be required to protect its citizens and to defend the State itself against its internal enemies. The first requirement of civil peace is an efficient and sufficient police force. One of the gravest criticisms to be made against successive governments (but especially Labour governments) in Britain in recent years concerns their readiness to allow the police to decline in numbers and morale (and therefore efficiency). In this field, as in that of the armed services, the State is the only legitimate employer, and it is the responsibility of the State to offer rates of pay and conditions of service and of retirement that will attract the best entrants in sufficient numbers. The resources freed by the drastic reduction in the economic involvements of the State would be so huge that even with sweeping cuts in income tax, ample funds would be released to fulfil this first requirement of the State.

With the restoration of morale and proper incentives, it would become relatively easier to stamp out corruption (which has become a problem in Britain, though to nothing like the same degree as in America). A parallel requirement would be a judicial policy appropriate to the problems facing the police. The death penalty should be restored, where it has been abolished, for acts of terrorism and for certain categories of treason, including espionage involving vital secrets. It is normal to punish espionage with death in wartime, and with appropriate gaol sentences in peacetime; but the supposition that the world is at peace is a mistaken one. As I tried to demonstrate in some detail in my book *Strategy of Survival*, the Soviet Union has been waging a war of a new kind on all countries not already under Soviet control ever since the end of the Second World War. There is therefore no ground for peacetime leniency in the punishment of spies.

I shall return to this aspect later. As regards terrorists, I believe the case for the death penalty is overwhelmingly strong. It is outrageous, for instance, that people guilty of the kind of horrors which the *Brigate Rosse* in Italy or the *Rote Armee Fraktion* in Germany have inflicted on innocent people should become guests of the State for years. The real case for the death penalty, however, is that it is the only way to eliminate a whole category of supplementary acts of terrorism—involving the capture of hostages to be exchanged for incarcerated terrorists.

Terrorism is internal war: a violent war waged by a tiny group of fanatics against society as a whole. Psychologically, terrorists court death; but that is not sufficient reason to deprive them of their secret wish. A dead terrorist is a challenge removed. A dead terrorist cannot be the cause of a campaign to turn him loose. A dead terrorist is a cause for relief. A dead terrorist cannot be freed by the misguided 'compassion' or weakness of the authorities, to resume his acts of terror.

A successful anti-terrorist campaign requires police and sometimes military skills of a high order: marksmanship; unarmed combat; the patience to sit out a siege; expert knowledge of arms and explosives. These skills may transcend those at the disposal of the ordinary police. The requirement may be either an elite squad within the police, or the creation of an armed and paramilitary force—a halfway house between the police and army.

Another requirement is reliable information and intelligence. And this again means the kind of money which the Welfare State can ill spare, but which the Minimum State would have in abundance.

The real basis for an appropriate security policy, however, would be the written Constitution I advocate. An Oath to the Constitution would have to be taken by all whose job it was to serve or defend the State—for what is the sense of entrusting the institutions of the State to those who are disloyal to it? All members of the profession of politics would be required to take the oath; and so would all members of the armed forces and police, and all civil servants.

But this alone would not be enough, for the security of the State may be threatened (and is in fact threatened in all Western countries) in other quarters: in the schools and universities; in the media. In the Federal Republic of Germany, teachers in State schools and universities are required to declare their support for the Constitution (and as mentioned earlier, the West German security service is aptly named the *Bundesamt für Verfassungsschutz*, or Office for the Protection of the Constitution), and there seems no very good reason why the same principle should not be adopted by other Western countries.

The Media

And the media? Are journalists, including television journalists, not supposed to be free and independent of all State control? Is it not their normal role to criticise, and even if necessary to stand up to the State? These questions raise difficult issues. In my Charter of Rights, I included that of 'free inquiry and advocacy'. The choice of words was deliberate. Journalists (and others) should be free to inquire and to advocate. But the freedom to inquire does not necessarily imply the freedom of access to State secrets; nor should it. And the right to advocate does not mean the right to distort, smear and subvert.

Such rights should never be unlimited. I do not favour censorship, which invariably creates anomalies and is useful to the State only when it has a monopoly of the means of information and coercion: a Soviet-style State, for example. For a democratic State, it tends to be counter-productive. But freedom from censorship does not necessarily carry with it a freedom from all restraints, including voluntary ones. The capacity of the media (but above all, of television) to exaggerate, distort, obfuscate, and misrepresent is notorious. Television is not invited to record the violence of terrorists, but has a wide licence in democratic countries to present the police and security forces in a bad light.

In Britain and other countries there is virtually no editorial control on television and the producers, many of them militant Marxists, are a law unto themselves, systematically smearing democratic institutions and remarkably lenient to totalist dictatorships (which of course deny them the freedom to operate).

In the absence of any coherent security policy, the press (especially in America) and television (again especially in America, but in Britain and other countries as well) have exercised an unjustifiable and irresponsible power. Unelected, uncontrolled and self-appointed, their power for destruction has grown beyond tolerable bounds. The right to advocate does not, or should not, extend to the excessive and gratuitous presentation of revolutionary or subversive views. Nor is it a permit to manipulate images and comment for subliminal purposes.

It may be too much to require an Oath to the Constitution of personnel in the press, radio and television. But it is not too much to require greater efforts at objectivity, responsible editorial control, and the elimination of Marxist–Leninists and other extremists, whose influence on the content of programmes, in Britain and other countries, is grotesquely disproportionate.

The Trade Unions

In Britain, more than in any other country with the possible exception of Argentina, the trade unions not only exert an intolerably excessive influence on the conduct of public affairs, but serve as a highly effective vehicle for subversion of the State. In the UK, they *own* the Labour Party, in effect. For many years the British Communist Party, which in terms of membership is negligible (about 25,000 at the time of writing) and in terms of electoral appeal a nullity (no Members of Parliament elected for three decades or so), has set about, single-mindedly and successfully, penetrating the most important trade unions. Their object has not, of course, been purely industrial, but political. They reasoned that if they controlled or heavily influenced the main trade unions, they could correspondingly influence the Labour Party in the direction of Marxist–Leninist policies.

This reasoning made sense, and one need look no further for the Left-ward lurch of the Labour Party in recent years. Who pays the piper calls the Marxist tune. Give or take a percentage point or two, the trade unions contribute 90 per cent of the Labour Party's funds and carry 90 per cent of the votes at the annual party conference. If the unions want Marxist–Leninist prescriptions written into the party manifesto or programme, in they go. The result, especially after Edward Heath's disastrous confrontation with the coal-miners early in 1974, has been a series of laws drafted specifically for the trade-union pressure group.

I am not here concerned with the ruthless and arrogant exercise of trade-union power, or even worse of trade-union weakness, when groups of workers hold the public to ransom without the official sanction of their leadership. But this is undoubtedly an aggravating factor.

The problem that exercises us here is: how to check and prevent subversion and penetration of the trade unions. Ideally, this is a problem to be dealt with by trade unionists themselves. That they are capable of doing the necessary was decisively shown in the executive committee elections in the Engineering Union (AUEW), when the moderates ousted the Leftists. What can be done in one union can be done in others; and I dare say that, in time, the workers themselves will see where their best interests lie and wrest control of their own affairs from the ideological intruders.

When, and if, this happens, the moderate leaders of trade unions may see the need for the measures which the Minimum State will have to take to protect itself from the excessive and subversive use of union power. It will be seen that I have used two adjectives: excessive and subversive. In terms of union power, it is possible for it to be excessive but not subversive; or subversive but not excessive; or of course both excessive and subversive. The ultimate difficulty may reside in the attachment of human beings to power once they have achieved it. Trade unionists, whether or not they are subversives, may actually *enjoy* their unfettered right to strike and the stranglehold they have achieved over the labour market. They may find it harder, therefore, to see the need for some of the measures I propose, to the extent that these are aimed at curbing excessive and arbitrary, rather than subversive, union power.

These, then, are the measures necessary to defend the Minimum State against abusive union power:

1. This provision is inherent in Articles 9 and 17 of the Charter of Rights of the Minimum State, rephrased with specific reference to trade unions: All citizens shall have the right to belong, or not to belong, to a trade union or professional organisation. Their employment shall in no way be conditional upon such membership.
2. Strikes shall be legal, with the following specific exceptions:
    (i) In essential services: food, transport, power; armed services, police, firemen; postal services; civil service. (All persons in essential services, in compensation for their inability to strike, would have indexed-linked wages or salaries at above the national average. The term 'food' shall include the handling of food consignments, for example at the docks.)

(ii) Political strikes: that is, strikes that serve no discernible industrial ends and are clearly designed for political ends, including systematic disruption or the weakening of the Minimum State for subversive ends.

(iii) Strikes in sympathy with those involved in industrial or especially in political disputes to which the workers proposing to strike are not a party.

It should be noted that these exceptions are inherent in Articles 11 and 12 of the Charter of Rights.

3. All elections to executive office in the trade unions shall be compulsory, secret and subject to independent scrutiny.

(If the Tories had gone for this single measure instead of the comprehensive and provocative Industrial Relations Act, they could have broken the power of the subversives *and* avoided a confrontation; but this is wisdom after the event.)

The Secret Services

The savings implicit in the creation of the Minimum State would free ample funds for defence forces in any State which had previously neglected defence in deference to Keynesian economics. But adequate defence forces are only one element (though a very important one) in a general security policy. Another, equally important, is the secret security and intelligence services. All States need the former to defend themselves against espionage and subversion (however that term is defined). All States of a certain size and beyond also need the latter (intelligence) if they wish to play an international role consistent with their importance. The questions to be determined are how far should their powers go, and what their guiding principles should be.

The powers of the secret services, and their size as well, need to be kept within bounds. It would defeat the objects of the Minimum State to make them too large and too powerful. On the other hand, their resources have to be sufficient and their mandate wide enough to deal with both foreign and home-based espionage and subversion (including the violent sort known as terrorism). It is essential that both security and intelligence services in major Western countries should have an offensive and counter-offensive capacity; that is, that their function should not be limited to the provision of information and intelligence. These, then are the essential requirements and guidelines:

Security Services

—It is proper in a democracy (which the Minimum State would be) that the intelligence function should be separated from the power to arrest. (In Britain, the Security Service, usually known as MI5, has the duty to inform the Home Secretary and Prime Minister, but the power of arrest is reserved for the police Special Branch.)

—However, the intelligence function, in itself, is not sufficient to deal with subversion. There should therefore be a *counter-subversive* capacity: whether this capacity should be under the control of a security service, or attached to an appropriate ministry (such as Defence or the Interior, or even External Affairs), or come under the direct control of the Prime Minister or President, is largely a matter of administrative convenience.

—Citizens of the Minimum State should not automatically be exempt from security and counter-subversion operations: the notion that subversion is committed by foreigners only is unfortunately untrue. It follows that telephone taps may be needed, and that files on the activities of subversive or potentially subversive groups must be maintained. Such procedures should be allowed, however, only under safeguards against abuse, including the production of *prima facie* evidence of subversive intent or practice.

In the United States, as the delayed result of Watergate and as the direct consequence of the recent Privacy Act, it is now illegal for the Federal Bureau of Investigation to tap telephones or to keep files on subversive organisations unless they commit an offence. This clearly makes it impossible to anticipate and prevent such offences. It is not an exaggeration to say, at the time of writing, that in consequence of such well-meaning follies, the US is a country without security. Thus one of the fundamental requisites of the State is no longer being fulfilled, to the benefit of the enemies of the USA and of its democracy, and to nobody else's benefit.

Intelligence Services

—The prime function of an intelligence service will always be the acquisition, by any means, of well-founded intelligence about actual or potential enemies of the country. This intelligence needs to be objectively analysed and assessed if it is to be useful.

—All major intelligence services, however, should also have an *operational* capacity, for offensive or counter-offensive use.

Although secret operations of this kind, if exposed, can lead to official embarrassment and even cause grave damage to public confidence and morale, they are far cheaper in resources than military operations, and far less costly in lives. For obvious reasons, it is only the failures that hit the public eye; the more numerous successes remain secret. It should be clear that secrecy is the prime requisite in such activities, and that if secrecy is not guaranteed, it is better not to launch an operation. The supervisory requirements (such as clearance by Congressional committees) imposed on the American CIA after Watergate had the simple effect of making secret operations impossible, to the benefit of the Soviet KGB and other enemies of the USA and its democratic system, and to the benefit of nobody else.

Parties in the No-Party State

Is this not a contradiction in terms? Well, no—not necessarily. The creation of political parties is implicit in Articles 14 and 17 of the Charter of Liberties of the Minimum State. All that is proposed is that political parties should be deprived of the right to compete for political power. Even if a No-Party State were set up, and if this were done according to Minimum State principles, political parties could be created, or continue to exist. They would have the unrestrained liberty of advocacy. In other words, they could constitute pressure groups, but would not be allowed to usurp the political function reserved to the profession of politics.

Parties in the Minimum State

All the objections to the political parties that have been stated, in various forms, in this book remain, whole and entire. Their very existence stands in the way of the Minimum State. If, however, a political party under intelligent and determined leadership understood the need for the Minimum State and found itself in power, the achievement would lie within reach. But even a party as sensible as that, and as determined on a worthy objective, would still be a political party, with the defects inherent in the concept. It would be unlikely, therefore, except in the kind of catastrophic crisis discussed elsewhere, to wish to abolish itself along with its rivals.

Could the Minimum State survive if political parties also did? The answer must be a conditional Yes. There would be no chance of survival if a rival party, determined to destroy it, were given the chance to come to power and do so.

The preservation of the Minimum State under a party system lies, therefore, in two directions: a suitable written constitution, and the professionalisation of the parties.

I have already discussed the constitutional requirements. A libertarian constitution, embodying the requirements of the Minimum State, including (not least) the economic prerequisites of political freedom, if passed by Parliament or Congress, and preferably submitted to a referendum, would undoubtedly, even in a country so reduced to apathy as Britain, attract a substantial majority. If then the members of political parties were required to take an oath of acceptance of the new constitution, the majority of subversives would automatically eliminate themselves. Those who dissembled would, if it could be shown that they were working to destroy the constitution, lay themselves open to appropriate charges. The parties could then survive, offering not radically incompatible ideologies, but alternative teams for office. The effect need be no more drastic than the alternation of Republicans and Democrats in the United States.

Although the creation of a profession of politics is ideally suited to the alternative democracy of the No-Party State, the concept is by no means incompatible with the continuance of the party system. One of my major criticisms of party democracy, as at present practised everywhere, is that apart from arbitrary and variable age criteria, and proof of literacy in countries with a large proportion of illiterates, no qualifications are required of legislators.

Does democracy reside in the people (i.e. the voters) or in those elected by the people? Surely the requirement of universality is more aptly applied to the former than to the latter. There is no very good reason why a profession of politics should not be set up, even under a party system, with the kind of rigorous requirements I have outlined elsewhere. Members of existing parties who could meet these requirements would be admitted to the profession, and therefore allowed to compete for political power.

This reform alone would greatly raise the quality of the legislators, and therefore the quality of debate and legislation. Who would shed genuine tears over the exclusion of the foolish and the incompetent, or indeed of the occasional rascal?

If this reform were successfully introduced, and combined with some of the ideas of Lord Hailsham and of Wilfrid Sendall analysed elsewhere, many (although not all) of my objections to the party system would be removed. It would indeed become the next best thing to the No-Party State, to which it would probably lead naturally and in due course.

THREE

DISMANTLING THE WELFARE STATE

If you are old, poor and sick, you need help. If you are old and rich and well you don't. If you are poor and mentally retarded, you need help. If you are poor, healthy and intelligent, you probably don't; or at any rate not much. If you are ill but a high earner, you don't need 'free' medicine and 'free' doctors and 'free' hospital beds.

All this is simple common sense. By throwing common sense to the winds in the interests of an untenable theory of equality, the Attlee government from 1945 on created a monstrously inefficient Welfare State, the costs of which go on escalating year after year with no end in sight. And the result is *less* Welfare, not more. It stands to reason that if you make benefits available to all, regardless of whether they are needed or not, you are perpetuating inequalities instead of levelling them out, and in the stupidest possible way. The wastefulness of such a system is of staggering proportions and the cost to the people as a whole is far higher than the relevant statistics suggest. The untrammelled Welfare State contributes to the permanent inflation problem in Britain and other countries; absorbs resources that could be put to better use; discourages initiative and hard work; demands an army of unproductive bureaucrats who could be better employed; and starves medicine of badly needed funds for research and equipment, resulting in lower standards. Moreover, it drives energetic and able doctors abroad to seek a living in more sensible countries.

The issue is not Welfare as such, nor is it compassion. It is not compassionate to give 'free' benefits to those well able to fend for themselves, but a misguided disservice to them and their families. To offer 'free' health to the fit is to foster a nation of expensive hypochondriacs. To tax people and companies to the hilt to pay for these unnecessary services is a giant disincentive. Most of the ills of the absurd semi-socialist State created since the Second World War may be attributed to 'Welfare' (the rest may be blamed on the nationalised industries).

The Welfare State is the antithesis of the Minimum State, and makes it impossible. The three criteria of the State are neglected because Welfare absorbs the funds that should be going to protecting the population at home and defending them against enemies from abroad. Nor can money be expected to preserve its value if the resources are hogged for Welfare. The Welfare State is not the boon it is supposed to be: it is an undigested lump on the collective stomach, constipating the entire nation. It must go.

In the Minimum State, the three criteria are satisfied *first*. When they are satisfied, those in power work out what is left, and see how much can be spared for essential education, essential benefits, essential health treatment. Above all, they work out how much of our collective needs can legitimately, and far more efficiently, be entrusted to private enterprise. And if some of the rest does logically and sensibly fall to the State, they will work out a more sensitive and sophisticated way of meeting the cost than the insensitive bludgeon of taxes. They will be lucky, moreover, for the brainwork has already been done for them—reasoning and sums—by Arthur Seldon, Editorial Director of the Institute of Economic Affairs, London, in a book with the pithy title of *Charge* (Temple Smith, 1977). I shall return to Mr Seldon's remarkable work later. But first, some facts and figures about Welfare States.

The Price of Folly

It is customary (still) among British Labour politicians to boast that Britain's National Health Service is 'the envy of the world'. I can think of no evidence to justify this claim. If it were true, one would expect other countries, or at the least one other country, to have copied its principle of universal benefits chargeable to the tax-payer. Yet it remains unique: the only folly of its kind. No wonder we are proud of it.

There can be no doubting the burning sincerity of the men who launched the NHS on 5 July 1948. Health for all: it was a dream about to be realised. With their idealism went a naïve hope—that in time we would all become so healthy that our need for the National Health Service would decline (much as the State was supposed to wither away in post-revolutionary Russia). The opposite has been true. The British have always loved their Health Service, but their love does not diminish: their appetite for pills grows with the swallowing. Within the first few years, the demand for free dentures and free spectacles proved so gigantic that a charge of sorts had to be introduced—a breach of the principles of freedom and universality that offended and worried the purists.

What the social engineers never understand is that human nature (though not necessarily human behaviour) goes on unchanged by collectivist schemes. The more we have the more we want (if the product is 'free' or appears to be so because it comes out of taxes). It has been worked out in real terms—that is adjusting the figures for inflation—the NHS now costs nearly four times as much as it did when launched thirty years earlier.* In 1976, the last year for which full statistics were available when these lines were written, the annual cost in inflated pounds was £6,215 million—sixteen times as much (1,700 per cent) as the starting figure in relatively uninflated sterling. And the figure was running at £6,938 million for 1977/78.

The benevolence of the NHS is universal in that it even extends to tourists who come to London for their operations, and to immigrants who have barely landed. Inevitably, the machine is overloaded and overworked. More and more, although its benevolence is undimmed, it simply cannot deliver the goods. During the past three years well over a hundred hospitals have been closed down in Britain, because it is easier and cheaper to close a hospital than repair crumbling buildings or replace obsolete equipment. The queues for hospital beds lengthens: 600,000 were on the waiting list in 1978. Some of the 600,000 (how many, no one can tell) probably didn't need hospital treatment and could just as well have been looked after at home, but hospital treatment was their entitlement, or so they thought with the backing of their harassed local general practitioner. Others needed access badly and were going to die before a kidney machine was available. Mild or incipient cases were going to become acute while the queue lengthened.

The standard of attention and treatment available varied enormously according to the fortunes or misfortunes of habitation. In some districts of London the standards would be very high; in some northern industrial slums, crowded, strained and inadequate. All NHS doctors were busy; some were under impossible strain and could scarcely spare the time to look at their patients before putting pen to a prescription form so that the nurse in attendance could say, 'Next, please.'

Britain's doctors were overworked and (in comparison with their European or North American colleagues) grossly underpaid. Many were emigrating, taking their expensive and painstakingly acquired skills elsewhere, to be replaced by immigrants, largely from India, Pakistan and Bangladesh—once they had demonstrated their capacity to qualify all over again in the English language. Their mastery of

* See David Moller, 'The Haemorrhaging Health Service' (*Reader's Digest*, UK ed., February 1978).

the alien tongue was not always immediately apparent to their patients, but no matter: the show went on.

Dr Tony Smith, Medical Correspondent of *The Times*, had words of praise and blame for the NHS in a commemorative article in his newspaper on 5 July 1978. He recorded dramatic achievements, principally in the reduction of infectious diseases. In 1948, it appears, tuberculosis and poliomyelitis between them accounted for 23,000 deaths. Now they are pretty well extinct. Only a hundred or so young women now die in childbirth, or undergoing abortions or of the complications of pregnancy: thirty years earlier, the figure was ten times as high. Rickets and other dietary deficiency diseases used to have a literally crippling effect on the young, and these too have almost vanished—though how far the National Health Service can take the credit, and how much of this success is simply the result of a general rise in living standards, is hard to determine.

The infant mortality figures are interesting. They show that far more British babies survive their first year than in 1948; but they also show that this is true of other countries, some of which have jumped ahead of us in the race. In 1948, France, emerging from German occupation, had an infant mortality rate of fifty-one per thousand, compared with twenty-four in England. By 1975, the French rate had dropped to fourteen; the English rate had also dropped, but only to sixteen. The Swedes, at peace throughout, held the world's record in 1948 with only twenty-three; they still held it in 1975, with a mere eight babies in a thousand lost in the first year. Also ahead of the English were the Swiss and Dutch (eleven each) and the Finns and Norwegians (ten each).

It is not accidental that the British Health Service is financed entirely by direct taxation, whereas in a number of countries with better health facilities, individual health insurance schemes cover most of the costs, allowing the market some say in determining the price of the service to the consumer. Sweden, Germany and France all have much higher gross national products per head of the population, and it is therefore not surprising that they should spend more on health than the British. What is more surprising is that they actually spend a higher percentage of their income on health: 7 per cent or more, compared with only 5·5 per cent in Britain.

The Great Tax Protest

An item of the first importance will never reach the official statistics. It is a pity, for it would tell us more about the failure of socialism and the longing for a Minimum State than all the other statistics put together. But the econometricians will have to do without it, and the political scientists and the polemicists will have to use guesswork. I refer, of course, to the global incidence of tax-dodging.

Nicholas Ridley, MP, a Conservative and a staunch defender of private enterprise, did some serious research on the subject and gave us the benefit of his researches in the *Reader's Digest* (UK edition) of July 1978. The only indicator is the figure for fines inflicted for underpayment of income tax. In ten years, says Ridley, fines for tax-evasion in Britain doubled, to £27 million. Allowing for inflation, the rise is hardly as steep as one would expect. Ridley himself quotes estimates ranging up to £2,000 million in lost tax-payments—about 10 per cent of the total income-tax yield. The problem is that nobody really knows, and by definition the answer is unknowable.

Ridley calls tax-evasion 'one of the few growth areas in our sluggish economy'—a wry comment on the counter-productive consequences of three decades of Welfarism in what was once the leading industrial country in the world.

In France, the income-tax scale starts at 5 per cent; in Britain at 25 per cent. In France a married couple with two children do not pay tax until their income reaches the equivalent of £2,959; in Britain the starting figure is £1,735. At the top end, the business executive, already much more highly paid in France, Germany and Holland than in Britain, keeps far more of what he earns. The top rate for income tax in the Federal Republic is 56 per cent, and in France 60 per cent. The Dutch high flyer suffers, with 72 per cent creamed off by the tax collector, but his sufferings are mild compared with the punishment inflicted on the successful Britisher, who is allowed to keep only 17 per cent of what he earns at the top end. Small wonder that the ambitious young man starts shopping around for a suitable market in which to sell his penalised talents.

If the estimate Ridley quotes is near the truth, 15 per cent of Britain's top managers seek, or have found, jobs abroad. The market is there, all right. The incentive to work hard lies not only in the spending-money left after taxes, but in the knowledge of high comparative rewards. A French chief executive will earn more than twenty-two times as much as the average industrial wage. The German is less well off, with only twelve times. But the German is rich compared with the British, who brings home only five and a half times the earnings of a semi-skilled industrial worker. Is there much point in working one's way to the top?

But the lower end is no better than the top, for all the egalitarian talk of the past thirty years. French or German workers earn much more than their British counterparts. And, of course, they produce far more too: man for man, the British car worker produces half as much, or in bad cases only a third as much, as his Continental counterpart in a given time. Over-manning is highly characteristic of the centralised State.

Healthy in Chile

A fascinating case, far from Europe, is that of Chile, before, during and since the ill-fated Allende experiment. Under the pragmatic, though much reviled, military leaders who rid their country of a dangerous demagogue, Chile could well become the first country in the world to discard a collectivised medical service. The experiment is worth watching.

The standard of medical practice has always been high in Chile. The Chilean Medical College, with disciplinary powers roughly equivalent to those of the British Medical Association, kept a check on quality as well as behaviour. Many of Chile's top medical men studied at the best schools in Europe and America. And many of the best medical professors from Germany and France taught at Santiago University's Faculty of Medicine. Typically, the oldest Spanish-language medical journal in the world is that of the Santiago Medical Society.

Until 1938, Chilean physicians used to charge good fees to those who could afford it, and nothing to those who couldn't. The poor went to church hospitals, where treatment was free. This was charity in the Christian sense. But 1938 brought a Popular Front government to Chile, in which the Health Minister was a certain Dr Salvador Allende who had lately entered the Senate as a rising young politician. Dr Allende (whose degree was a medical one) introduced the Maternal and Child Care Act, bringing free health services to Chile's mothers and their children. He was naturally applauded for his humanitarian approach to the health problem. And Chile's young women and their children, present and to come, sought attention at the tax-payer's expense, not that of private and Christian charity. Naturally, the demand for treatment increased as it always does when the State appears to be providing something for nothing. But mothers and children are only part of the population and the damage done was thus limited.

In 1952, General Ibáñez (see Part II, Chapter 4) was back in power with an overwhelming popular vote. Chile's traditional links with Britain meant in those days that if the British were doing something, it was probably good. What Britain was doing at that time included the National Health Service, launched four years earlier. It was too early to judge whether it was going to be a success in the long run, but one thing certain about it (at that time) was that it was popular with the consumers. General Ibáñez decided that what the British enjoyed the Chileans should also enjoy. So medicine was nationalised.

What this meant in practice was that all hospitals now belonged to the State, and any doctor wishing to practise in a hospital had to sign on part-time or full-time for the Chilean NHS. About one-third of the Chilean population, at that time, were covered by a health insurance organisation called Sermena. Their premiums, as well as their taxes, now went to finance health for all. The duplication of the British experience reflected itself in the economic consequences as well as in the original conception. Taxes went up, hospitals became crowded, waiting lengthened, the standard of treatment declined (except in private practice), doctors on full-time NHS work were ill-paid, and those on part-time contracts were better off only to the extent that their private practices flourished.

But the doctors' grouses were not confined to low remuneration. Working norms were another cause for complaint. The bureaucrats in their wisdom laid down that pediatricians must see ten patients an hour. It was difficult to defeat the bureaucrats, for by now there were so many of them. A General Directorate of Health had been set up under the Health Ministry. The country had been divided into twelve Health Regions, each of which had to work to minutely drafted directives. For a population of 10 million, the administrative burden was tremendous.

Clinics opened at 8 a.m. and the queues started forming at 5. Many of those queueing weren't particularly sick, but the service was available, so they joined the queue. Those who really did need treatment would be sent to a hospital, where they would have to wait another four or five hours, after a day of shuffling forward at the clinic. But those who needed emergency operations were the ones in trouble, as waits of twenty-four hours were common. Time for an inflamed appendix to burst.

If a patient decided he had better have a grumbling appendix or troublesome tonsils out, he or she would have to wait up to a year, or even more: another point in common with the British NHS.

And then there was the second coming of Dr Allende in 1970. The former Health Minister was bursting with collectivist zeal. One of the first things he did was to denounce the existing NHS as 'class-ridden' and to announce the banning of all private practice under a new Unified Health Service, with Cuba as a model. The new service was to be fully politicised and not merely nationalised. Thus each district would have its Lay Health Chief, each a registered member of the Popular Unity coalition which henceforth governed Chile. It was up to the Lay Health Chief to decide whether or not a patient needed treatment. From now on, Health would be democratised as well as politicised and nationalised. Away with qualifications: new 'working-class' doctors would be produced in four years of part-time study (two hours a day on tiresome things such as anatomy and pathology, plus a hefty dose of political indoctrination). This compared favourably with the class-ridden past of six years at medical school plus three years in hospital. Now the party would rule: the head of the Workers' Committee attached to each clinic and hospital would give the orders on all matters medical.

As always in his term of supreme power, Allende had tried to move too fast. Meetings of doctors all over Chile overwhelmingly rejected the new plan, and threatened to strike if Allende went ahead. The plan remained a dead letter.

Medical standards nevertheless deteriorated sharply, simply because everything did as a result of Allende's headlong rush to collectivism. By 1973 inflation was running at 1,000 per cent a year and shortages of all kinds plagued households and hospitals alike. Malnutrition invaded the cities. In the three years of the Allende experiment, infant mortality soared by 36 per cent.

These past five years (as these lines were written) Chile has been learning to get along without Allende and without socialism. The unpredictable violence of streets and country lanes has gone. Unemployment has been halved, from 20 per cent to 10 per cent, and inflation slashed from 1,000 per cent to 60 per cent. Taxes have been cut and industries that had been seized by Allende in the name of 'the people' have been returned to their private owners. There were 500 of them. The private banks were providing credit and creating jobs. Most important of all, government spending was being drastically reduced. At the height of the Allende nightmare, the government was spending about 46 per cent of GNP (about 12 per cent *less*, incidentally than Britain under Labour, but Chile was poorer to start with). Allende had run up foreign debts of $1 billion, and the despised junta was paying them off fast.

The junta called in the doctors and sought their advice. They in turn consulted the membership of the Medical College, who did not hesitate for long. They had seen a unified health service in action, and they did not like what they saw. They thought fees should be restored, for patients who could afford to pay. Above all, they wondered whether the great health bureaucracy was really necessary. On reflection the sensible military agreed: so the entire General Directorate of Health was abolished. Overcrowding diminished fast, and with it queueing and waiting. The health budget is much smaller but more is done than with the swollen collectivist budget of the recent past.*

Welfare of Other Kinds

I have given a good deal of space to health because it is probably the single element in the Welfare State that most universally impinges on people's lives: even education only affects those being educated, or themselves in education, or with children to educate. But there is more to the nanny State than hospitals and schools. There is also Social Security, itself to be subdivided into supplementary benefits, pensions, family allowances, sickness benefit and the rest. And there are school meals and subsidised housing. Moreover, if one is to stray beyond the limits of 'Welfare' in the strict sense, one may include in one's expectations of 'free' services from the State land drainage and coast protection, street lighting and roads, parks and recreation grounds, libraries, museums and art galleries, not to mention sewage and the disposal of refuse. The list seems endless.

To what extent these manifold services are properly to be performed by the State is a legitimate subject for debate. Apart from Welfare, however, and some of the other things listed above, the greatest area of official failure has been the nationalised industries. The British experience constitutes one of the most striking indictments of party democracy, for if the original sin was certainly committed by the Labour Party, the Conservative Party is almost equally guilty in its timid acceptance of the harm done. Together (though in supposed opposition to each other) the two great political parties have ruined Britain in three decades.

Many of us shared in the original sin. It seemed clear to us in the 1930s that 'capitalism' had failed, that it produced misery and unemployment, that it was ready to compromise with fascism and nazism, and even that it was incapable of defending the country. The hermetical sealing-off of the USSR blinded us to the crimes and infinitely greater miseries of the socialist experiment in Russia. Although Churchill had been the great popular hero of the war, his party did not share his popularity and it seemed natural to drive

---

* The facts in this account of the Chilean Health Service are culled from an article by Llewellyn H. Rockwell, Jr, in the American medical journal, *Private Practice* (September 1977).

it out of office when the war ended. I was among those who thought that way, and who voted Labour in 1945.

Clement Attlee, that efficient, waspish, committee chairman, embarked on his well-known programme of Welfare (accepted by all three political parties), and 'public ownership' (in which Labour stood alone). His government nationalised the coal-mines and railways, gas and electricity, steel and road haulage and parts of civil aviation, and not least the Bank of England (which had entered popular demonology as one of the culprits in the Great Depression). When Churchill and his Tories came back to power in 1951, they denationalised steel and road transport, but left everything else in the hands of the bureaucrats. And so the misbegotten thing known as 'the mixed economy' was born. The social democrats of the Labour Party (whose spiritual or ideological leader was the late Anthony Crosland) were pleased with it initially, for it brought them the kind of mild 'socialism' they needed to feel they were helping suffering humanity. The majority of the Conservatives accepted it for a number of reasons: timidity and inertia, incomprehension of economic laws, but above all the desire for a consensus, so that the two-party system could be made to work, or seem to work. The hybrid 'Butskellism' (meaning something acceptable both to R. A. Butler as the arch-exponent of the new Toryism, and to the moderate Hugh Gaitskell when he led the Labour Party in opposition) was the perfect expression of the reigning consensus.

Gaitskell, sensible man that he was, wanted his party to reject Clause 4 of its constitution, which was (and remains) a commitment to full-scale socialism. He was defeated by a coalition of Leftists, sentimentalists and opportunists, in which the leading figure was Harold Wilson, who took over the leadership of the party on the death of Gaitskell in January 1963. Back in power under Wilson in 1964, Labour renationalised steel and took over a score of private road-transport companies. But the Heath government (1970–74) did little to unscramble the mixed economy. All it could do was to denationalise Thomas Cook, the travel agents, and a brewery, while allocating certain air-routes to private enterprise. When Rolls-Royce found itself in difficulties, the Tory government, despite much earlier talk about not helping 'lame ducks', moved in with public money. After the disastrous confrontation between the Heath government and the trade union movement early in 1974, came the minority Labour government which nationalised the giant British Leyland car conglomerate, Ferranti and the British National Oil Corporation. The aircraft and shipbuilding industries were also nationalised. Thus each Labour government took the country further towards collectivism, and each Tory government acquiesced in the deathly drift.

The overall performance of the nationalised sectors of the economy has been dismal: mostly the losses are heavy, but at times there are inordinate profits, the benefits of which are not necessarily passed on to the consumer. Thus the nationalised Electricity Council (for England and Wales) announced a profit of £133 million on 27 July 1978; and the Post Office showed a profit (mainly on the tele-communications side) of nearly £368 million for 1977/78. But the consumer's expectation that such figures would lead to price cuts was disappointed. As for service, there is no comparison between the prompt service and attention given to American users of the private and competitive telephone companies, and the inefficient and frustrating performance of Britain's State system; just as there is no comparison between the standards of the pre-war gas and electricity companies and the nationalised services.

But the black spots are undoubtedly steel and coal. In 1976–77, the Japanese steelworker's average output during the year was 340 tons; in Britain, it was only sixty-two tons. (In between came the Americans, with 247 tons per man year, the Germans with 161 and the Italians with 158). And Britain's steel industry was losing £2 million a day by mid-1978. Britain's coal-miners (perhaps rightly from some points of view) are the pampered ones of industry, with union muscle behind them, much Welfare and more capital invested per man than anywhere else. Yet output fell by about 50 per cent to 108 million tons between 1945 and 1976.

From Rhodes Boyson's stimulating book, *Centre Forward: A radical Conservative Programme* (Temple Smith, 1978, p. 84), I borrow these significant facts:

Price rises, January 1948–December 1970
Nationalised sector	245%
Private sector	135%
Return on capital, 1948–68 (at 1958 prices)	
Nationalised sector	7%
Private sector	24%

Collectivism—including State ownership or control of industries—is a *political* evil in that it restricts the area of free choice, in employment as well as for the consumer. But the essence of the evil lies in the creation of State monopolies. I have never understood by what logic Marxists pretend to solve the evils of private monopolies by creating State monopolies. Private 'monopolies' are rarely complete, although the tendency toward monopoly is deplorable whether the forces creating it are in the private or the public sector. But in

Britain, nationalised industries have mostly, though not invariably, been total monopolies (as they always are in Russia). Where nationalised industries have been forced to compete with private companies, the inherent evils of nationalisation are greatly reduced. One need only mention the healthy French Régie Renault, a long-nationalised concern which goes on producing cars which people want to buy because it is competing with Peugeot–Citroën and the rest. The trouble with nationalisation, British-style, is that it is either monopolistic or does not allow genuine competition—as in the case of British Leyland, which would have been driven out of business within months if the government had not continued to top up its subsidies.

If the Minimum State is ever to be created in the United Kingdom, the mixed economy will have to be dismantled, along with the Welfare State.

The Swedish Model in Trouble

For several decades social democrats in many countries looked wistfully in the direction of Sweden. What they yearned for, the Swedes seemed to have achieved. Welfare was universal, yet no one was poor. It was not only the British Labour Party that was fascinated by this Scandinavian example: I vividly remember President Bourguiba of poverty-stricken Tunisia telling me that his regime looked to Sweden, not Yugoslavia, as the model for a suitable form of socialism.

Today, the Swedish example has turned sour; as a model it is in deep trouble. It is worth asking why.

The most important difference between social democracy Swedish-style and British-style is that the Swedes have never seen the need for sweeping nationalisation of industry, whereas the Labour Party was always a prisoner of its absurd Clause 4. The Swedes thus kept the productive base for their surge into prosperity largely intact, whereas the British handicapped themselves from the start out of doctrinal obstinacy.

Sweden had other and more natural advantages: rich deposits of high-grade iron ore; huge forests to feed the pulp industry; abundant water power; and a small population of hard-working and unexcitable people. Moreover, the Swedes have enjoyed a pro-tracted period of neutrality and peace. In this their case recalls that of the Swiss; and like them, the Swedes have an earlier history of poverty, violence and war. And again, like the Swiss, the Swedish workers and employers settled their differences—in Sweden's case in the famous Saltsjöbaden agreement of 1938, which repudiated strikes without actually outlawing them. Ever since then, both sides of industry have settled their differences quietly, and in general without government interference.

Six years earlier, in the depth of the Depression and with nearly a third of the work force unemployed, the Social Democratic party had begun its lengthy reign, which was to last forty years until it was narrowly defeated by a centre-Right coalition in 1976. During those decades Sweden was totally transformed, achieving the highest, or nearly the highest, living standard in the world and an almost unique social stability.

One of the most remarkable aspects of Sweden's undeniable economic and social achievements was, or so it seemed, that it had remained a democracy. Indeed in a party sense this proposition was proved by the elections of 19 September 1976, which unseated the apparently immovable Social Democrats. But in a deeper sense it is hard to sustain the argument that Sweden remained a democracy. Certainly individual freedom as I have used the term in this book died somewhere along the road to the perfect Welfare State.

Some years ago an acute observer of Sweden, Roland Huntford of the *Observer*, shattered the myth of this ideal society in a book of startling power, *The New Totalitarians* (New York, 1972). In it, Huntford compared Swedish society, not with that of the Soviet Union, not with George Orwell's totalitarian nightmare, *1984*, but with that totalist nightmare of a different kind, Aldous Huxley's *Brave New World*. Outwardly there was no repression in Sweden; no tortures, no concentration camps. But every detail of life was regulated by myriad pressures, by a generalised conditioning of the mind to passive acceptance, by a pervasive customary conformity. To step out of line was either literally unthinkable or in practice impossible, and in any case morally unacceptable to the community. The Swedes had exchanged economic well-being for social and political servitude.

In Sweden, the concept of security transcended mere economic success and Welfarism. It was subsumed in the untranslatable Scandinavian word *trygghet*, meaning both safety and security: 'the safety of a harbour in a storm, and the security of the womb', as Huntford puts it (p. 169). So deeply is the idea of *trygghet* implanted, and so completely had the Social Democrats appropriated it, that it was virtually impossible for Swedes to oppose what was happening and what the party was doing to their country. Huntford quotes several cases of Swedish Conservatives who were against the Social Democrats but could not actually bring themselves to vote against them in elections for fear of disturbing *trygghet* and losing it, for themselves and others.

In the end, *trygghet* was disturbed partly by causes beyond the control of the Swedish government. The terms of trade—that is, the relative prices of exports and imports—turned against Sweden during the period from 1974 to 1976. Other sources of iron ore were proving more attractive to the world market. The world demand for shipping fell and Sweden's shipbuilders were hard hit. Above all, the great oil crisis hurt Sweden badly, sending the annual bill for imported oil up from 3,500 million crowns to 11,500 million crowns. The balance of payments ran into trouble and the standard of living—for the first time in decades—actually stagnated. Whatever the reasons, it seemed that the Social Democrats could no longer infallibly deliver prosperity. So they were voted out.

The distinguished Swedish diplomat and business man, C. H. von Platen, explained what had happened in an interesting article in *The Times* on 15 February 1978. He told a tale of inordinately high taxes, of huge subsidies to inefficient State enterprises (the Social Democrats having yielded to the temptation of economic meddling), absenteeism, and waste in the national health service—all the British symptoms, attenuated of course by the long years of prosperity for a small population.

Ambassador von Platen went more deeply into the problems of socialism, Welfare and government in a speech from which I quote the following extract:

> ... most available evidence shows ... that as a rule governments are less capable of handling trade and industry, than private enterprise is. And most available evidence indicates that a lack of competition and choice in state-run education, social welfare and medical care tends to make these services more wasteful and less efficient than they could be in a flexible system.
>
> Supersized bureaucracy and public spending will, if allowed to develop unchecked, increasingly reduce economic progress and counteract social welfare. For evidence let us look at two countries that are comparatively poor in natural resources—Japan and Switzerland. Switzerland's current government expenditure is approximately 26% (1975) of its Gross Domestic Product and Japan's is about 16% (1973). Switzerland had the highest per capita income in the world, or $6,970. Japan had about $4,130 and a formidable growth rate up to the recent depression. These two countries may be compared with for example the Netherlands, with government expenditure running at over 46%, and a per

capita income of $5,110, in spite of the wealth that the gas fields have brought to Holland. The corresponding figure for the United Kingdom is 60% (1976) with a per capita income of only $3,370.

It is useful that words of such wisdom should come from a Swede.

The German Miracle

So much has been written about the German *Wirtschaftswunder*: can anything more usefully be said? I believe it is useful, in the context of this book, to recall at least the bare facts. For the German case remains, with Japan's, the classic example of the prodigious economic stimulus of the market economy after the total devastation of war. The market economy is the true creator of wealth and the natural basis for the freedoms of the Minimum State.

The Third Reich had been utterly destroyed, and the German people, who had been told they were invincible, were confused and demoralised. Industry was at a standstill and the cities were in ruins. There was a Reichsmark, but it was valueless: the money economy had yielded to barter, with cigarettes and lighters as the units of exchange. There was famine and there was a rampant black market. Moreover, millions of refugees flowed in from the territories seized by Poland under the Potsdam decisions. On top of all this, there was no German State as such: four occupying powers had divided the country between them, each responsible for its own zone. The Russians alone knew exactly what they wanted: to destroy the free economy and incorporate their zone of Germany into a people's republic under Soviet control.

The Western allies had no very clear idea whither they wished Germany to go. President Roosevelt's friend, Henry J. Morgenthau, Secretary of the Treasury, had pressed upon the President the plan that bore his name for the destruction of German industry and the reduction of Germany to a pastoral economy. Fortunately, he resigned shortly after Roosevelt's death and the plan was laid aside. One thing the Allied Commission was agreed upon, however, whether from East or West: price controls were necessary in the desperate conditions of post-war Germany. At least one Allied decision, however, does them credit: they picked an able economist, apparently untainted by Nazi associations, to rebuild industry in the Nürnberg–Fürth area. In 1948, they gave him the job of Director of the Economic Council for the joint Anglo-American occupation district.

Dr Ludwig Erhard startled and displeased his masters by immediately sweeping away most price and wage controls and by abolishing rationing. Scandalised cries were heard from socialist-minded economists, but Erhard stood his ground. He called in the old Reichsmarks and issued new Deutschmarks.

He was right and his critics were wrong. In no time the factories were in production, the black markets vanished and the shops filled up with goods. Within a year, the national income in real terms was back to the 1936 level. Unemployment did increase, but only temporarily. From its high point of 11 per cent in 1950 it declined steadily to only 0·8 per cent in 1961.

Having started on the right lines, and proved his point, Erhard went on gradually doing away with the enormous apparatus of controls which Hitler (a National *Socialist*, let us not forget) had imposed on his country, and which the Allies had initially sustained. Rent controls went, and down went income tax. Over the years from 1949 to 1977, West Germany maintained the lowest inflation rate among industrial countries—at 2·7 per cent even less than Switzerland (3·1) and the United States (3·4). At the other end of the scale, France averaged 6·1 per cent and Britain 6·4.

It was sometimes said that West Germany's miracle owed much to the availability of cheap labour from the East, and to the absence of an arms burden during the early post-war years. The second argument is not without force, but the first is absurd and easily discounted. If West Germany had not had Erhard and his 'social market economy', the 14 million refugees from the East would have constituted an intolerable burden for a poverty-stricken country to absorb. It was the currency reform and de-control policy that brought prosperity, and in this context the 14 million helped because the booming economy could absorb them.

How to Dismantle a Welfare State

Except in Chile, where the experiment was gathering impetus when these lines were written, no country has yet set out systematically to dismantle the Welfare State. And yet, the need to discard a system that is costly, wasteful and inefficient is patent and urgent. As I have said, it is not Welfare that needs to be discarded, but the indiscriminate provision of Welfare for all at the expense of the taxpayer. As Lenin said in another context: What is to be done?

The American economists of the Chicago school, of whom Milton Friedman is the foremost, and of London's Institute of Economic Affairs under Ralph Harris, have given us the answers, at least in economic terms. The best statement of the case for dismantling the Welfare State and of the economic ways of doing it, so that it yields more Welfare for those who need it at a lower cost to the country as a whole, is Arthur Seldon's book, *Charge*, which I have already mentioned.

The economic principles involved are essentially those enunciated two centuries ago by Adam Smith in *The Wealth of Nations*. But they have been made unfashionable for so long by socialist theories accepted or acquiesced in by non-socialist parties, that they now sound distinctly unfamiliar and unconventional. All goods and services have a price, which somebody has to pay. In a free market, the price is infinitely adjustable and is determined by the individual decisions of sellers and buyers. The seller can withhold his goods if an insufficient price is offered. The buyer can take his custom elsewhere if the price required is too high; or he can save his money.

Welfare services, too, have a price. The trouble is that when they are run by the State and financed out of taxation, the element of choice is removed. The consumer, whose taxes pay for the services, will tend to use them whether or not he really needs these services. There is therefore waste and inefficiency, and in the end the services themselves are starved of requirements—for instance, hospitals and equipment, or the skills of doctors. We have seen a number of examples in this chapter.

The problem, then, is to restore the price mechanism and the element of personal choice. There are various ways of doing it. One is the voucher system: every adult is issued with vouchers to a certain value, to cover, for instance, £150 worth of education or health care, leaving it to the individual to choose where to use it—which school to send children to, which doctor or hospital to use. Beyond a certain sum, the individual would have to find the money to pay the difference.

Individual needs and risks are best catered for by insurance schemes, whether private or public. Such schemes are far more prevalent in the United States (where medical costs uncovered by insurance can be crippling) than in Britain, where they also flourish but on a smaller scale—for instance, to ensure private beds and private treatment for those covered. As for the poor, the best answer to their needs is 'reverse income tax'. Instead of paying tax, the poor should receive a sum from government funds to bring their incomes up to the level that would enable them to exercise the choice which dismantling the Welfare State would create. The disabled and the mentally handicapped constitute a special section of the population for whom special arrangements would be necessary.

The effects of restoring the pricing mechanism in health, education and related matters, would be immediately and enormously beneficial. The economy as a whole would be galvanised. The apathy and inertia and mediocrity of the false egalitarianism of our times would vanish. People would be happier because they would have greater freedom of choice than they now have. They would regain, or acquire for the first time, a sense of initiative. Taxes would be much lower, especially income tax, the great destroyer of enterprise and incentive. Gigantic sums would be freed for constructive investment. There would be jobs instead of unemployment, growth instead of stagnation. And if the principles of the Minimum State were rigorously applied, money would regain its value, and keep it.

The best arguments for dismantling the Welfare State are thus moral as well as economic. In the old days, every poor street was full of unpaid social workers, quaintly known as good neighbours, ready to take in the washing or look after the children or tide a family over a crisis. Today social workers are trained, housed and salaried. Socialism benefits, but charity suffers.

What about the political problems? Arthur Seldon disposes of them in his book. I need only say that a policy that is good in itself will be popular if properly and intelligently presented. It is necessary, for example, to explain that the poor will not suffer if health and education are largely or wholly de-bureaucratised. The only sufferers in the dismantling of the Welfare State will be those who abuse the privileges on offer, the 'scroungers'. (The chairman of the Supplementary Benefits Commission in the UK, David Donnison, disclosed in an article in the *Daily Telegraph* on 14 June 1976 that the government employed nearly 400 special investigators and hundreds more officials for the discovery or prevention of fraud. About 46,000 cases of fraud were unearthed every year, although many of these were 'trivial or tragic rather than seriously criminal'; there were some 15,000 prosecutions a year, most of them resulting in convictions.)

Having presented the case fairly but intelligently, a government in power would need to show boldness, courage and dispatch. In *Centre Forward*, that energetic and eloquent politician, Rhodes Boyson, a Conservative MP as these lines were written, put it this way:

Day one, taxes would be reduced for all, with a top rate of 50 per cent. Day two, a declaration that government expenditure would be cut by 5 per cent a year in real terms each year of the five-year term of government. Day three, the statutory monopoly of the nationalised industries would be ended and existing national-ised industries would be both offered for sale and opened to internal and international competition. Day four, all exchange controls would be repealed and a pledge made to let the pound continue to find its own level. Day five would see the announce-ment that the present Welfare State would give way to a system of topping up individual spending-power by money or specific vouchers to put the consumer in charge of all the welfare services. Day six, increase police pay and numbers, and declare war on crime and the moral pollution of our cities. Day seven, rest like creator and stroll in our gardens apart from attending the funerals of socialist suicides for whose widows we must care.

Dr Boyson, be it noted, is a former member of the Labour Party, and the former headmaster of Highbury Grove Comprehensive School, one of the largest in the country.

Leaving aside the note of frivolity, there is a core of solid sense in Boyson's prescription. In the end, the only way to create the Minimum State or at least to move towards it is by rigorous budgetary discipline: each year the government has to set rigid ceilings on expenditure for all government departments, except those that have long suffered from demagogic neglect, such as the police and armed forces. Unlike the Utopian revolutions, which promise a paradise never yet delivered, this revolution in reverse could be *guaranteed* to work, for Germany shows the benefits of the market economy, and Switzerland the blessings of good government. Emulation is better than envy when the Minimum State is the target.

FOUR

DISASTER SCENARIOS

The passing of the party system is no cause for mourning. In historical terms, political parties are a very recent phenomenon and cannot claim the sanctity of long-established tradition. The cliques that gathered around noblemen in the early nineteenth century yielded in time to parties based upon ideas and programmes. The notions of democracy, the general will and universal suffrage called for some device to make them appear to be workable: political parties fulfilled this purpose. I have tried, in this book, to demonstrate that they have failed utterly to provide good government, with the solitary exception of the Swiss Confederation which, for that reason, deserves the closest study.

The problem of the legitimacy of political power is unsolved, and perhaps of its nature insoluble. The ancients ascribed the origins of power to myths, such as the Roman myth of Romulus and Remus, the Cretan myth of Minos, or the East Asian myths of the divinity of Emperors. In an elegant description of the insoluble problem of government, James Burnham wrote (in *Congress and the American Tradition*, 1959, Chapter I):

> The central truth is the insight that there is no adequate rational explanation for the existence and effective working of government, much less for good or fairly good government. . . . Moreover, apart from a few gross and almost self-evident cases, no one has found a purely rational theory to explain why some governments, though very different from each other, do well, whereas others, though closely similar, do badly. When you drop scientist ideology, it becomes clear that you cannot explain the success of some and the failure of other governments without including a non-rational factor that we call, according to our metaphysical habits, chance, luck, accident, magic, or Providence.

Democratic theory purports to have solved the problem by finding legitimation in the popular vote. But any despot, from Louis Napoleon to Hitler or Stalin, can find such legitimacy. Nor are the assumptions behind the counting of heads or hands in any sense rational. Burnham again:

When we believe that a specified political group can make valid
political decisions by taking a poll among its members, we are
implicitly assuming that with respect to political decisions all the
individuals belonging to the group are qualitatively identical, and
thus equal: differing only quantitatively, only as one numerical
unit from another. Without this assumption, in fact, we could not
add up the vote. You cannot add two oranges plus three apples,
two monkeys plus three horses, or two carpenters plus three
merchants [Chapter XXV].

He goes on:

Considered philosophically, the assumption of qualitative political
identity is very radical indeed. When it is carried out all the way
to its logical limit, as in the democratist drive towards an unlimited
franchise, it implies that no qualitative differences whatever among
human beings—not knowledge, sex, education, wealth, experience,
religion, race, talents, colour, character, reputation, intelligence—
have any relevant bearing on their ability and right to make
fundamental political choices.

I do not want to labour such arguments. The point I have in mind
is simply that neither historically nor philosophically is there any
rational justification for the view that the party system (or any other
system) is 'legitimate'. If, as I believe, it has had its day, then the
time has come when men and women of goodwill should sit down
together and work out alternatives that might preserve the virtues
and shed the defects of 'democracy' as we have known it. I have
suggested a system which, with certain safeguards, might do just this.
We need at all times to bear in mind the present alternatives:

1. A pluralist and representative system.
2. An authoritarian system.
3. The collectivist or totalist final solution.

The debate is essential and indeed has become urgent. I confess to
profound scepticism about the proposition that men and women of
goodwill should sit down and work out a better system than the
given one, although it is not impossible that they could come
up with improvements on the existing model (for example on
the lines suggested by Lord Hailsham). What is far more likely
is that the existing systems will collapse, either gradually or in
turmoil. Then, if the dreadful third alternative can be avoided,
the authoritarian interlude could be used (if the strong man or woman

has wisdom as well as strength) to think, and to prepare for a restoration of liberties with a suitable residue of authority to avoid a return to the inherent chaos and vulnerability of the unsatisfactory present.

Political prophecy is notoriously fallible. The Communists are still waiting for 'capitalism' to collapse; and Soviet citizens for the State to wither away. I am reconciled to the probability that the party system will outlive me. But as I have just entered my seventh decade, my expectation of further life is statistically limited.

It is not difficult to construct 'scenarios' of collapse or disaster leading to authoritarian rule in each of the major democracies. Nor is it difficult to charter the consequences of drift and inaction, which could be a good deal worse. In France, for instance, a scenario in reverse is an instructive exercise. In historical fact, a majority of the French people were sensible enough to prove the prophets of doom wrong in March 1978 by voting in favour of the existing political line-up, thereby excluding the Communist–Socialist alliance. If they had not been so sensible, a predominantly Marxist government would have come to power with six or seven portfolios in the hands of Communists.

There would have been a programme of sweeping nationalisation, leading to a grave social and economic crisis. The President of the Republic, in the last two years of his mandate and lacking a parliamentary majority, would have been powerless to intervene. Supposing, however, that the army had decided to take over, as it so nearly did in May 1958 and again ten years later. Supposing, more-over, that it botched the job, so that on Day 2 it controlled only part of Paris, with the leading ministers taking refuge in the Hôtel Matignon, protected by a militia of Left-wing troops. The immediate response to an attempted army *coup* would have been a call for a general strike by the Communist-controlled CGT trade unions, with the probable support of the Catholic and Socialist union con-federations. At this point, the Marxist government (legally elected and threatened by military force) would perhaps have appealed to the USSR for 'fraternal assistance'. Then one of the following alternatives would have been in prospect:

1. Soviet forces land at key points, counting on American apathy, and get away with. Collapse of NATO.
2. Soviet intervention sparks a nuclear war.
3. More likely, the Soviet Union decides on balance that it is unwilling to risk war and with it, the lucrative 'detente' relationship with the United States.

If the third alternative prevailed, the army would have its victory with the collapse of the general strike and the surrender of the ministers. Thereafter, the real question would be what to do with the successful *coup d'état*? There is no point in taking the scenario further, since none of these things happened. But France came uncomfortably close to these gloomy alternatives, by the inexorable logic of the party system. In France, too, men and women of goodwill ought to be thinking of a post-disaster system.

In Italy, in the late summer of 1978, there was a state of incipient civil war. In some other countries, faced with Italy's problems, fighting would already have broken out, but the immemorial capacity of the Italian people to manage to live outside the official system and despite the worst that government could do, preserved an uneasy peace. But it is common knowledge that a military *coup* was narrowly averted in 1964. The question needs to be asked: what would happen in Italy if the Soviet Union occupied Yugoslavia after Marshal Tito's death? What if the Italian Communists, by that time, had a share of political power in Rome? What if powerful sections of the armed forces, the Carabinieri and the police decided to do something about 'ungovernability'? It is easier to ask such questions than to answer them.

In Spain, too, is it unthinkable that the army, outraged by chaos, economic drift, permissiveness, 'Eurocommunism' and the general decline of respect for the symbols of authority, might again take over? It is too late now for 'Francoism without Franco', but in the face of predictable hostility from the USA, from the UN and from the European Community, what alternative would there be to prolonged military rule?

In the United States, a military take-over is of course 'unthinkable'; or is it? Supposing, over the next two years, that the Soviet Union gains control over the strategic minerals of Southern Africa; that the Royal House of Saudi Arabia falls (as the Shah of Iran has fallen) and is replaced by a Marxist government subservient to Moscow; that the Russians present Western Europe with the prospect of zero supplies of oil, and blackmail the European members of NATO into showing their American ally's forces the door. Already, the American military are deeply alarmed at the strategic drift tolerated by a weak and indecisive President, and by his apparent readiness to allow the US to accept a position of permanent inferiority to the USSR. If the drift is not reversed, is a military intervention to be ruled out, even in the USA?

What of Britain? The general election of 3 May 1979 was crucially important, in that it gave the British people a chance to regain lost or eroded rights and liberties, instead of being driven ever more swiftly to an irreversible collectivist hell. In the event, they chose freedom, by giving Mrs Margaret Thatcher's Conservative Party an absolute majority of more than 40 seats. In several respects, it was an exceptional election in that the voters, instead of being asked to choose between parties sharing a general consensus (details apart), were given a clear choice of a socially fundamental kind. For Mrs Thatcher had made it clear beyond doubt that she was aware of the dangers and had the will and determination to do something about them. Her victory would have been impossible unless many voters who normally supported Labour had realised that the party was ceasing to be a democratic one and had largely fallen into the hands of totalitarians.

Although this famous victory gave Mrs Thatcher, her party and the British people as a whole the chance to dispel the totalist nightmare, it did not mean that Britain's troubles were over. In one sense, they were just beginning, for we had travelled so far on the wrong road that to go into reverse was bound to be difficult, painful and perilous. There would be hazards and man-made obstacles on the way back to sanity.

It seemed probable (writing these lines within days of the election) that the totalists would try to break Mrs Thatcher if she tried seriously to implement her campaign promises, by reducing taxes, slashing government expenditure, yet spending more on the police and armed forces—that is, in general, moving towards the Minimum State and away from collectivism. The unusually vicious and damaging strikes of the long winter of early 1979—when patients were turned away at hospitals, corpses went unburied, and refuse uncollected for weeks on end—could well prove a dress rehearsal for a concerted trade union attempt to make it impossible for Thatcher-style Toryism to govern the country.

Further speculation would be unprofitable in this book. In choosing Mrs Thatcher, the first woman Prime Minister in Europe, the voters had not chosen the soft option. In the event of a violent confrontation designed to frustrate the people's choice of a way of life, it would be up to the people, including the great mass of normally intimidated or apathetic trade unionists, to give her government the muscle power to defeat the extremists once and for all.

The alternative could only be a victory for the totalists and their 'moderate' appeasers. It was a time for boldness and courage, not for pliancy and timidity. And perhaps out of the chaos and inevitable suffering of a confrontation which only the extremists seek, a sensible alternative to the system that enabled the extremists to gain excessive power could yet emerge.

The road to the Minimum State is bound to be arduous, but journey's end would bring its own reward.

SHORT READING LIST

This book is neither a political treatise nor a text-book: it is a philosophical but activist polemic. Accordingly, I have compiled only a very brief list of books which I found relevant to my theme. Where appropriate, I indicate the chapter or chapters on which a book has a particular bearing. Authors are listed in alphabetical order.

Boyson, Rhodes, *Centre Forward—A Radical Conservative Programme* (Temple Smith, London, 1978), III, 3.

Crossman, Richard, *The Diaries of a Cabinet Minister, Vols 1, 2 and 3* (Hamilton and Cape, London, 1975–77), I, 2.

Crozier, Brian, *A Theory of Conflict* (Hamish Hamilton, 1974), I, 1 and throughout.

Fairlie, Henry, *The Life of Politics* (Methuen, London, 1968), I, 2.

Fernández de la Mora, G., *La Partitocracia* (G. Mistral, Santiago de Chile, 1976), I, 2 and 5.

Gilmour, Ian, *The Body Politic* (Hutchinson, London, 1969), I, 2.

Hailsham, Lord, *The Dilemma of Democracy—Diagnosis and Prescription* (Collins, London, 1978), III, 1 and 2.

Haseler, Stephen, *The Death of British Democracy* (Elek, London, 1976), I, 3.

Hughes, Christopher, *Switzerland* (Benn, London, 1975).

—— *The Parliament of Switzerland* (Cassell, London, 1962), II, 6.

Lakeman, Enid, and Lambert, J. D., *How Democracies Vote* (Faber, London, 1970), I, 4.

Moss, Robert, *The Collapse of Democracy* (Temple Smith, 1975), I, 3; II, 5.

Nollau, Günther, *Wie Sicher ist die Bundesrepublik?* (Bertelsmann, Munich, 1976), III, 2.

Peyrefitte, Alain, *Le Mal Français* (Plon, Paris, 1976), II, 2.

Seldon, Arthur, *Charge* (Temple Smith, 1977), III, 3.

Somary, Felix, *Krise und Zukunft der Demokratie* (Europa, Zurich, 1952), I, 5.

Wyatt, Woodrow, *What's Left of the Labour Party* (Sidgwick & Jackson, London, 1977), I, 3; III, 1.

INDEX